AF571776

# TREASURES OF THE
# WHITE HOUSE

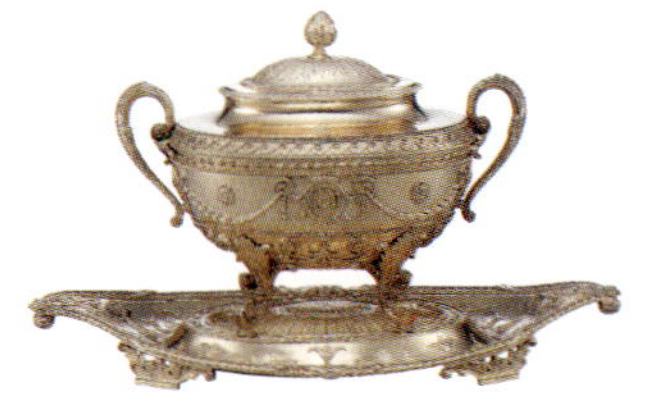

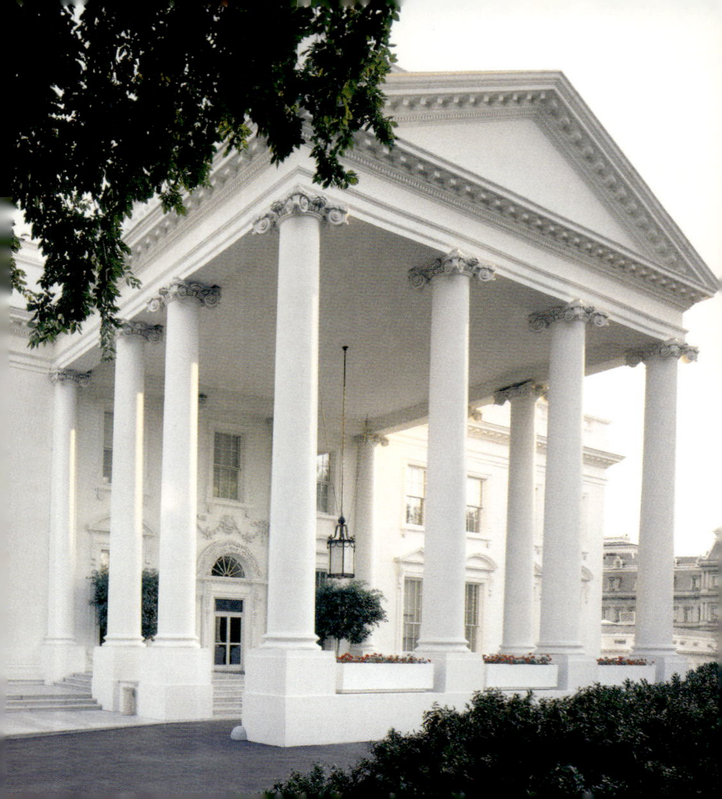

# TREASURES OF THE WHITE HOUSE

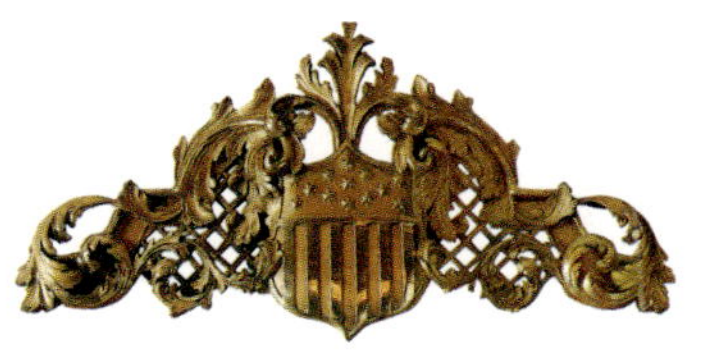

*By Betty C. Monkman*

*Principal Photography by Bruce White*

A Tiny Folio™

ABBEVILLE PRESS PUBLISHERS

New York London

Front Cover: *The Blue Room, with French furnishings purchased for that room in 1817 by James Monroe.*
Back Cover: *The State Dining Room, north wall.*
Page 1: SOUP TUREEN · *James Young · London, 1779*
Page 2: *The North Portico of the White House*
Page 6: PLATE (detail) · *Job & John Jackson · Burslem, England, 1831-43?*
Page 8: *The Red Room with early 19th-century neoclassical objects—an Italian marble mantel installed in 1819, Paris porcelain vases, New York furniture, and a late 18th-century French musical clock.*

ABBEVILLE PRESS
Project Manager: Susan Costello
Editor: Walton Rawls
Designer: Patricia Fabricant
Copyeditor: Marian K. Gordin
Production Manager: Louise Kurtz

THE WHITE HOUSE OFFICE OF THE CURATOR
Curator: Betty C. Monkman
Assistant Curators: William G. Allman, Lydia S. Tederick
Collections Manager: Donna Hayashi Smith
Administrative Assistant: Barbara D. McMillan

WHITE HOUSE HISTORICAL ASSOCIATION
The White House Historical Association is a nonprofit organization, chartered on November 3, 1961, to enhance understanding, appreciation, and enjoyment of the Executive Mansion. Address inquiries to 740 Jackson Place, N.W., Washington, D.C. 20503; whitehousehistory.org
President: Neil W. Horstman
Director of Publications: Marcia Mallet Anderson
Photo Archivist: Harmony Haskins

# Contents

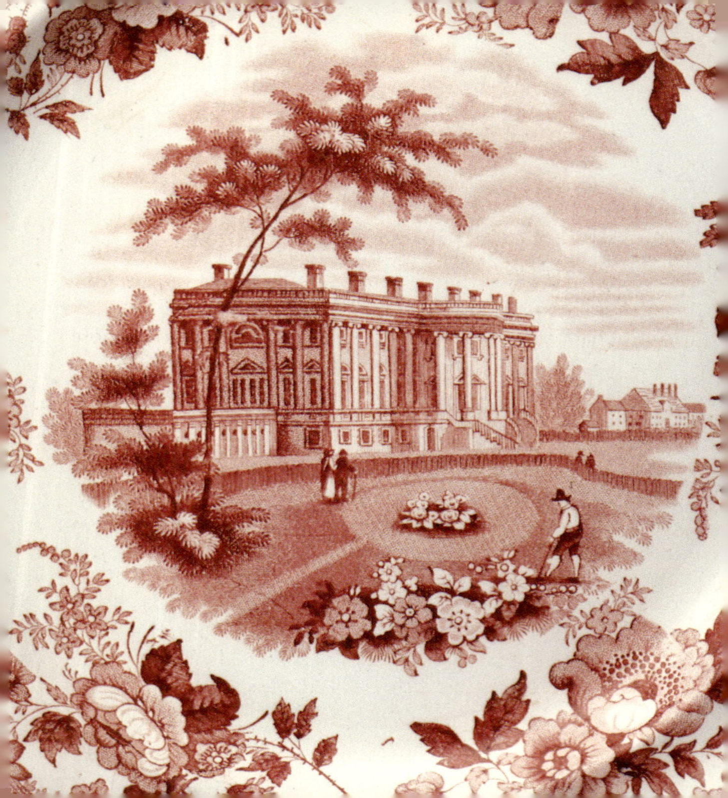

# FOREWORD

*HUGH S. SIDEY, CHAIRMAN*
*The White House Historical Association*

Here is a colorful and graphic catalog of America, the collected fragments of two centuries of life in the White House. Put together they form a stunning historical narrative of our national taste and a reflection of those who lived in the White House and the times in which they served and how they helped to shape our culture. Every painting and every table and candlestick has its own story, almost always brought proudly by a president or his family to the national stage that was and is the White House. Let history speak. There is a decanter that felt the sinewy grip of Andrew Jackson, the great Lincoln Bed that was ordered for him but never used by him, the plush, flamboyant décor from Chester Arthur, and Jackie Kennedy's soothing touches that made the White House a living museum. In every room, in every corner and niche, on every porch, there is a story of men and women contending with the great issues of war and peace for the United States and also dealing with those smaller things that make up most of each individual life, even those of presidents and first ladies—comfort, beauty, friends, food, and children.

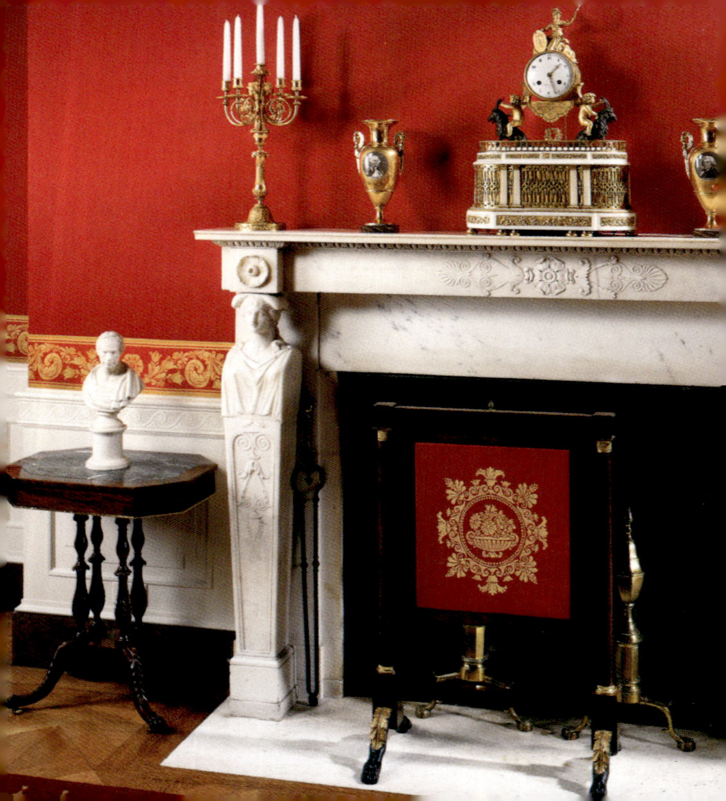

# INTRODUCTION

*BETTY C. MONKMAN, CURATOR,*
*The White House*

Built to be the residence of America's presidents and their families, the White House has been a symbol of the nation since 1800. Within its sandstone walls, presidents have led both public and private lives, and the house has also served as the president's office and as a setting for ceremonies of state. Today the White House is as well an important museum of America's history and art. Open to the public since 1801, it now receives more than a million visitors each year. No other house in America has been so accessible.

In meeting the residential needs of first families, the office functions of the president, and the continuous demands of ceremony and entertaining, the White House has accumulated over the years a special collection of paintings, sculpture, and decorative objects. Many have historical associations with occupants of the house, and others were acquired as examples of the highest quality in American and European fine and decorative arts. Until the mid-twentieth century, the art collection consisted primarily of portraits of presidents and first ladies, but it has grown to include images of America and its people. The historic furnishings reflect and document the tastes and daily life of White House residents, who, from diverse backgrounds and various regions of the country, helped shape the collections. These objects resonate with meaning, imparting inspiration and a glimpse into past presidential lives and significant White House events for each new first family. They are also evidence of changes in the nation's taste in art and technology, its styles of decoration, and an increasing interest in the country's history and its cultural heritage.

As most first families moved in and out every four or eight years, the furnishings and decorations of the nineteenth-century White House were in constant flux, and the heavy demands of large-scale entertaining necessitated regular refurbishing of the state rooms. As early as 1797, when George Washington left office, Congress viewed most presidential furnishings as expendable utilitarian items of little historic value and authorized disposition of "decayed" pieces through local auctions. This practice continued until 1903 when a final sale dispersed most of the remaining nineteenth-century furnishings—with the exception of James Monroe's gilded bronze treasures from France, the elegant silver from Andrew Jackson's era, objects that had come to be identified with Abraham Lincoln, and a few other pieces still in use, such as furniture from the Ulysses S. Grant-era Cabinet Room. In recent decades, many of the items bought at those public sales, and treasured because of their provenance, have been returned to the White House. Donations have included pieces of the gilded French furniture suite purchased by Monroe for the Oval Room in 1817 and sold at auction in 1860.

Until public awareness of America's history was heightened by the 1876 Centennial Exposition in Philadelphia, there had been little sense of the historic value of objects associated with the White House. As this awareness grew, efforts were begun to identify and preserve articles that were associated with the lives of past presidents. First Lady Caroline Harrison, in the 1890s, began to assemble examples of surviving porcelain from the state table services ordered and used by earlier presidents. This first attempt to document a group of White House objects eventually resulted in the creation of the China Room in 1917 as a place to display historic china, glassware, and silver. However, much of what was known about the history of the pieces came from stories handed down by the staff.

No effort to systematically survey the art and furnishings was undertaken until 1931, at the urging of First Lady Lou Hoover, who also supported a proposal by the Frick Art Reference Library in New York City to prepare descriptive and historical records of each painting and to provide photographs to scholars and publishers. As interest in the White House grew, the National Park Service began a historical study of the President's House and proposed a cataloging system for its objects. The project was under way when President and Mrs. Truman vacated the house in 1948 for an overdue major renovation. As objects were carefully removed from the house for safekeeping, historians searched through the National Archives and other depositories for related documents and compiled files on individual pieces. Since government appropriations were expended to maintain the house and to purchase art work and furnishings until well into the twentieth century, there was a wealth of documentation. Supplementing the official record are descriptive accounts in diaries and letters by numerous White House visitors. Wood engravings used to illustrate nineteenth-century newspaper and magazine articles and vintage photographs of White House interiors, taken as early as the mid-1860s and 1870s, provide visual documentation of rooms and their furnishings at particular times.

In the later twentieth century, interest in the White House was increased through television tours conducted by President Truman in 1952 and First Lady Jacqueline Kennedy in 1962. Expanded media attention prompted by these tours brought the history of the White House and its collections to a broader audience. At the same time, American museums and historic sites began to recognize a new public appreciation for American art and the nineteenth-century revival furnishings that had dominated domestic interiors, including those in the President's House, in the last half of the previous century. With its well-documented interiors and collections, the White House has become a rich resource for the study of America's artistic heritage.

In 1961, Congress passed legislation to preserve and interpret the museum character of the public rooms of the White House and to provide for the permanent protection of its art and historic objects. Jacqueline Kennedy selected a curator, creating for the first time an office in the White House that would meet museum standards of documentation, care, and preservation for growing collections, and provide the research for future room restoration projects. The office was formalized in 1964 when President Lyndon B. Johnson issued an executive order instituting the permanent position of curator of the White House and the Committee for the Preservation of the White House to advise the president and first lady on the character of the public rooms and the collections.

Today, the White House continues to add portraits to the collection and to broaden the scope of its acquisitions in the fine arts by including works by leading American artists and scenes of regions of the country not previously represented. The historic objects in the house span a wide range of decorative styles, including those of late-eighteenth-century America and France, the early nineteenth-century neoclassical styles of the Federal and Empire periods, the revival styles of the Victorian era, and the Colonial Revival of the twentieth century. The foremost craftsmen and manufacturers of American furniture, silver, porcelain, and glassware are well represented. Many of the pieces were made in the urban centers of New York City, Philadelphia, Boston, and Baltimore, and in the new District of

Columbia at about the same time the President's House was under construction and first occupied. From the eras of James Monroe and Andrew Jackson, elegant furniture, silver, gilded bronze, and porcelain by the finest artisans of Napoleonic France also survive. Among the thousand pieces of gilded silver in the White House are handsome objects of the English Regency period. Eighteenth-century English lighting fixtures grace many rooms, and carpets from America, England, France, Persia, and Turkey cover the floors. While a historic group of objects remains from government purchases of the nineteenth and early twentieth centuries, the majority of works in the fine and decorative arts that are displayed in the state rooms have been donated by generous Americans and the White House Historical Association. These donations have assisted the nation's presidents and first ladies as they have worked to build a significant collection of American art for the White House.

As the White House has entered its third century and continues to serve as the home of presidents of the United States and their families, as well as the ceremonial center of the presidency, the collections will continue to grow and change to reflect each new era and the evolving cultural tastes of White House occupants and the nation, much as they have since John and Abigail Adams first took up residence in the President's House two hundred years ago.

CANDELABRUM · *Paris, c. 1817*

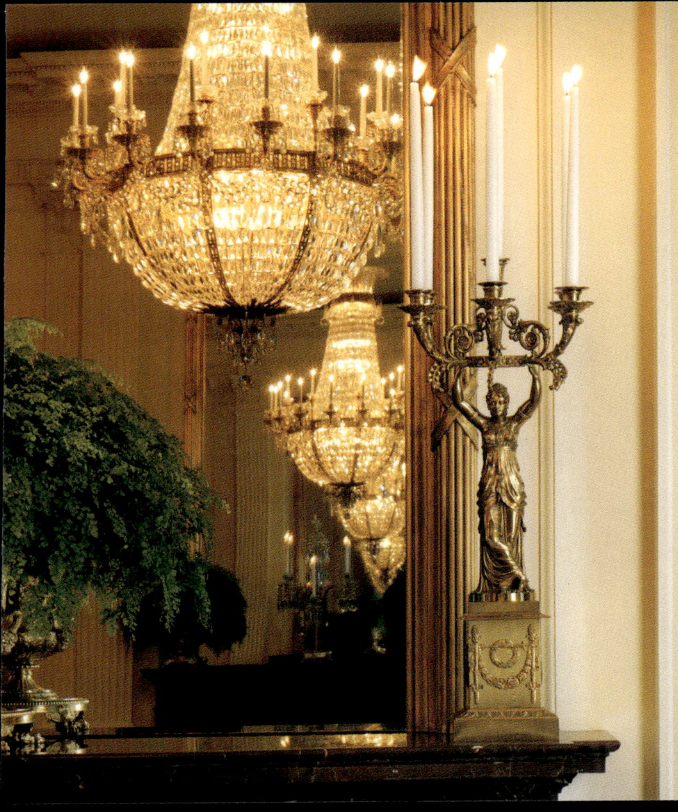

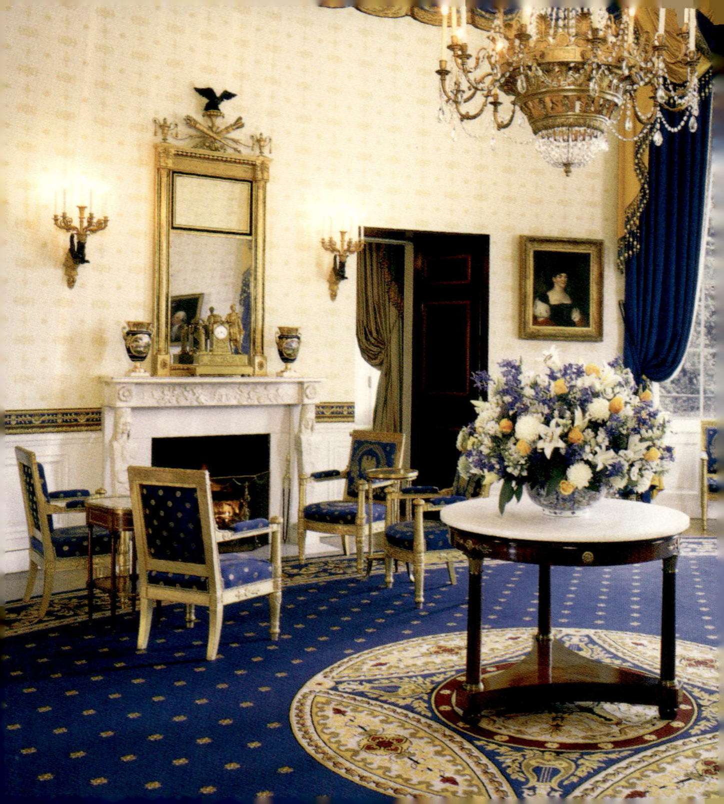

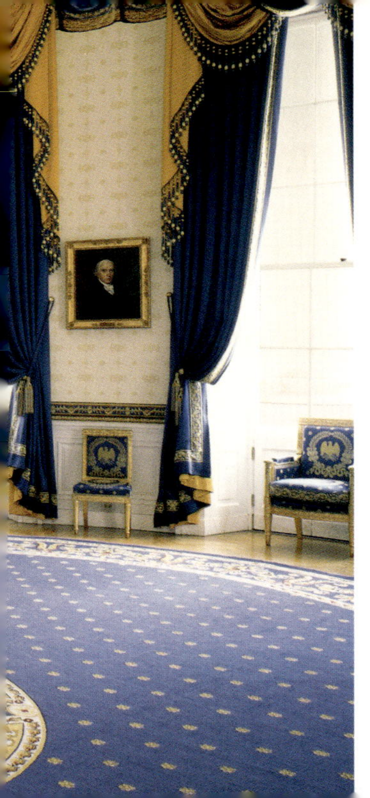

The State Floor:
The Blue Room, 2000

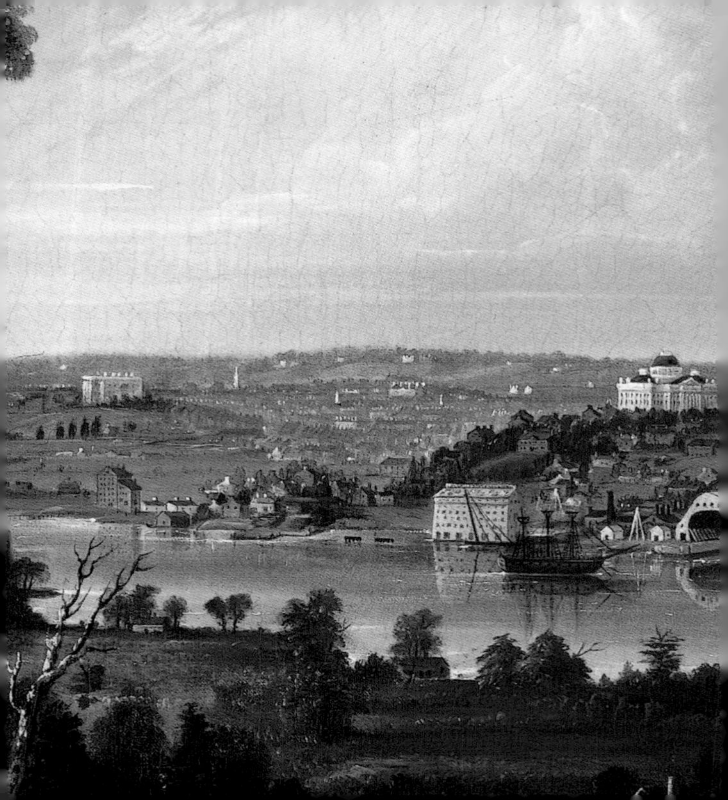

# THE FINE ARTS

The first work of art purchased for the new President's House was a full-length portrait of George Washington painted by Gilbert Stuart in 1797. It arrived at the still-unfinished mansion within days of its first occupant, John Adams, who moved in on November 1, 1800. Thanks to its famous rescue by First Lady Dolley Madison, it is the only object that has remained in the White House since before the British torched the building in 1814. In 1817, while James Monroe was refurnishing the President's House, he acquired the first pieces of sculpture—marble busts of Washington, Amerigo Vespucci, and Christopher Columbus by Giuseppe Ceracchi. During the next half century, the federal government had little impetus to assemble portraits of presidents or purchase other works of art for the rebuilt White House. Although the White House collection now holds hundreds of paintings, sculptures, and portraits by leading artists of the nation's early years—such as Charles Willson Peale, John

GEORGE COOKE · Detail of *City of Washington From Beyond the Navy Yard,* 1833 (see page 35)

Trumbull, and Rembrandt Peale—they were all acquired through twentieth-century donations.

In 1857 Congress recognized that the White House should have a portrait of each president and commissioned George P. A. Healy to paint several of them. The exhibition of the finished portraits was interrupted by the Civil War. The unframed paintings were stored in the White House attic, and discovered later by Martha Patterson, the daughter of Andrew Johnson, who had them displayed on the State Floor in 1867.

In 1869, Julia Tyler launched the first lady portrait collection when she donated her own 1848 portrait by Francesco Anelli. Lucy Hayes later urged Congress to commission a full-length portrait of Martha Washington to pair with the Stuart portrait of George Washington, her face based on a life portrait by the same artist. Beginning in the 1880s, both presidents and first ladies selected prominent artists to paint their portraits; Theodore Roosevelt was painted by the illustrious John Singer Sargent, and William Howard Taft by the distinguished Swedish artist Anders Zorn. In 1902, Edith Roosevelt turned the Ground Floor Corridor into a gallery of first ladies' portraits. Grace Coolidge sat for Howard Chandler Christy, one of the leading portraitists of the day in 1924. Lou Hoover introduced the genre of history paintings to the White House and continued to seek out presidential portraits. In 1947 the government purchased another Healy painting, *The Peacemakers* (1868), which recreated a historic meeting of Civil War leaders with Abraham Lincoln. Years later, with Patricia Nixon's support, eighteen portraits of presidents and first ladies were added to the collection, including portraits of President and Mrs. John Q. Adams by Gilbert Stuart.

Growth in the fine arts collection was further inspired by Jacqueline Kennedy, who in 1961 launched a program to bring America's history to life in the White House. The advisory boards she formed included a Special Committee for White House Paintings. The committee worked to expand and upgrade the presidential portrait collection by replacing copies with original portraits painted from life and also sought out representative landscapes and still-lifes by America's finest painters. It is a program that has continued to this day with the support and interest of the presidents and first ladies and the advice of the Committee for the Preservation of the White House, resulting in a collection that now numbers more than 450 works of art. Included are a broad range of paintings by such noted American artists as George Caleb Bingham, Albert Bierstadt, Thomas Eakins, Mary Cassatt, Thomas Moran, and Georgia O'Keeffe.

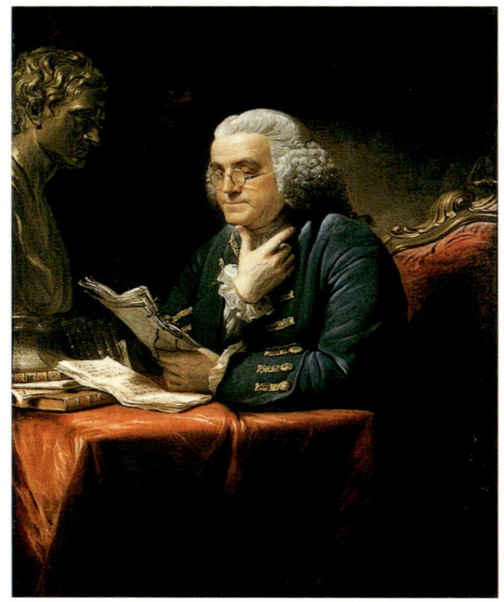

DAVID MARTIN (1737–1798) · *Benjamin Franklin,* 1767
Oil on canvas on panel, 50 1/16 x 39 15/16 in. (127.2 x 101.4 cm)

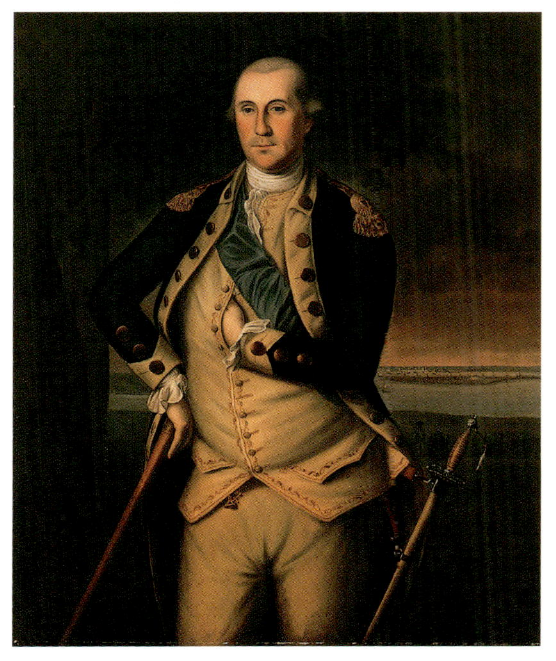

Charles Willson Peale (1741–1827) · *George Washington,* 1776
Oil on canvas, 50 x 39 15/16 in. (127 x 101.4 cm)

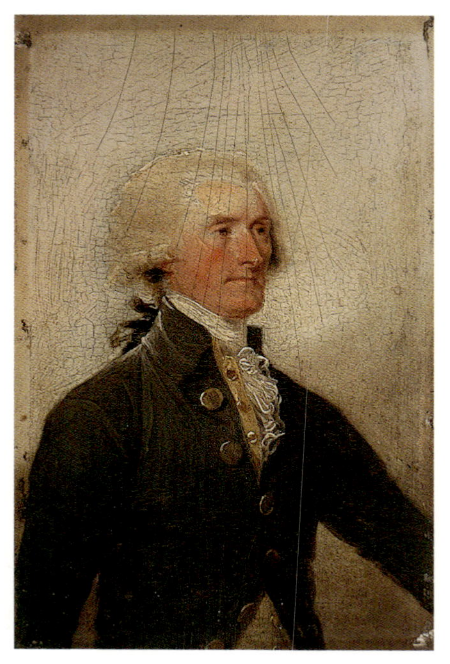

JOHN TRUMBULL (1756–1843) · *Thomas Jefferson,* 1788
Oil on panel, 4¾ x 3 in. (12.1 x 7.6 cm)

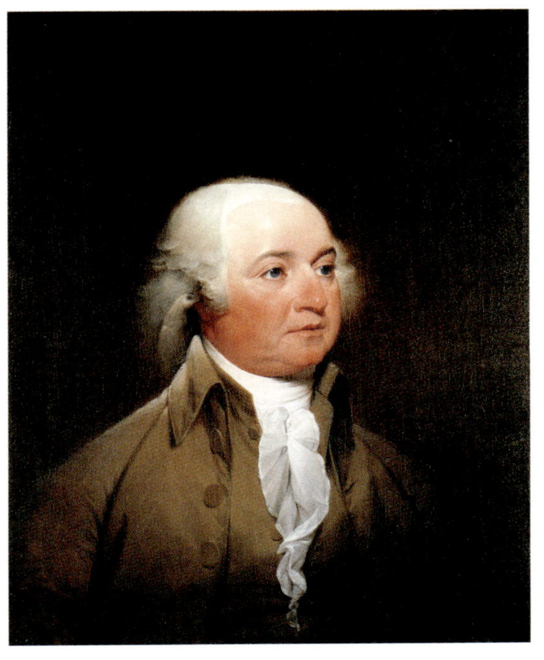

JOHN TRUMBULL (1756–1843) · *John Adams*, c. 1792–93
Oil on canvas, 30 1/16 x 24 in. (76.4 x 61 cm)

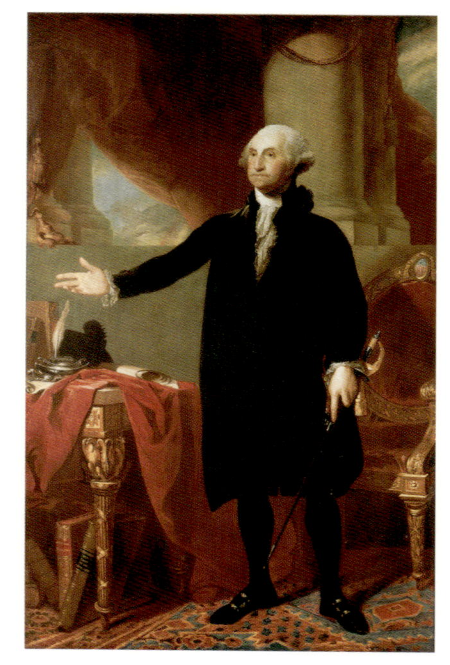

GILBERT STUART (1755–1828) · *George Washington*, 1797
Oil on canvas, 95 x 59 13/16 in. (241.3 x 151.9 cm)

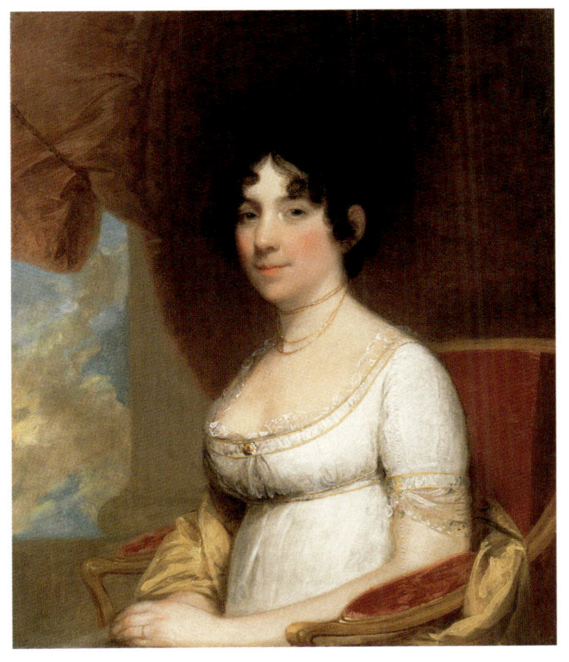

GILBERT STUART (1755–1828) · *Dolley Payne Madison,* 1804
Oil on canvas, 29 3/16 x 24 1/8 in. (74.1 x 61.3 cm)

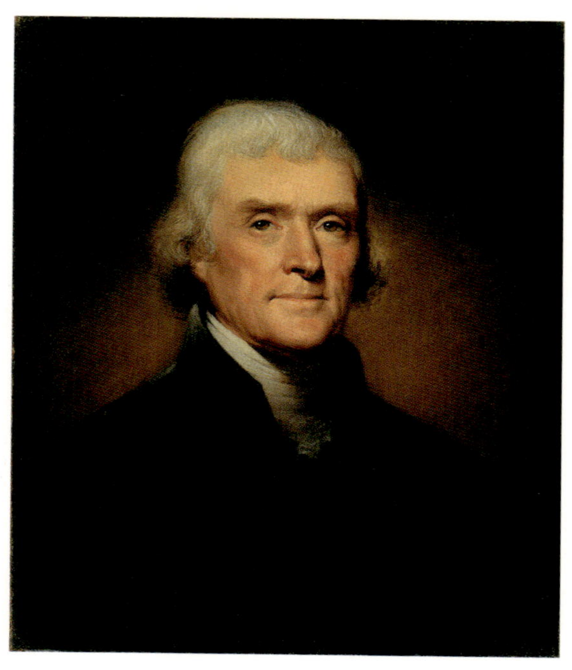

REMBRANDT PEALE (1778–1860) · *Thomas Jefferson,* 1800
Oil on canvas, 23 1/8 x 19 1/4 in. (58.7 x 48.9 cm)

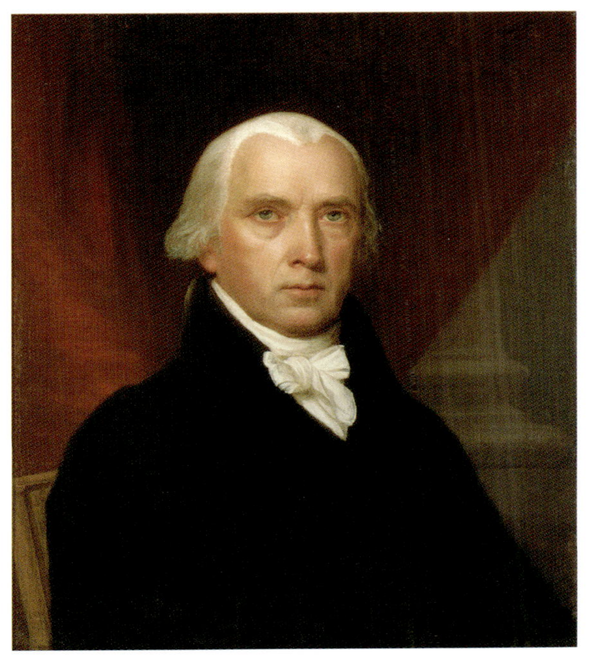

JOHN VANDERLYN (1775–1852) · *James Madison,* 1816
Oil on canvas, 26 x 22 3/16 in. (66 x 56.4 cm)

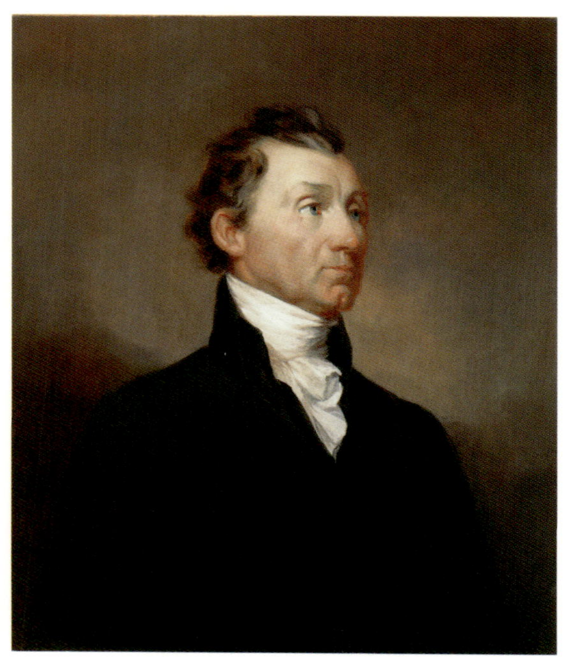

Samuel F. B. Morse (1791–1872)
*James Monroe,* c. 1819
Oil on canvas, 29 5/8 x 24 5/8 in. (75.2 x 62.6 cm)

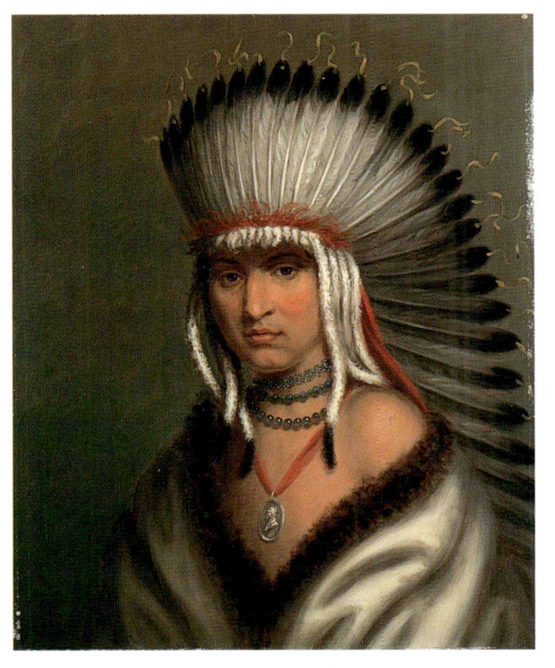

Charles Bird King (1785–1862)
*Petalesharro (Generous Chief), Pawnee,* c. 1822
Oil on panel, 17 1/2 x 13 13/16 in. (44.5 x 35.1 cm)

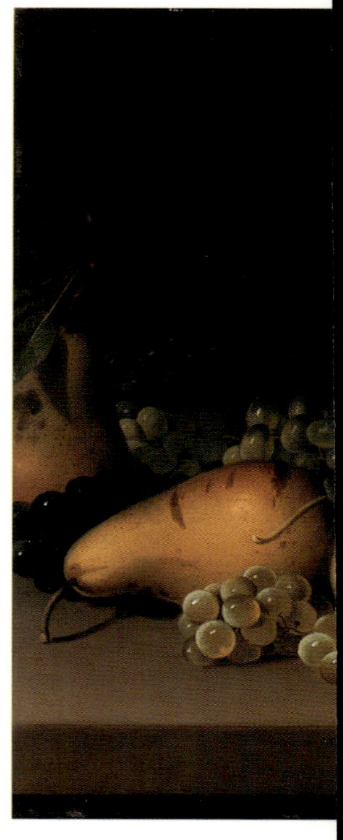

James Peale (1749–1831)
*Fruit in a Chinese Export Basket,* 1822
Oil on canvas on panel, 16 5/8 x 21 3/4 in.
(42.2 x 55.2 cm)

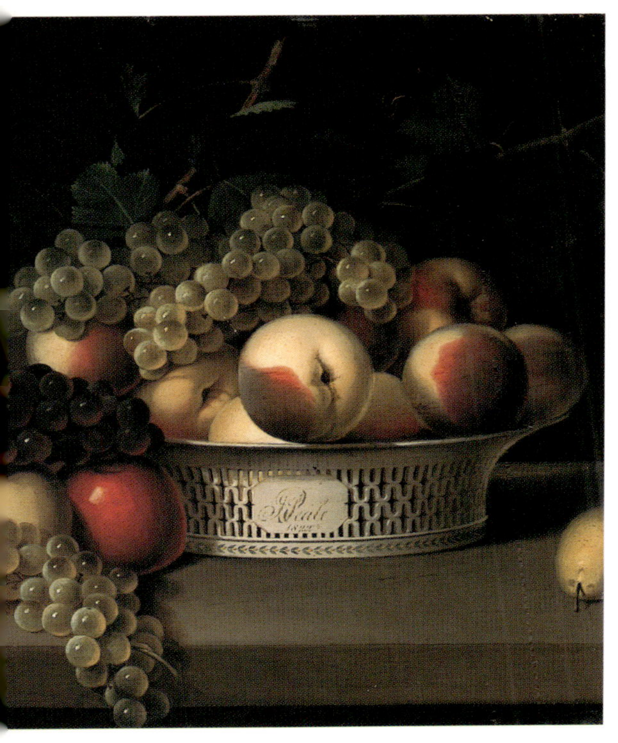

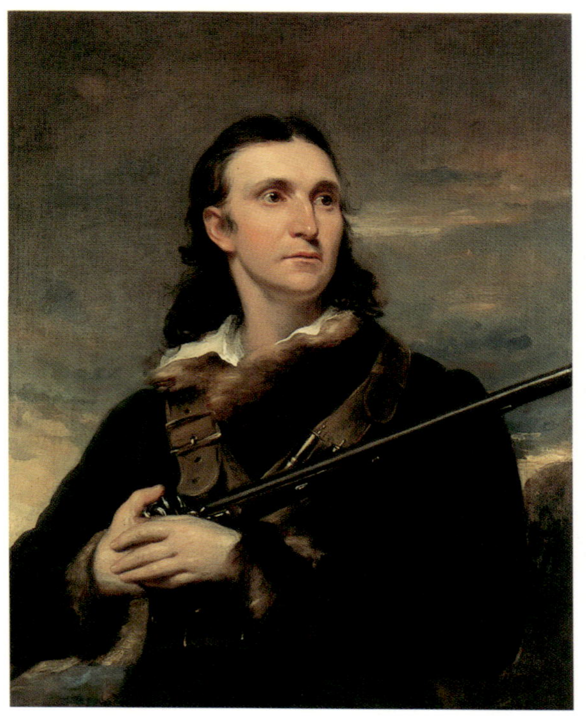

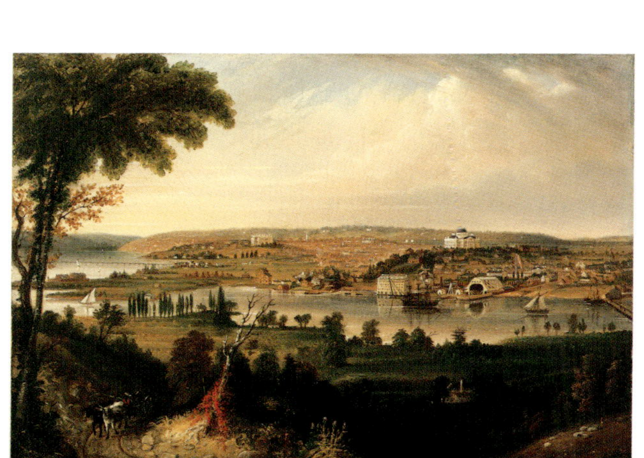

OPPOSITE: JOHN SYME (1795–1861) · *John James Audubon,* 1826
Oil on canvas, $35^{1}/2$ x $27^{1}/2$ in. (90.2 x 69.8 cm)
ABOVE: GEORGE COOKE (1793–1849)
*City of Washington From Beyond the Navy Yard,* 1833
Oil on canvas, 18 x 25 in. (45.7 x 63.5 cm)

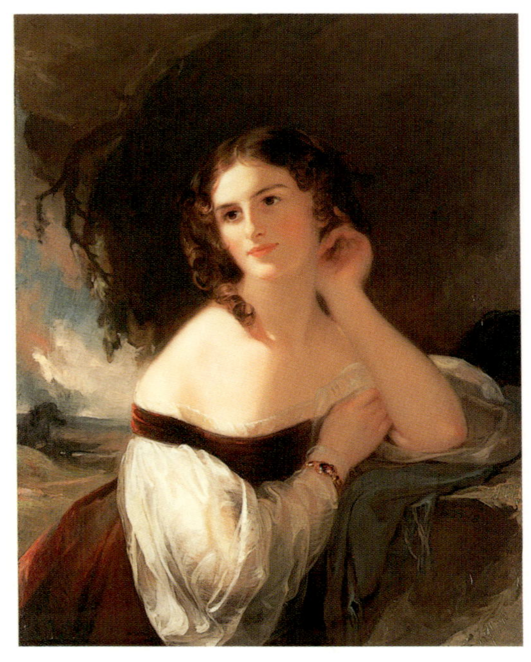

THOMAS SULLY (1783–1872) · *Fanny Kemble,* 1834
Oil on canvas, $36^{1}/8$ x $27^{15}/16$ in. (91.8 x 71 cm)

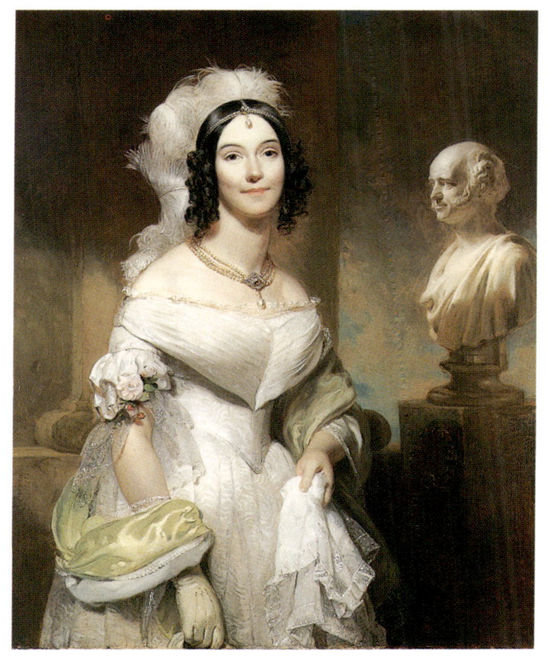

HENRY INMAN (1801–1846) · *Angelica Singleton Van Buren,* 1842
Oil on canvas, $42^{1}/_{4}$ x $33^{5}/_{8}$ in. (107.3 x 85.4 cm)

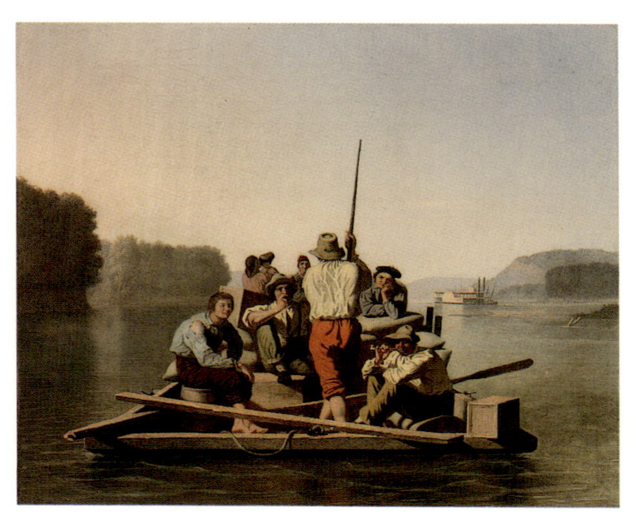

George Caleb Bingham (1811–1879)
*Lighter Relieving a Steamboat Aground*, 1847
Oil on canvas, 30 5/16 x 36 3/16 in. (77 x 91.9 cm)

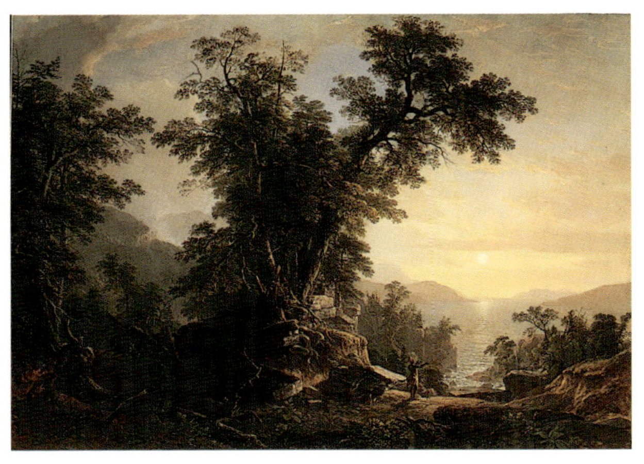

ASHER B. DURAND (1796–1886)
*The Indian's Vespers,* 1847
Oil on canvas, 46 1/8 x 62 1/4 in. (117.2 x 158.1 cm)

FREDERIC E. CHURCH
(1826–1900)
*Rutland Falls, Vermont,* 1848
Oil on canvas,
20 x 29¾ in.
(50.8 x 75.6 cm)

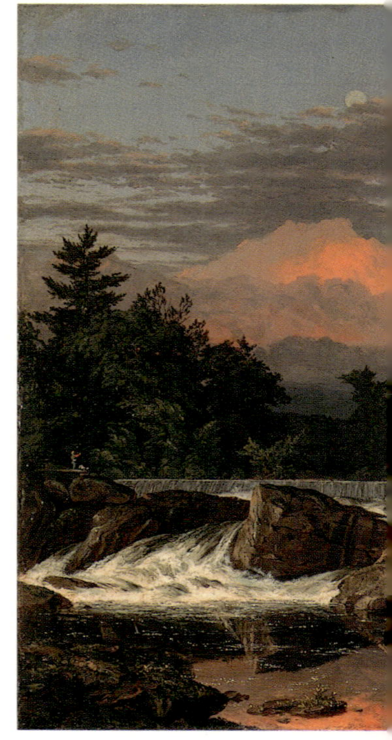

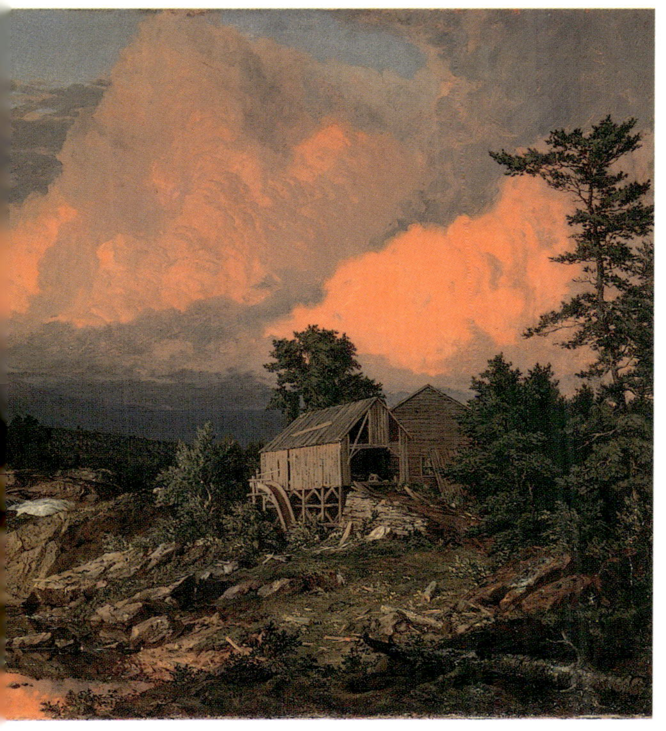

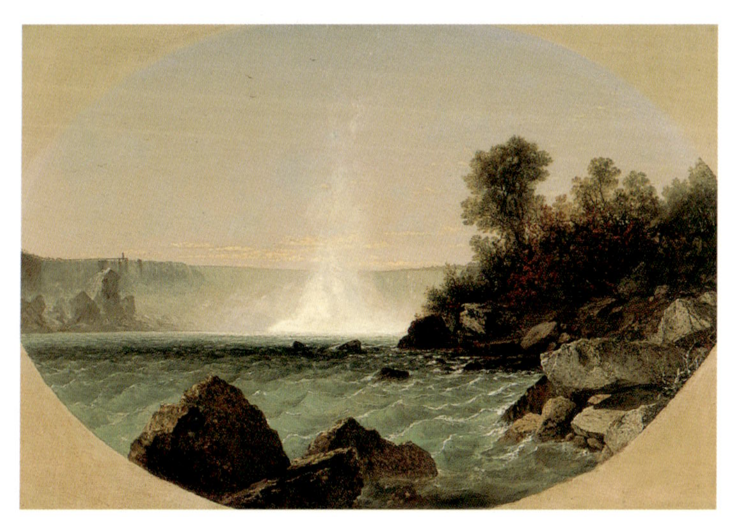

JOHN FREDERICK KENSETT (1816–1872) · *Niagara Falls,* c. 1852–54
Oil on canvas, 32 3/4 x 48 1/16 in. (83.2 x 122.1 cm)

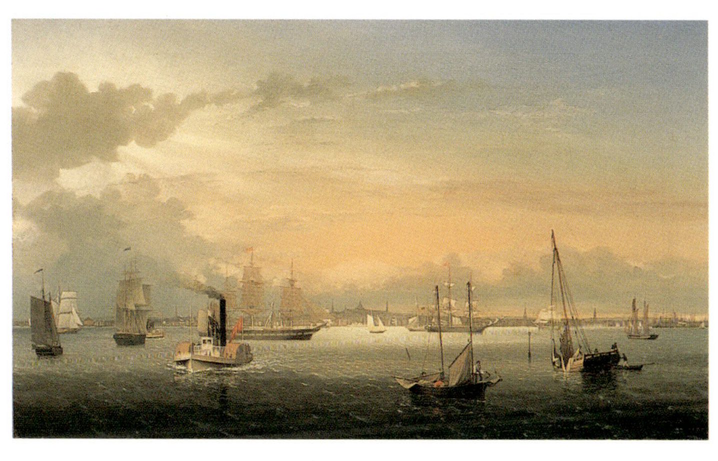

Fitz Hugh Lane (1804–1865) · *Boston Harbor*, 1854
Oil on canvas, 23 1/4 x 39 1/4 in. (59.1 x 99.7 cm)

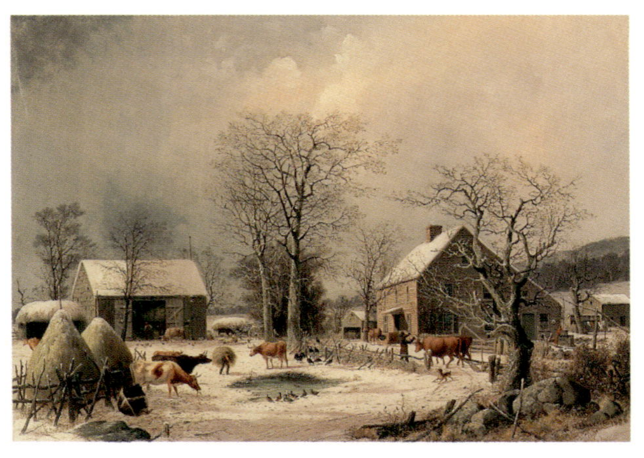

ABOVE: GEORGE HENRY DURRIE (1820–1863)
*Farmyard in Winter,* 1858
Oil on canvas, 26 x $36^{1}/_{8}$ in. (66 x 91.8 cm)
OPPOSITE: GEORGE P. A. HEALY (1813–1894) · *John Tyler,* 1859
Oil on canvas, 62 x $47^{1}/_{8}$ in. (157.5 x 119.7 cm)

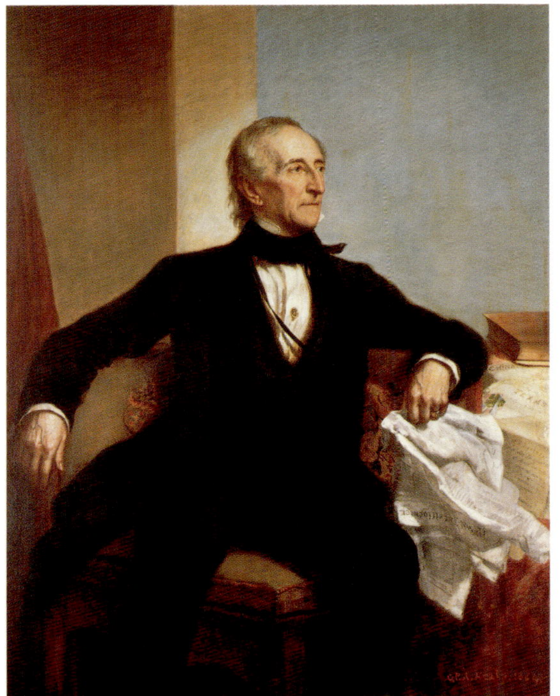

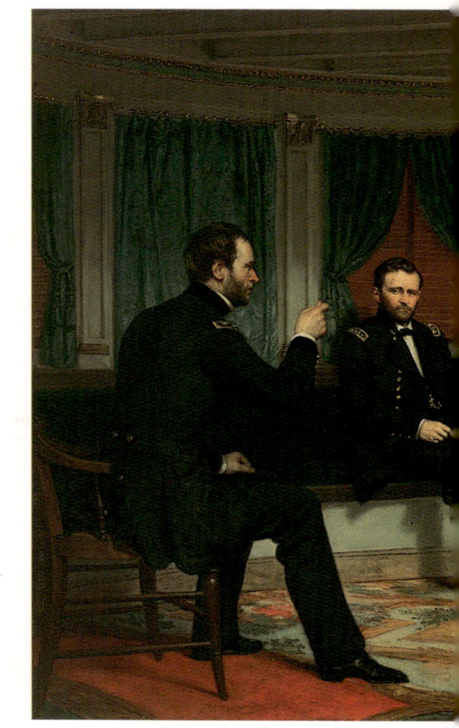

George P. A. Healy
(1813–1894)
*The Peacemakers,* 1868
Oil on canvas,
$47^{1}/8$ x $62^{5}/8$ in.
(119.7 x 159.1 cm)

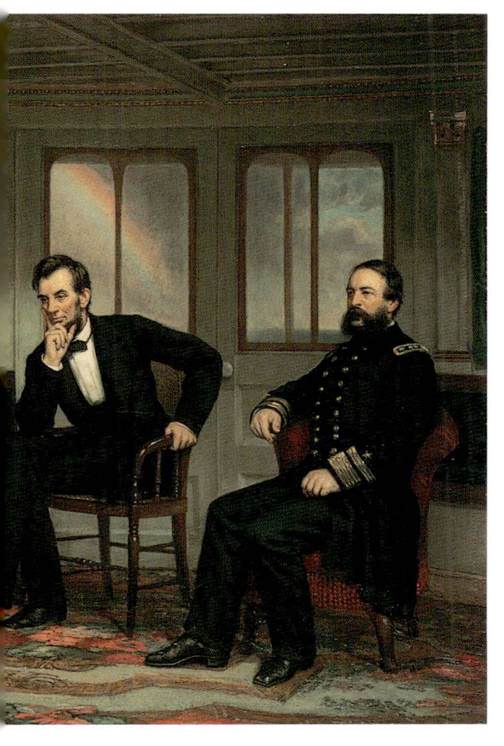

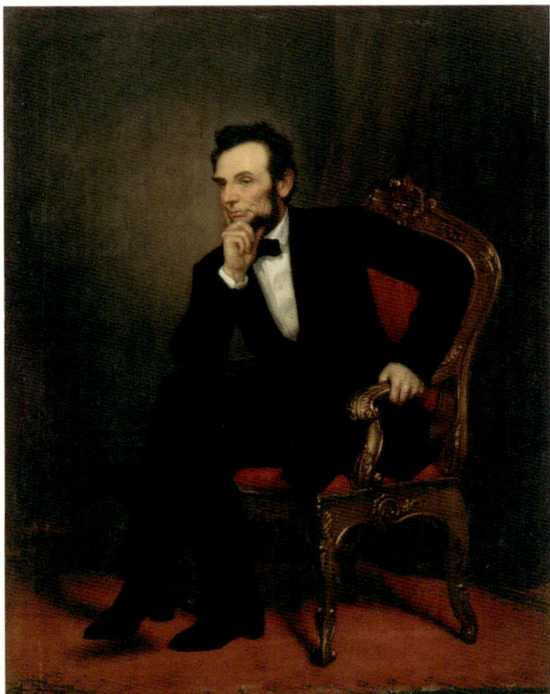

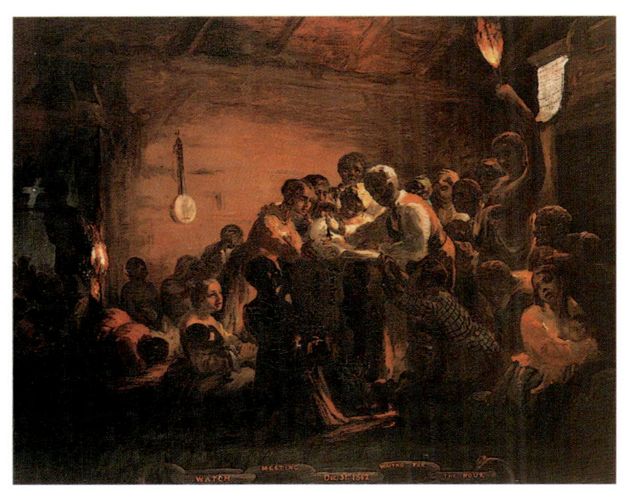


OPPOSITE: GEORGE P. A. HEALY (1813–1894)
*Abraham Lincoln,* 1869
Oil on canvas, 73¾ x 55⅝ in. (187.3 x 141.3 cm)
ABOVE: WILLIAM TOLMAN CARLTON (1816–1888)
*Watch Meeting—Dec. 31st 1862—Waiting for the Hour,* 1863
Oil on canvas, 29⅜ x 36¼ in. (74.6 x 92.1 cm)

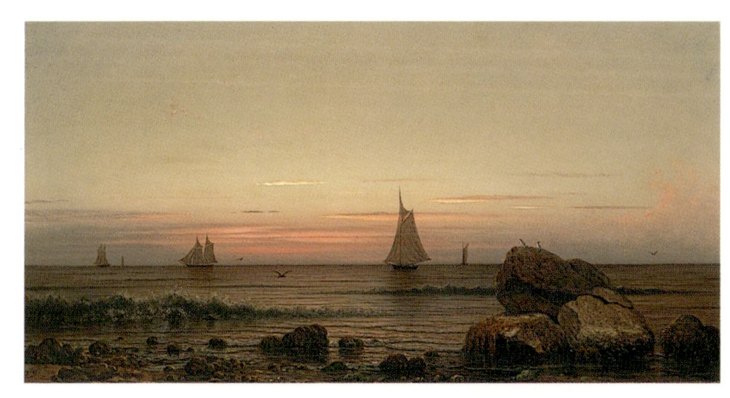

MARTIN JOHNSON HEADE (1819–1904) · *Sailing off the Coast,* 1869
Oil on canvas, 15 1/8 x 29 1/8 in. (38.4 x 74 cm)

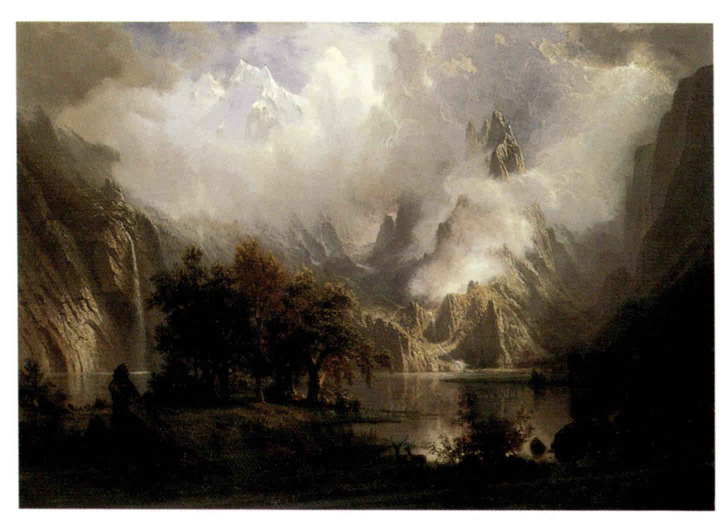

ALBERT BIERSTADT (1830–1902) · *Rocky Mountain Landscape,* 1870
Oil on canvas, $36^{5}/8$ x $54^{3}/4$ in. (93 x 139.1 cm)

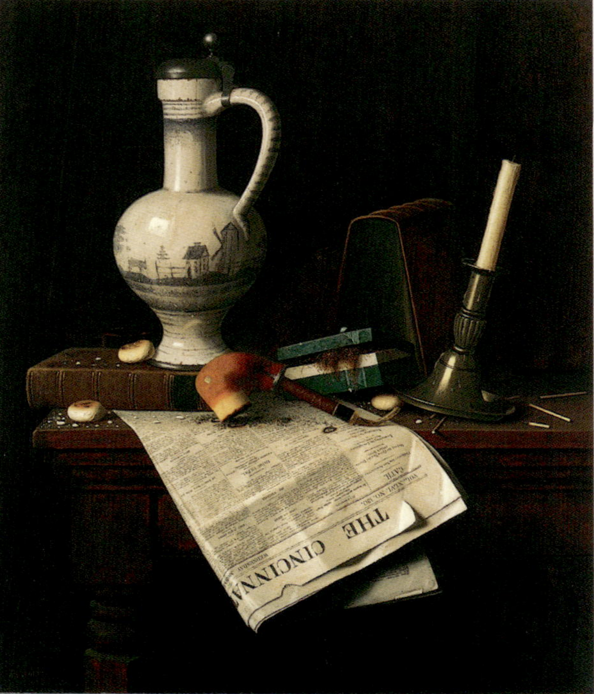

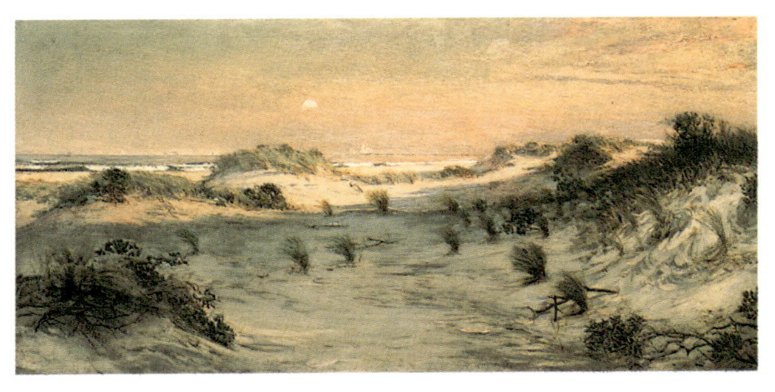

OPPOSITE: WILLIAM M. HARNETT (1848–1892)
*The Cincinnati Enquirer,* 1888
Oil on canvas, 30 x 25 in. (76.2 x 63.5 cm)
ABOVE: HENRY OSSAWA TANNER (1859–1937)
*Sand Dunes at Sunset, Atlantic City,* c.1885
Oil on canvas, 30 3/16 x 59 7/16 in. (76.7 x 151 cm)

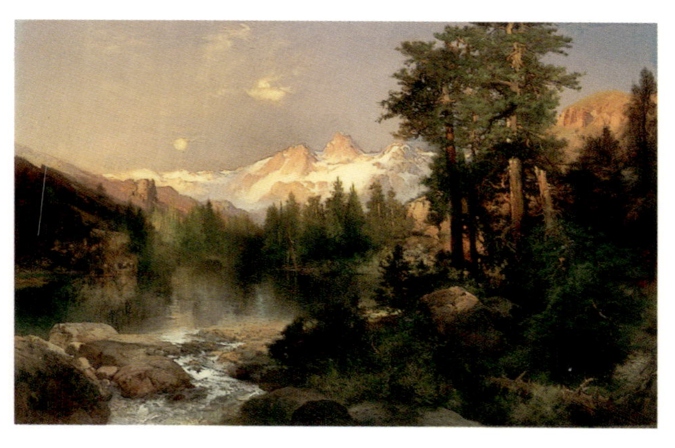

THOMAS MORAN (1837–1926) · *The Three Tetons,* 1895
Oil on canvas, 20 5/8 x 30 1/2 in. (52.4 x 77.5 cm)

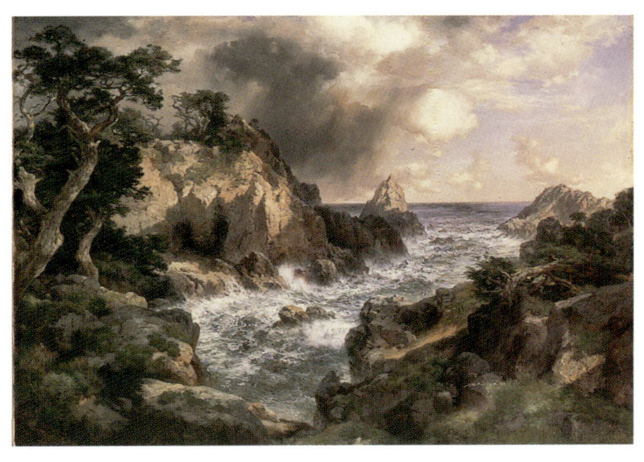

THOMAS MORAN (1837–1926) · *Point Lobos, Monterey, California,* 1912
Oil on canvas, 30 3/16 x 40 1/4 in. (76.7 x 102.2 cm)

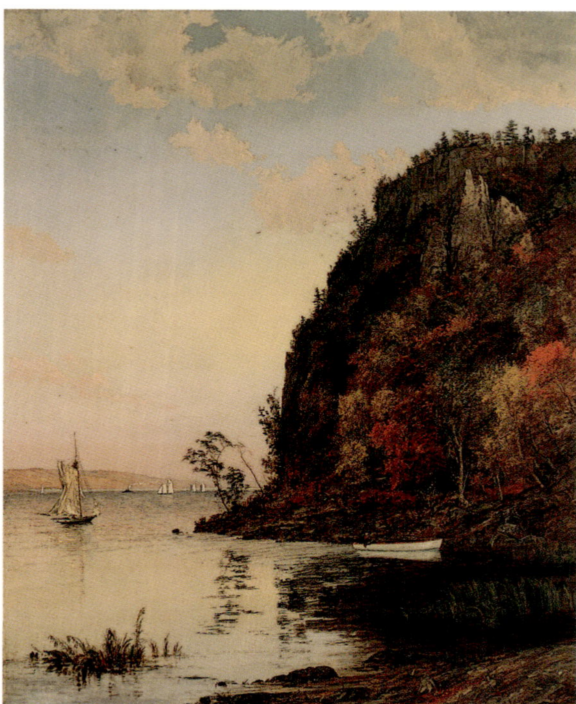

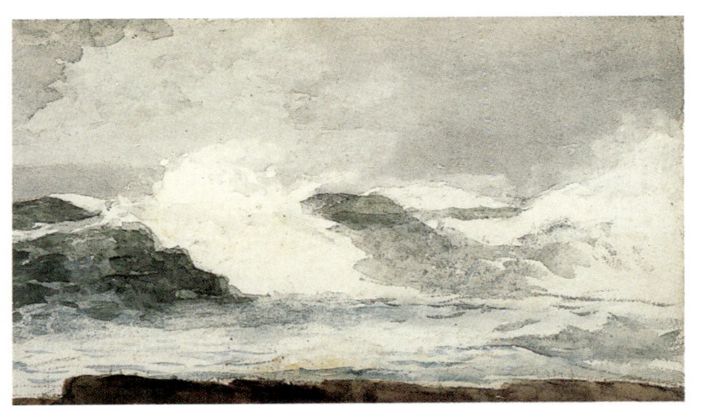

OPPOSITE: JASPER F. CROPSEY (1823–1900)
*Under the Palisades, in October,* 1895
Oil on canvas, 60 x 48 in. (152.4 x 121.9 cm)
ABOVE: WINSLOW HOMER (1836–1910)
*Surf at Prout's Neck,* c. 1895
Watercolor on paper, 12¼ x 21½ in. (31.1 x 54.6 cm)

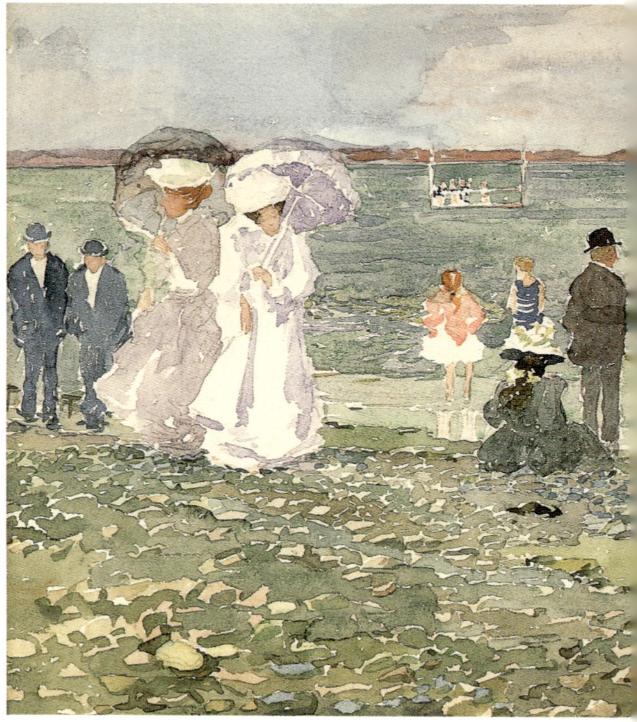

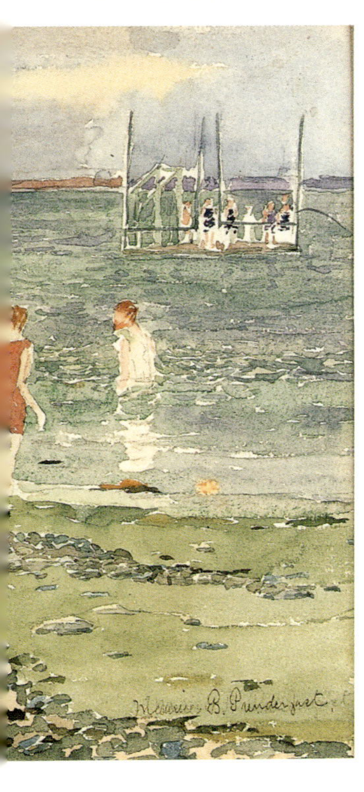

MAURICE B PRENDERGAST
(1858–1924)
*Revere Beach*, c. 1896–97
Watercolor and pencil on paper,
$9^{1}/_{2}$ x 12 in. (24.1 x 30.5 cm)

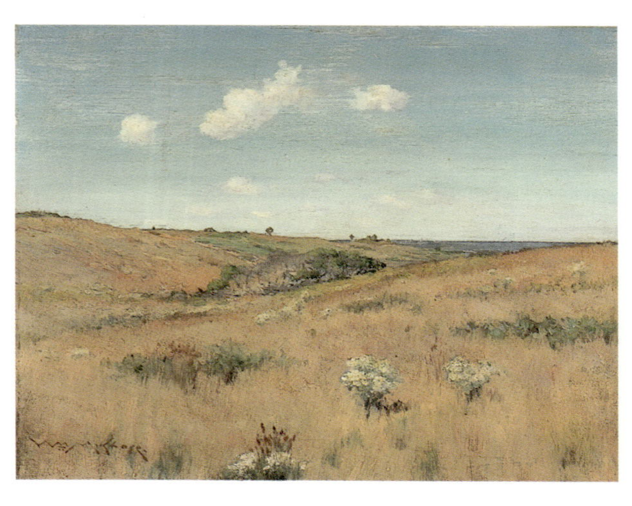

WILLIAM MERRITT CHASE (1849–1916)
*Shinnecock Hills, Long Island,* 1900
Oil on panel, $14^{1}/_{2}$ x $18^{5}/_{8}$ in. (36.8 x 47.3 cm)

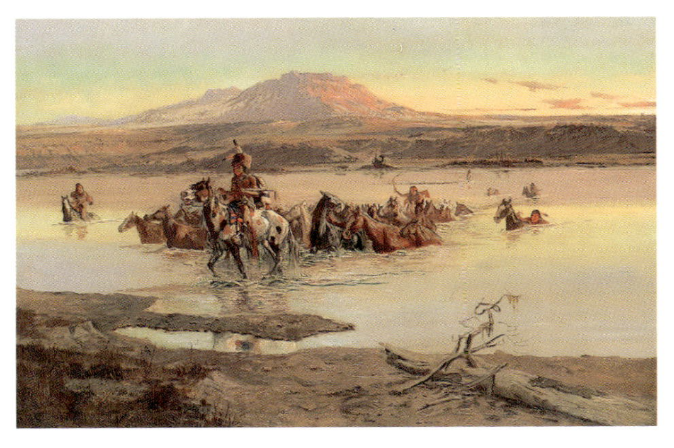

CHARLES M. RUSSELL (1864–1926)
*Fording the Horse Herd*, 1900
Oil on canvas, 24 x 36 in. (61 x 91.4 cm)

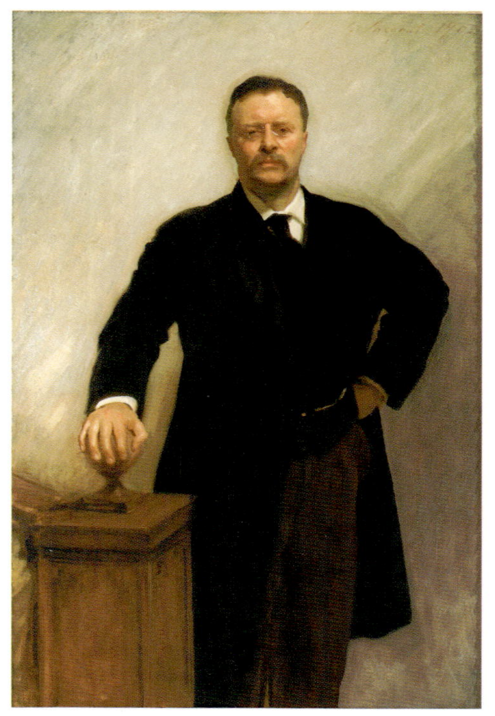

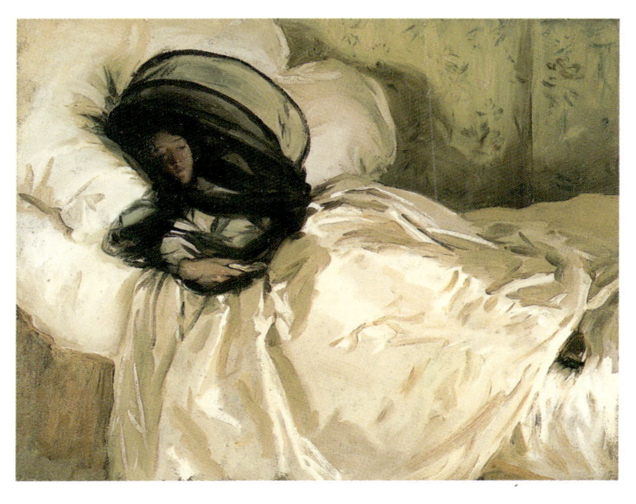

OPPOSITE: JOHN SINGER SARGENT (1856–1925)
*Theodore Roosevelt,* 1903
Oil on canvas, $58^{1}/8$ x 40 in. (147.6 x 101.6 cm)
ABOVE: JOHN SINGER SARGENT (1856–1925)
*The Mosquito Net,* 1912
Oil on canvas, $22^{5}/8$ x $28^{1}/2$ in. (57.5 x 72.4 cm)

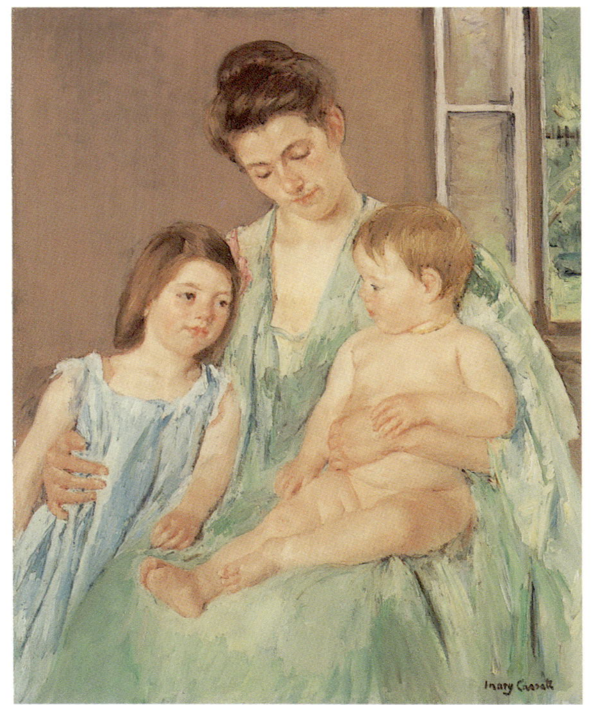
Mary Cassatt

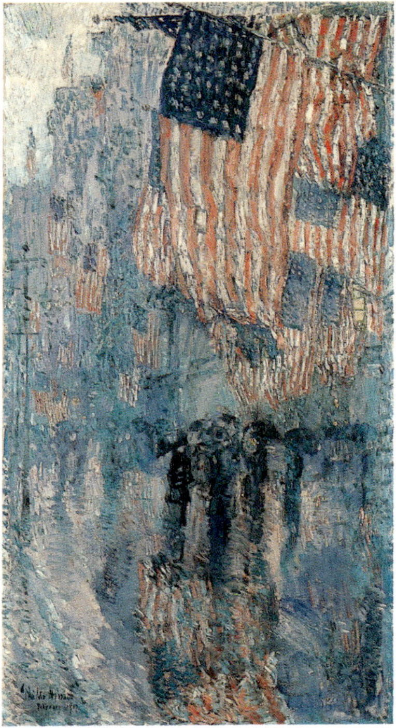

OPPOSITE:
MARY CASSATT
(1844–1926)
*Young Mother and Two Children,* 1908
Oil on canvas $36^{3}/_{8}$ x 29 in. (92.4 x 73.7 cm)
RIGHT:
CHILDE HASSAM
(1859–1935)
*The Avenue in the Rain,* 1917
Oil on canvas, 42 x $22^{1}/_{4}$ in. (106.7 x 56.5 cm)

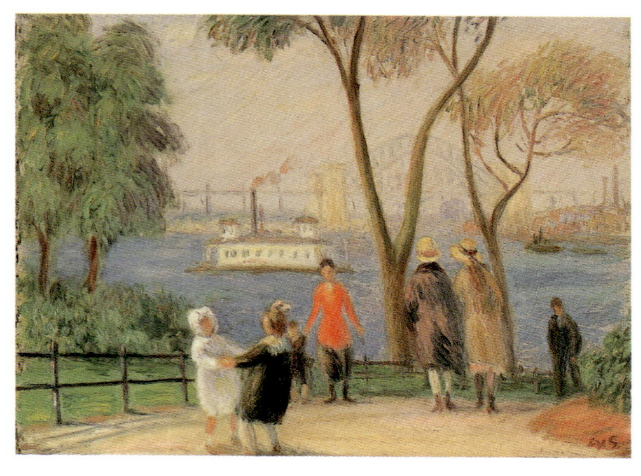

ABOVE: WILLIAM GLACKENS (1870–1938)
*Carl Schurz Park, New York,* c. 1922
Oil on canvas, 18 x 24 1/16 in. (45.7 x 61.1 cm)
OPPOSITE: THOMAS EAKINS (1844–1916) · *Ruth,* 1903
Oil on canvas, 24 3/16 x 20 1/4 in. (61.4 x 51.4 cm)

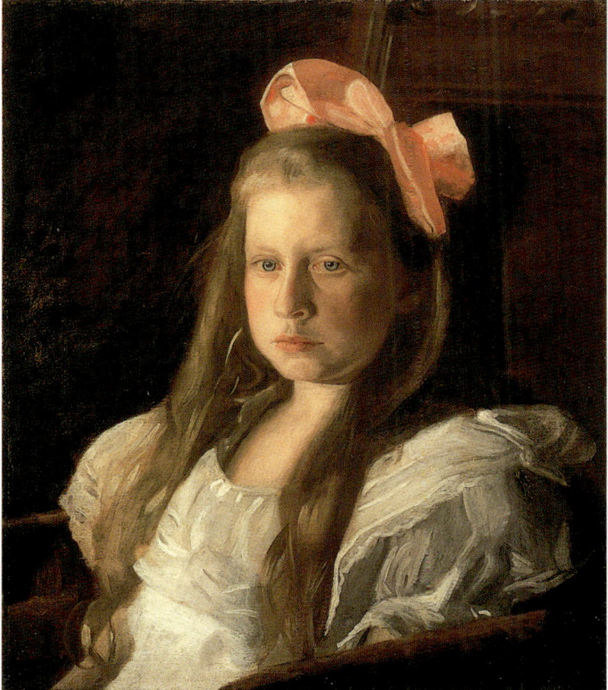

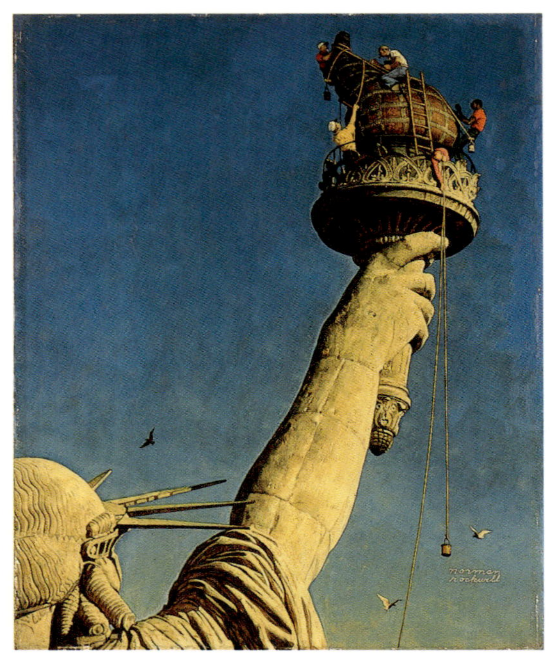


NORMAN ROCKWELL (1894–1978) · *Statue of Liberty,* 1946
Oil on panel, 21 1/2 x 16 15/16 in. (54.6 x 43 cm)

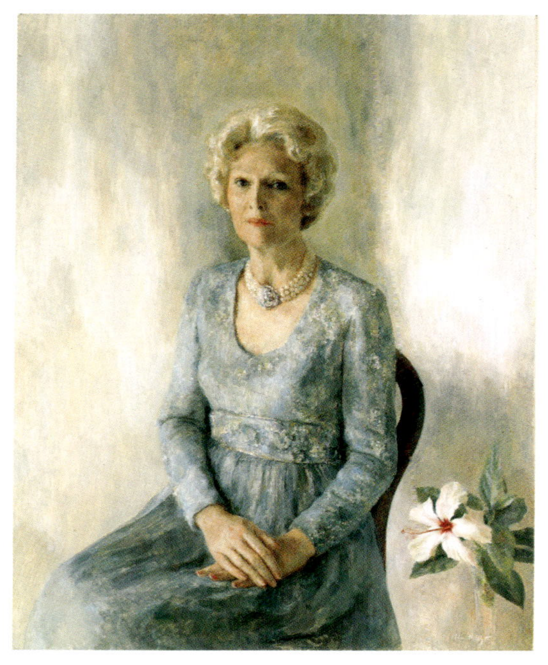

HENRIETTE WYETH (1907–1997) · *Patricia Ryan Nixon*, 1978
Oil on canvas, 45 7/8 x 36 in. (116.5 x 91.4 cm)

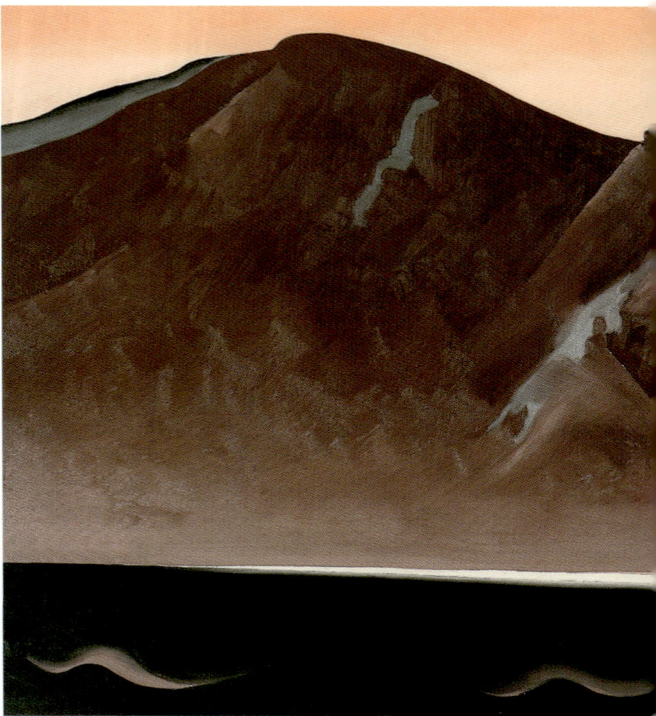

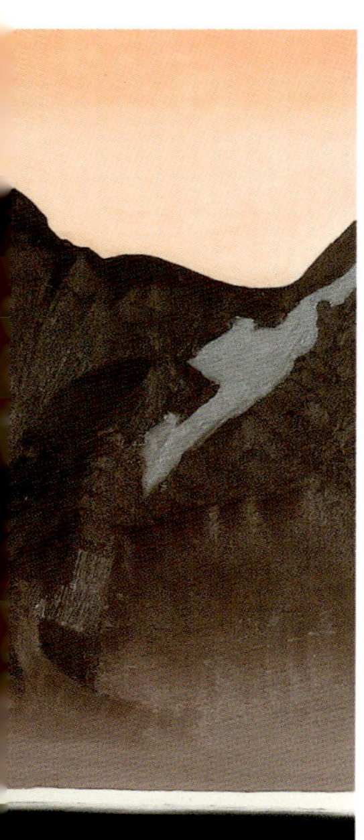

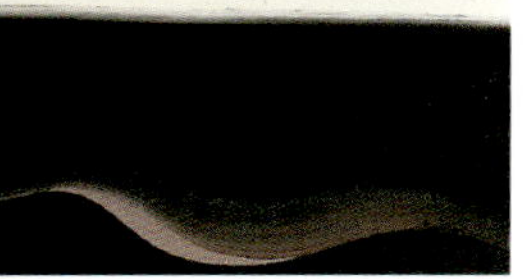

GEORGIA O'KEEFFE (1887–1986)
*Bear Lake, New Mexico,* 1930
Oil on canvas, 30 x 40 in.
(76.2 x 101.6 cm)

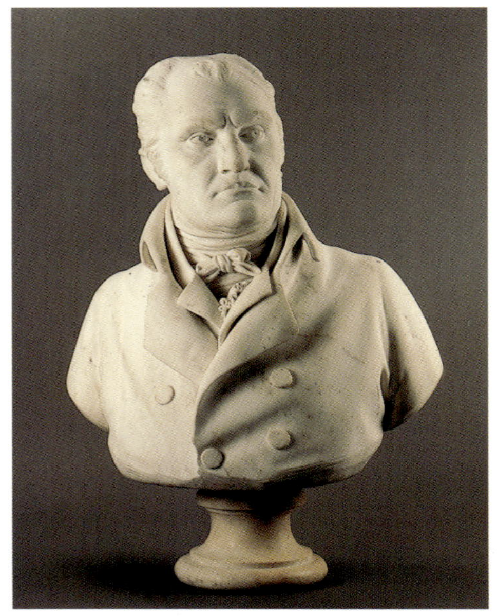

JEAN-ANTOINE HOUDON (1741–1828)
*Joel Barlow*, c. 1804
Marble, $27^{1}/2$ x 19 x $12^{1}/2$ in. (69.8 x 48.3 x 31.8 cm)

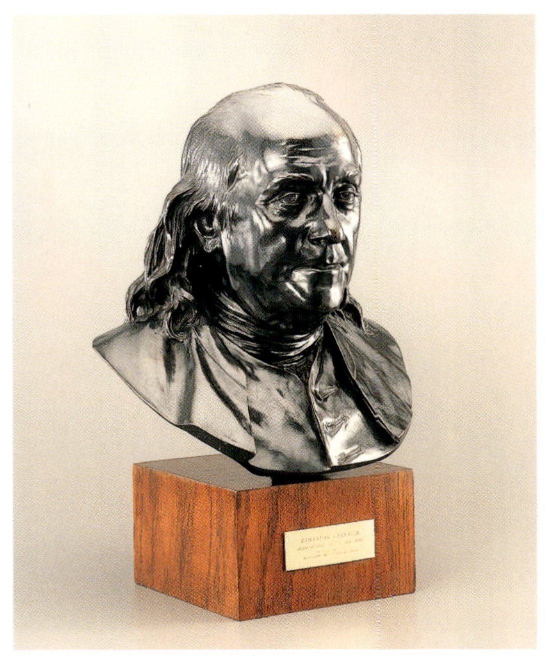

JEAN-ANTOINE HOUDON (1741–1828)
*Benjamin Franklin*, c. 1778–1828
Bronze, 15¾ x 13½ x 9 in. (40 x 34.3 x 22.9 cm)

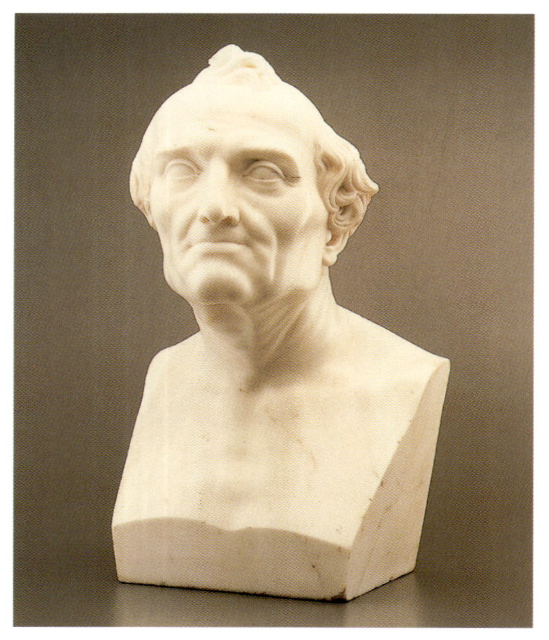

GIUSEPPE CERACCHI (1751–1801)
*Amerigo Vespucci,* modeled c.1790–94, carved c. 1815
Marble, 21 x 12 1/2 x 10 in. (53.3 x 31.8 x 25.4 cm)

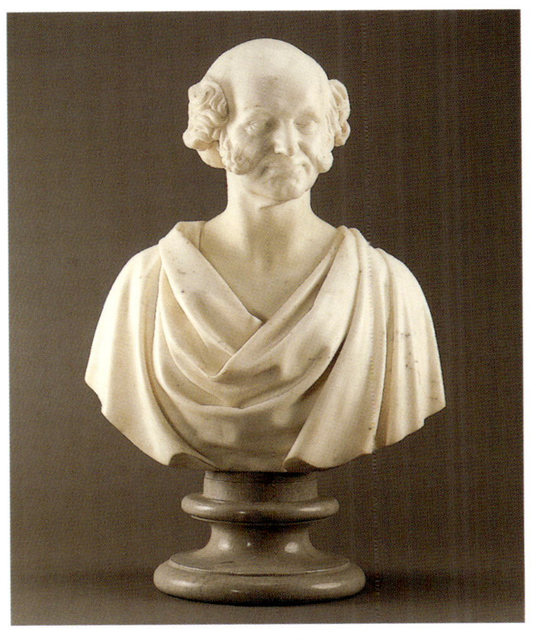

HIRAM POWERS (1805–1873)
*Martin Van Buren,* modeled 1836, carved 1840
Marble, $24^{1}/8$ x $21^{3}/8$ x $13^{1}/2$ in. (61.3 x 54.3 x 34.3 cm)

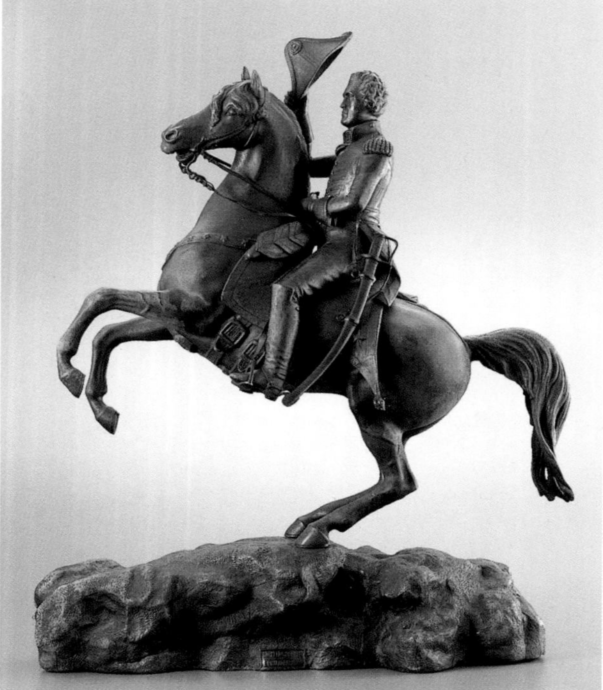

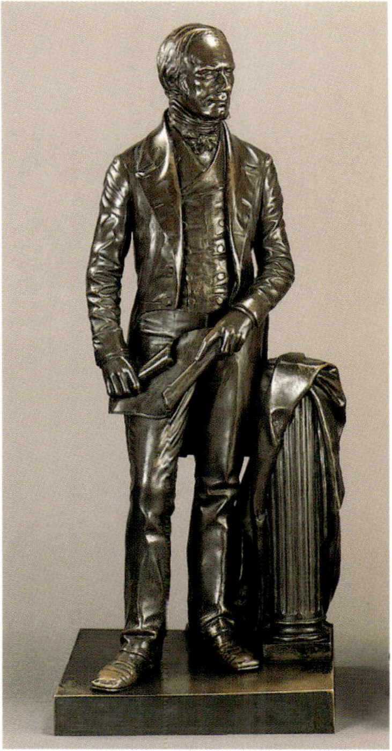

OPPOSITE:
CLARK MILLS
(1815–1883)
*Andrew Jackson,* 1855
White metal,
$23^{3}/_{4}$ x $19^{3}/_{4}$ x $7^{3}/_{4}$ in.
(60.3 x 50.2 x 19.7 cm)
RIGHT:
THOMAS BALL
(1819–1911)
*Henry Clay,* 1858
Bronze, 31 x 12 x $10^{3}/_{4}$ in.
(78.7 x 30.5 x 27.3 cm)

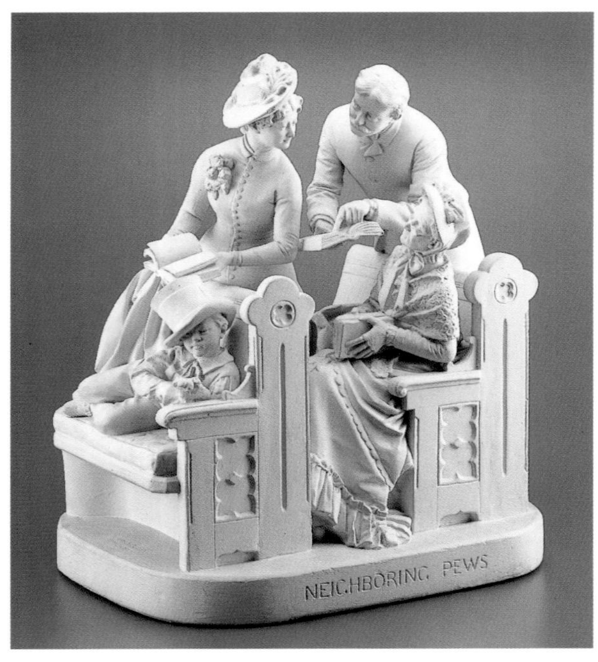


JOHN ROGERS (1829–1904)
*Neighboring Pews*, 1883
Plaster, 18¾ x 16 x 11½ in. (47.6 x 40.6 x 29.2 cm)

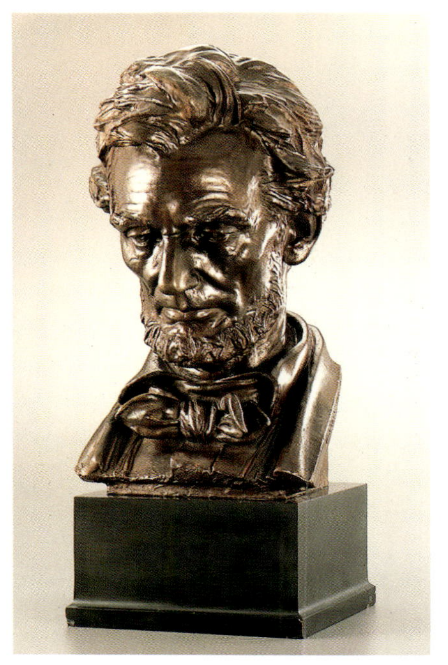

AUGUSTUS SAINT-GAUDENS (1848–1907)
*Abraham Lincoln,* late 19th century
Bronze, 20¾ x 10 x 11⅝ in. (52.7 x 25.4 x 29.5 cm)

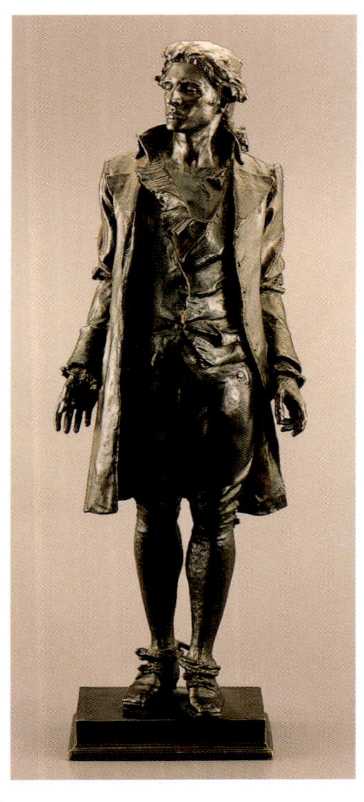

LEFT:
FREDERICK MACMONNIES
(1863–1937)
*Nathan Hale,* c. 1890
Bronze, 28 3/8 x 9 1/2 x 6 in.
(72.1 x 24.1 x 15.2 cm)
OPPOSITE:
FREDERIC REMINGTON
(1861–1909)
*The Bronco Buster,* modeled
1895, cast c. 1903
Bronze, 23 3/8 x 19 7/8 x 12 1/4 in.
(59.4 x 50.5 x 31.1 cm)

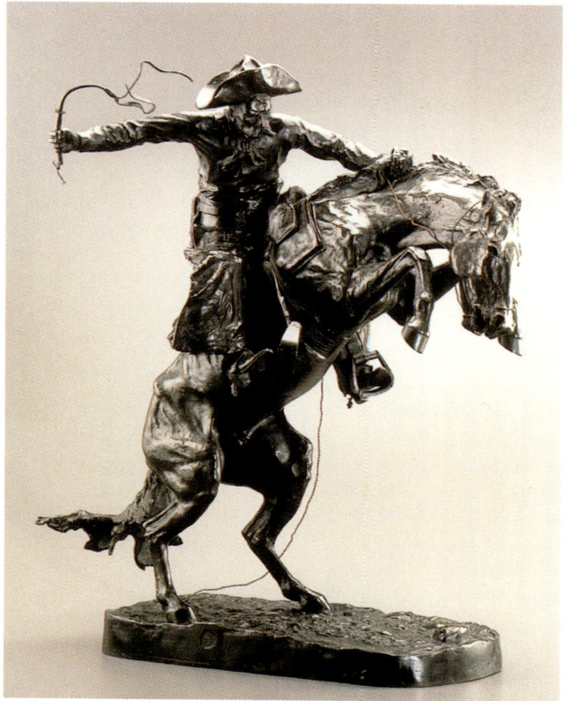

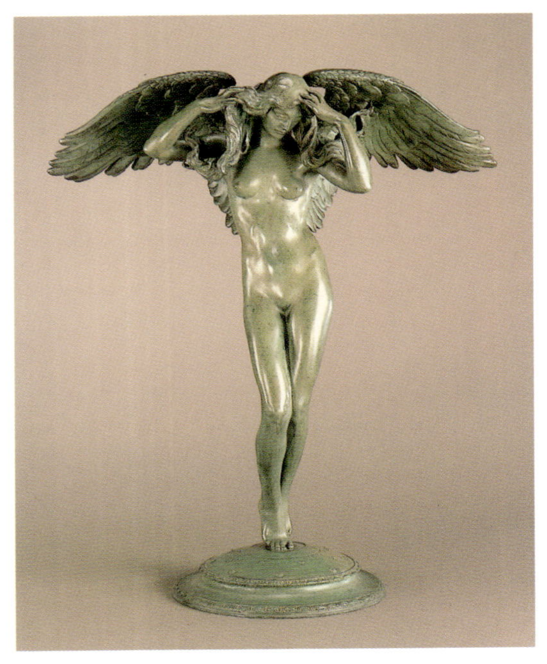

Adolph A. Weinman (1870–1952)
*Descending Night,* modeled c. 1914, cast c. 1915–23
Bronze, 25 1/2 x 21 3/4 x 10 in. (64.8 x 55.2 x 25.4 cm)

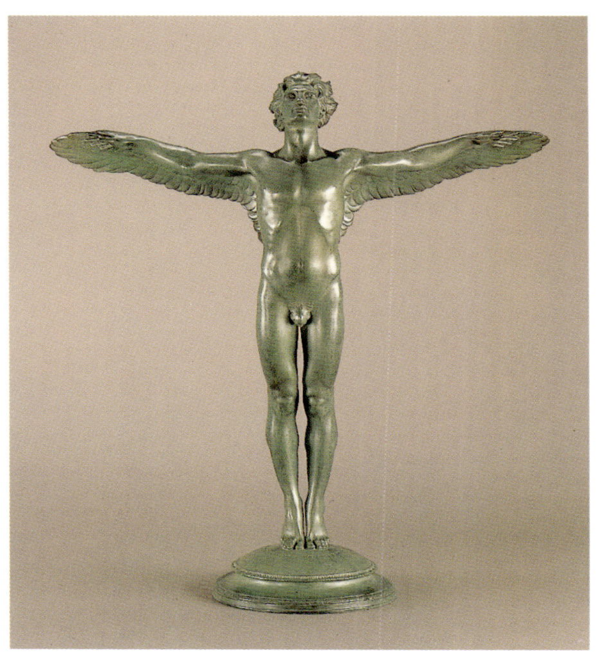

ADOLPH A. WEINMAN (1870–1952)
*Rising Day,* modeled c. 1914, cast c. 1915–23
Bronze, 26 3/4 x 24 7/8 x 9 1/4 in. (68 x 63.2 x 23.5 cm)

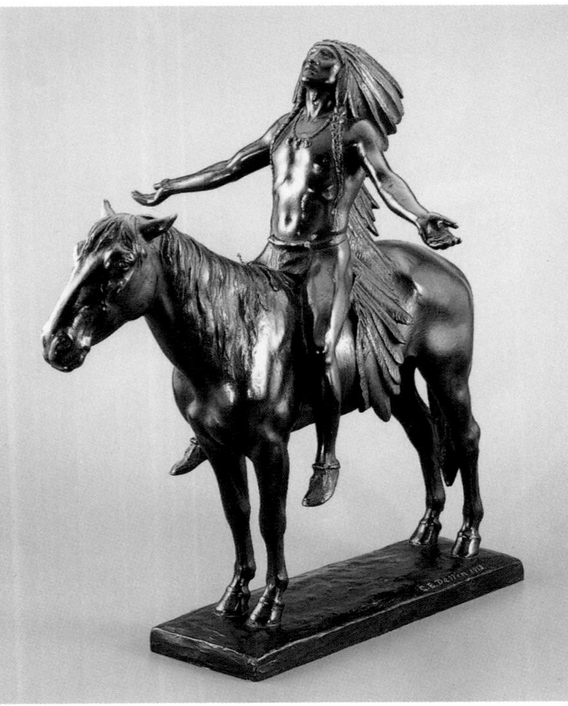
C.E. Dallin

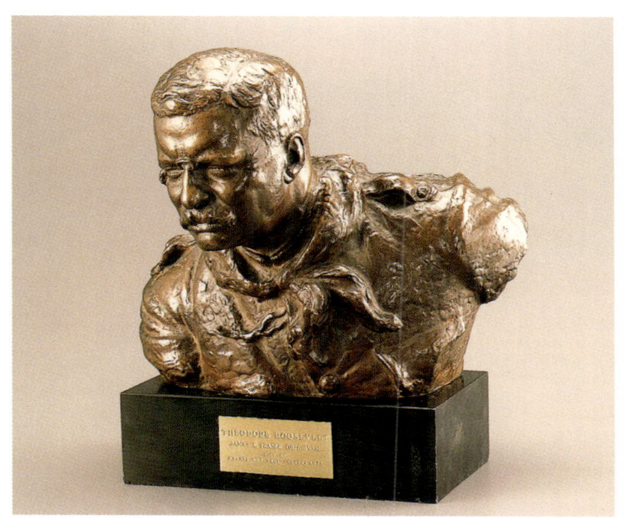


Opposite: Cyrus Edwin Dallin (1861–1944)
*Appeal to the Great Spirit,* c. 1916
Bronze, $21\frac{1}{4} \times 21\frac{3}{4} \times 14\frac{1}{2}$ in. (54 x 55.2 x 36.8 cm)
Above: James Earle Fraser (1876–1953)
*Theodore Roosevelt,* c. 1920
Bronze, $9\frac{1}{4} \times 10\frac{1}{2} \times 8$ in. (23.5 x 26.7 x 20.3 cm)

Overleaf: The State Floor: The Red Room, 2000

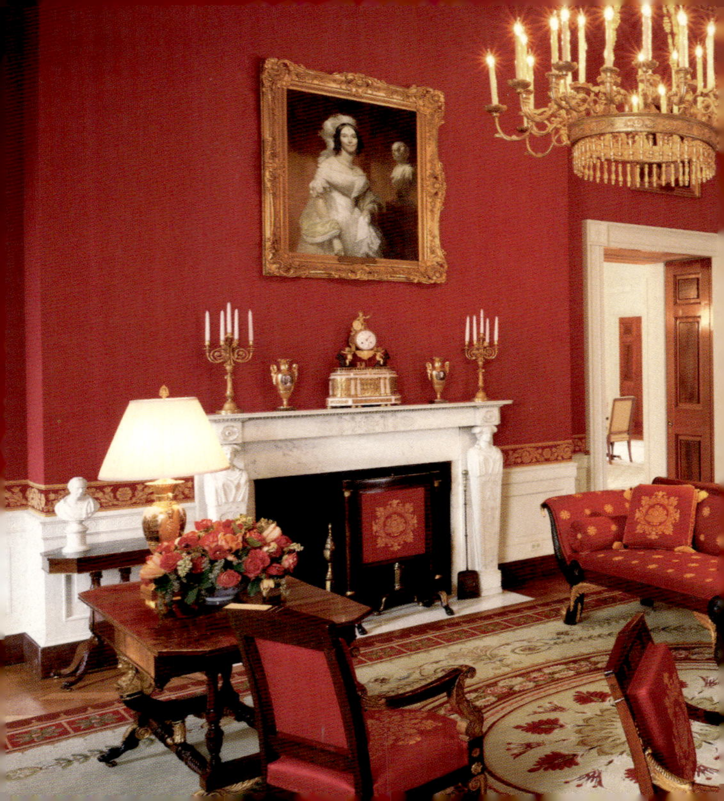

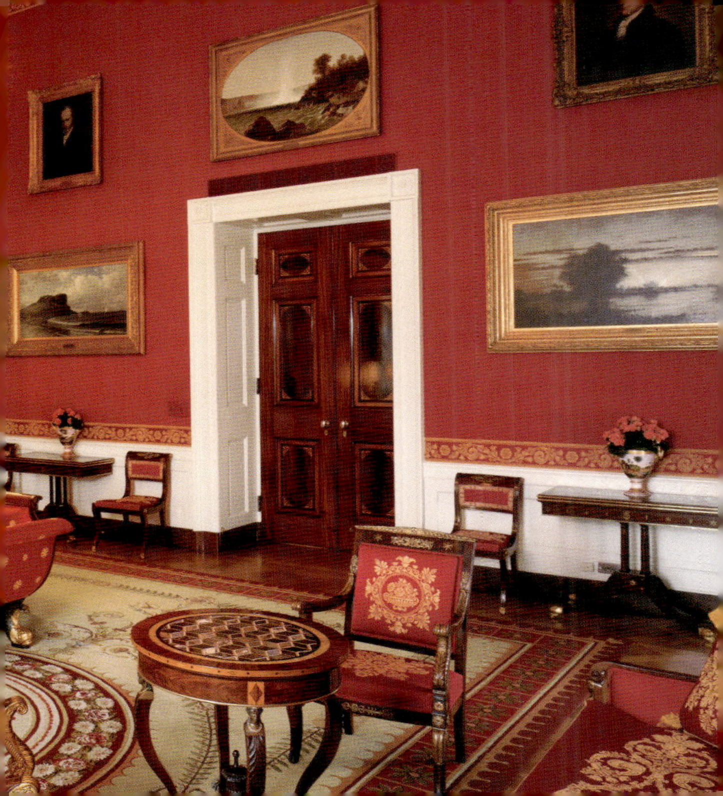

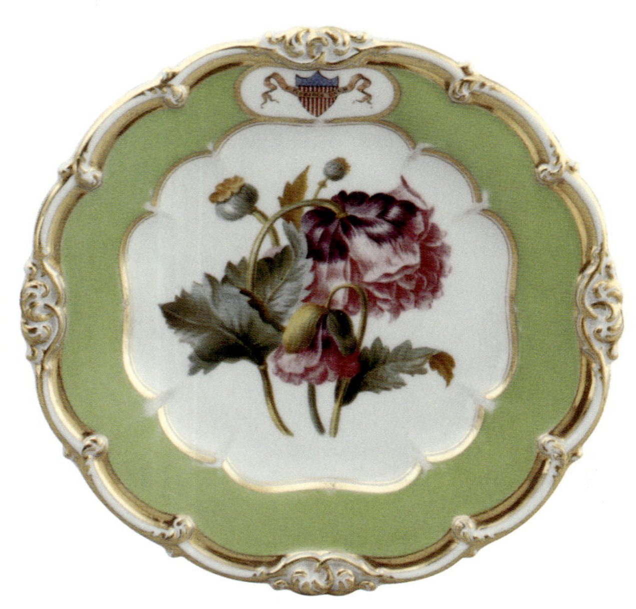

DESSERT PLATE · *1846 · James K. Polk Administration*
(see page 209)

# The Decorative Arts

The nation's presidents and first ladies have been instrumental in forming the White House decorative arts collection. Jacqueline Kennedy's well-known projects brought much attention to the collection, but it was an earlier first lady, Caroline Harrison, who, in the late 1880s, began to assemble historic White House objects. An artist and china painter, Mrs. Benjamin Harrison admired the old state table services she discovered in storage and began a program to preserve them, as well as historic furniture and other furnishings in the White House. Her efforts bore fruit in the McKinley administration, when the first research was begun on White House objects. Edith Roosevelt supported the documentation and put a selection of historic china on public display, prompting Theodore Roosevelt to suggest including pieces from every administration. In 1917, Edith Wilson created a special room off the Ground Floor Corridor for exhibiting the growing china collection, along with a representative selection of White House silver and glassware. There are nearly 900 pieces of nineteenth-century American glass preserved in the White House; the oldest service to survive was ordered by Andrew Jackson in 1829.

In 1814 everything in the White House acquired by the first four presidents, except for some family silver and a full-length portrait of George Washington, was destroyed when the British set fire to the house. It was James Monroe's task to refurnish the rebuilt White House in 1817. Monroe purchased furniture for the White House from American artisans, but it was to the finest French craftsmen of the Empire period that he directed his personal attention, ordering a gilded bronze centerpiece, clocks, candelabra, vases, silver tureens, porcelain dinner and dessert services and vases, and carved and gilded furniture. Many of these treasures remain in the house, including several pieces of furniture sold at auction in 1860 that have been returned to the collection during the last few decades.

In 1902 Theodore Roosevelt, working with architects Charles McKim and Stanford White, decided that the nineteenth-century accumulation of heavily ornamented decoration in the state rooms of the White House was not in harmony with the building's refined architecture. This led to a complete redesign of the public spaces and the last auction of White House objects. Many nineteenth-century pieces were disposed of in favor of more fashionable Colonial Revival items, which today remain in the State Dining Room and East Room.

Grace Coolidge had a strong appreciation for history and began to refurnish White House rooms with antiques in the 1920s. Reluctant to spend government funds on furnishings, she encouraged President Coolidge to persuade Congress in 1925 to pass a joint resolution that permitted the acceptance of gifts and authorized a committee to advise on furnishing the White House. This effort launched the first program to acquire objects by gift and was the beginning of a museum role for the White House. In 1960, Mamie Eisenhower accepted fine early nineteenth-century American furnishings for the Diplomatic Reception Room. This laid the groundwork for the efforts of Jacqueline Kennedy, who in 1961 launched a successful program to acquire historic White House furnishings as well as other excellent examples of American craftsmanship and of encouraging donations to the White House. A substantial acquisitions program in the 1970s was championed by Patricia Nixon. The support of each succeeding administration has further ensured that American decorative arts are collected, preserved, and interpreted in the President's House.

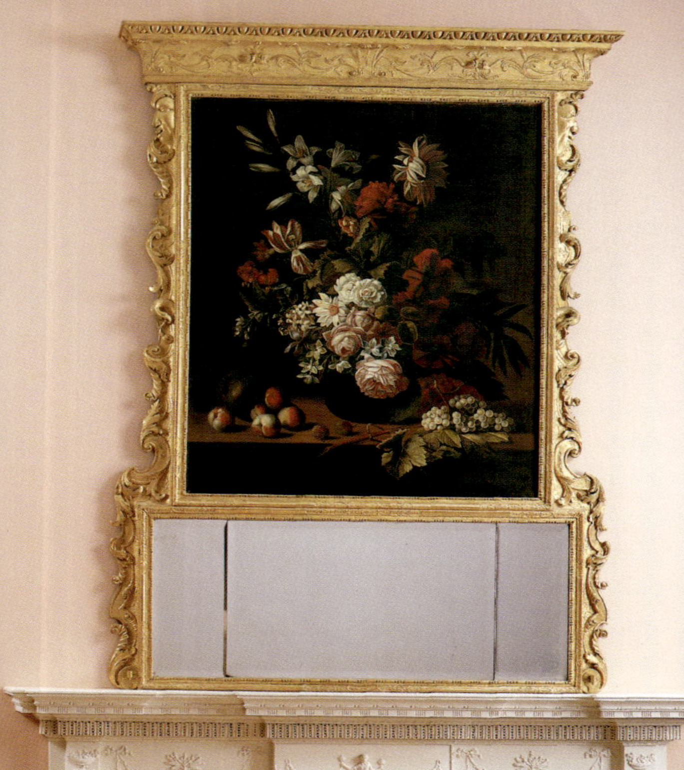

# Furniture

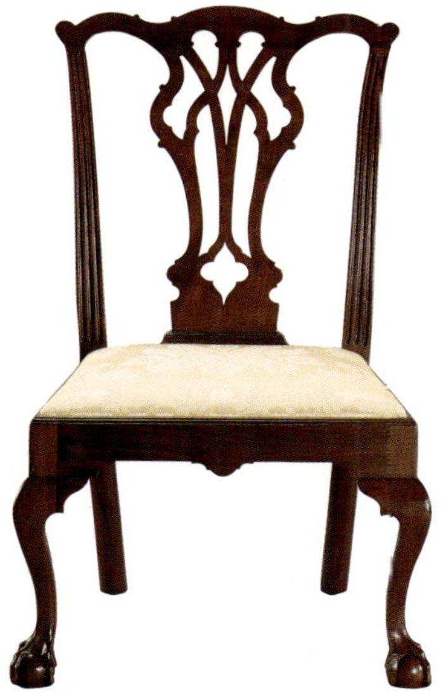

Opposite: Overmantel Glass with Painting · *England, c. 1695*
Gilded red pine, mirror/oil on canvas, 80 x 55 x 4 in. (203.4 x 139.7 x 10.2 cm)
Above: Side Chair · *Philadelphia, c. 1760–85*
Mahogany, 38 1/16 x 23 1/4 x 21 1/2 in. (96.7 x 60.1 x 54.6 cm)
*George Washington Administration*

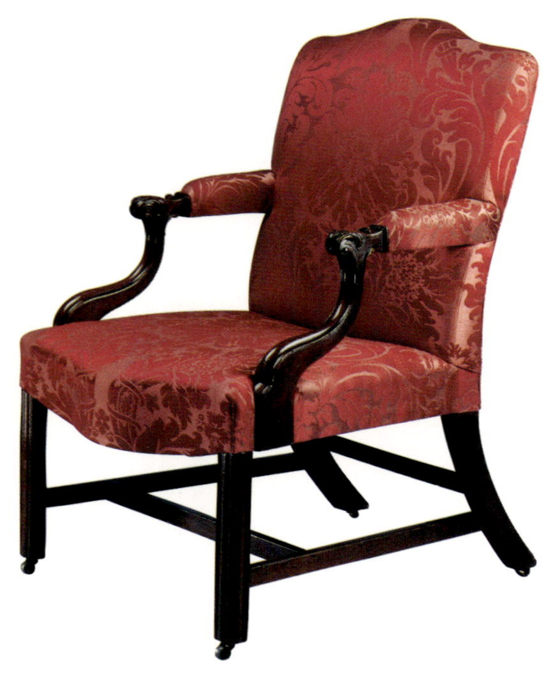

ARMCHAIR · *Possibly by Thomas Affleck (1740–95)*
*Philadelphia, c. 1765–75* · Mahogany
43 x 27 x 31½ in. (109.2 x 68.6 x 80 cm)

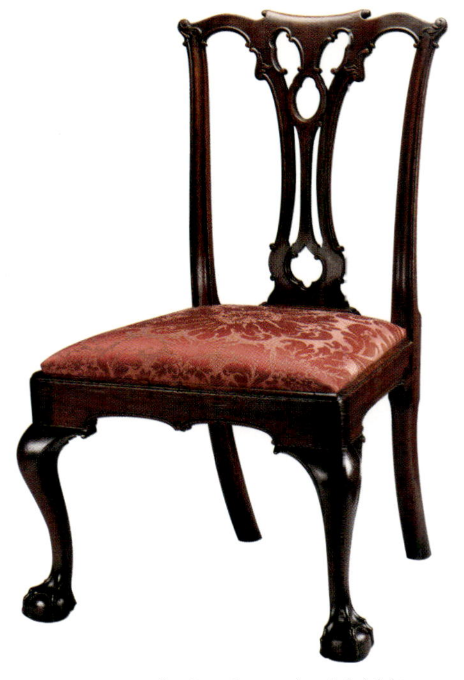

SIDE CHAIR · *James Gillingham (1736–81)* · *Philadelphia, c. 1768–73*
Mahogany, 38¾ x 23½ x 18½ in. (98.5 x 59.7 x 47 cm)

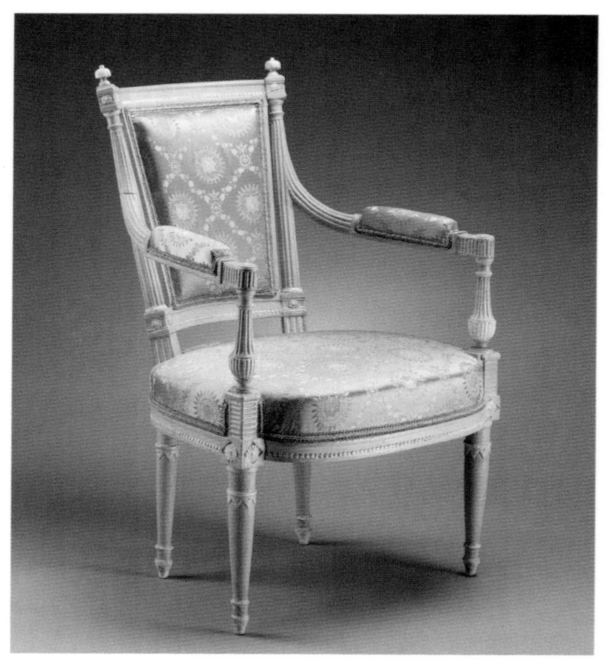

ARMCHAIR · *France, c. 1780–85*
Painted walnut, 34 x 24 3/4 x 23 in. (86.4 x 62.9 x 58.4 cm)
*Belonged to George Washington*

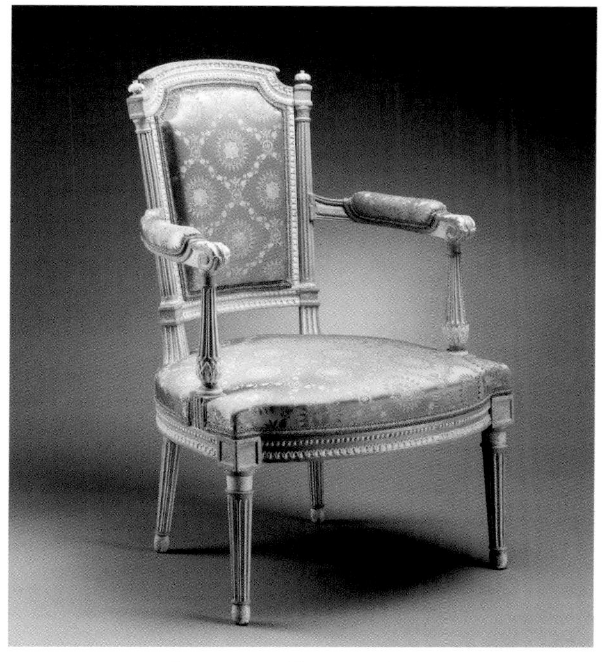

ARMCHAIR · *France, c. 1784–89*
Painted beechwood, 34½ x 23 x 23¼ in. (87.6 x 58.4 x 59.1 cm)
*Belonged to Thomas Jefferson and Dolley Madison*

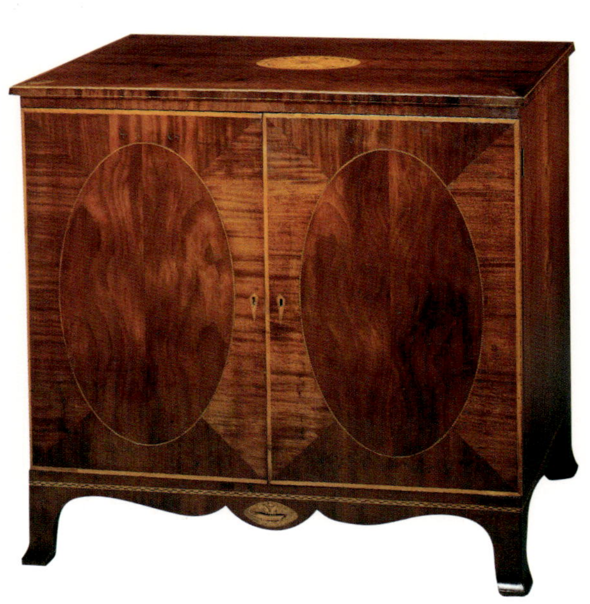

LINEN PRESS · *Annapolis, Maryland, c. 1790–1800*
Mahogany, 38 x 39 x 20 in. (96.5 x 99.1 x 50.8 cm)

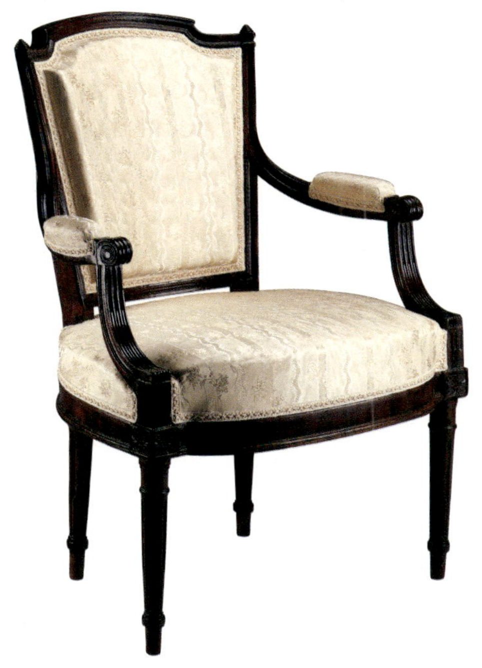

ARMCHAIR · *Attributed to Adam Hains (1768–after 1820)*
*Philadelphia, c. 1793–97* · Mahogany, 34 1/8 x 23 x 23 in.
(87 x 58.4 x 58.4 cm) · *Belonged to George Washington*

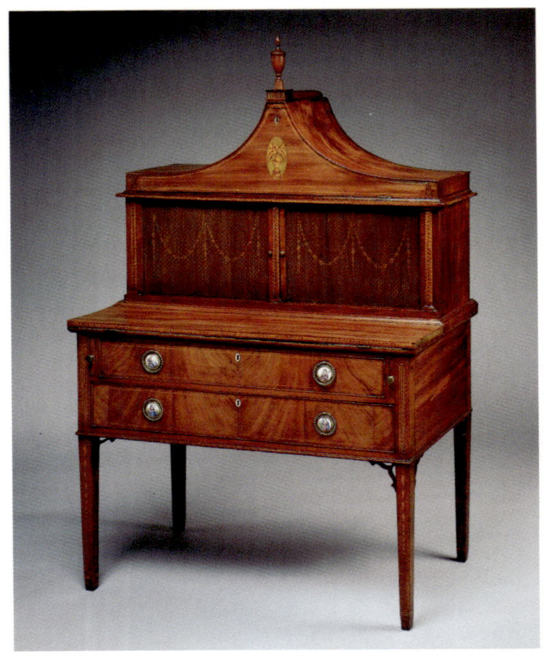

TAMBOUR DESK · *John Seymour (c. 1738–1818) and/or Thomas Seymour (1771–1848)* · *Boston, c. 1795–1810*
Mahogany, 59 7/8 x 38 x 19 5/8 in. (152.1 x 96.5 x 49.9 cm)

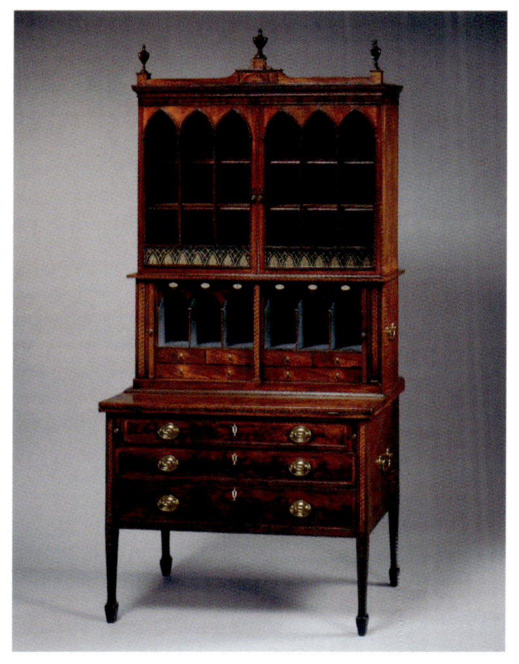

Tambour Desk and Bookcase · *John Seymour (c. 1738–1818) and/or Thomas Seymour (1771–1848) · Boston, c. 1795–1810*
Mahogany, 81 1/2 x 36 9/16 x 28 3/8 (open) in. (207 x 92.9 x 72.1 cm)

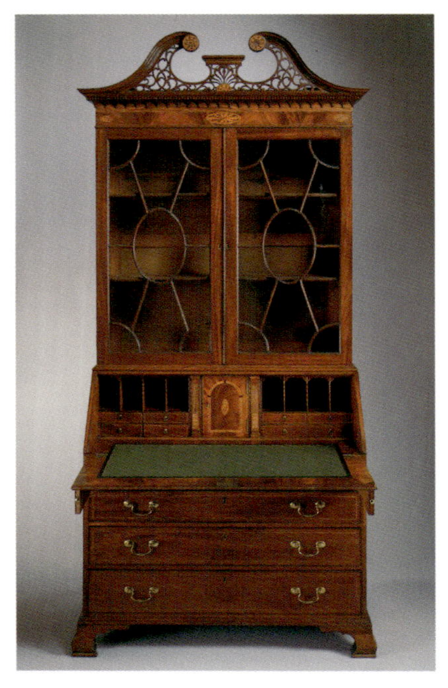

Desk and Bookcase
*John Shaw (1745–1829) · Annapolis, Maryland, 1797*
Mahogany, 98 5/8 x 45 3/4 x 36 1/4 in. (250.6 x 115.2 x 92.1 cm)

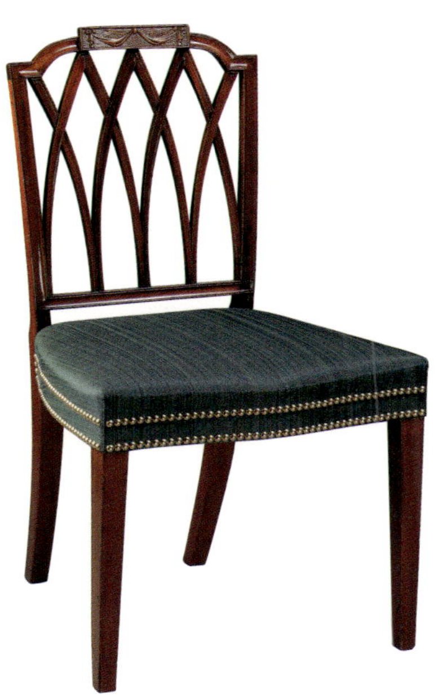

SIDE CHAIR · *Carving possibly by the workshop of Samuel McIntire (1757–1811) · Salem, Massachusetts, c. 1800*
Mahogany, 36 7/8 x 21 1/2 x 20 1/2 in. (93.7 x 54.6 x 52.1 cm)

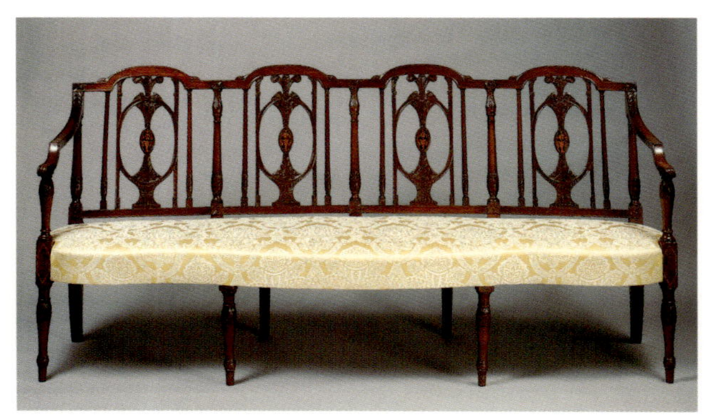

ABOVE: SETTEE · *Philadelphia, c. 1800–10* · Mahogany
36 1/2 x 75 x 23 1/2 in. (92.7 x 190.5 x 59.7 cm)
OPPOSITE: BOOKCASE · *Philadelphia, c. 1800–10* · Mahogany
107 1/8 x 73 1/2 x 21 1/2 in. (222.1 x 186.7 x 54.6 cm)

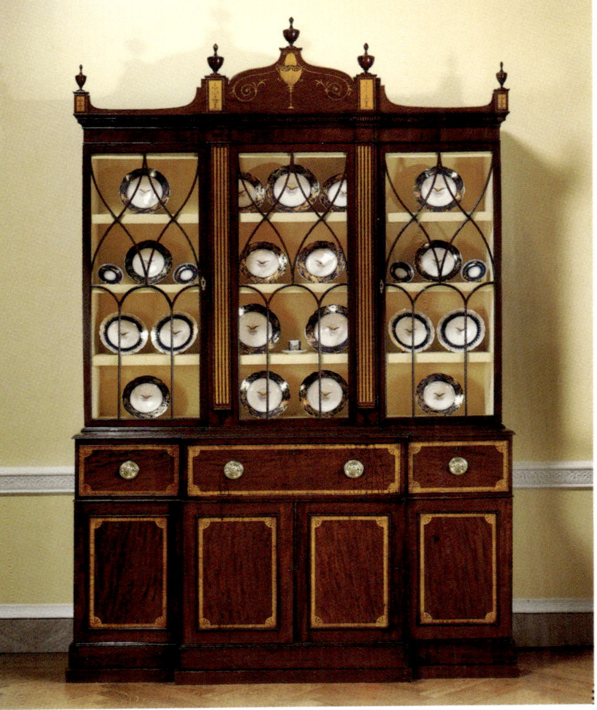

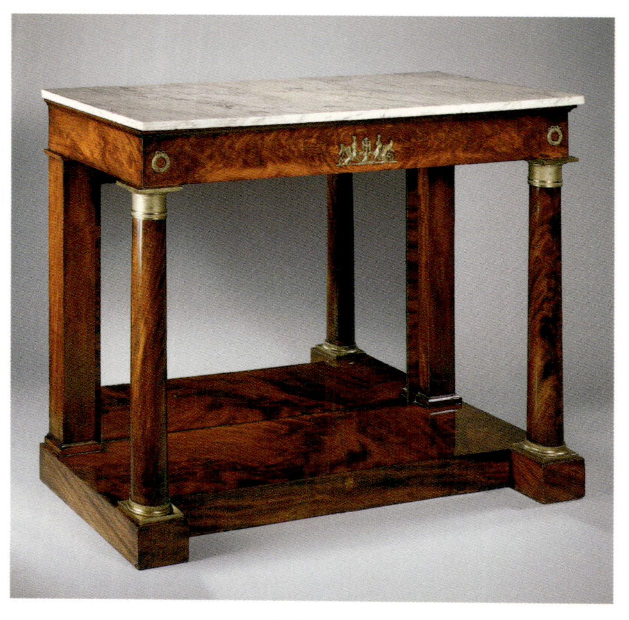

ABOVE: PIER TABLE · *Charles-Honoré Lannuier (1779–1819)*
*New York, c. 1805–10* · Mahogany, mirror, marble
35 x 41½ x 19 in. (88.9 x 105.4 x 48.2 cm)
OPPOSITE: CENTER TABLE · *Charles-Honoré Lannuier* · *New York, c. 1810*
Mahogany, marble, 29 ¾ x 26 in. (75.9 x 68.6 cm)

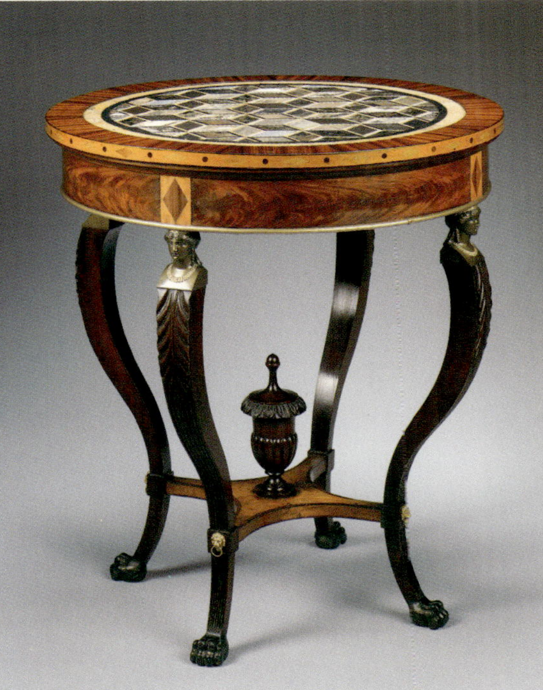

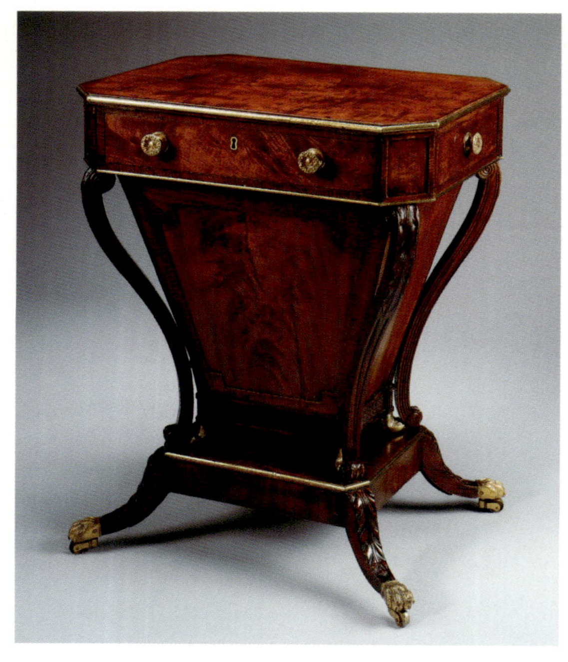

ABOVE AND OPPOSITE: WORK TABLE
*Attributed to Duncan Phyfe (1768–1854) · New York, c. 1810*
Mahogany, closed: 28¼ x 23 x 16 in. (71.8 x 58.4 x 40.6 cm)

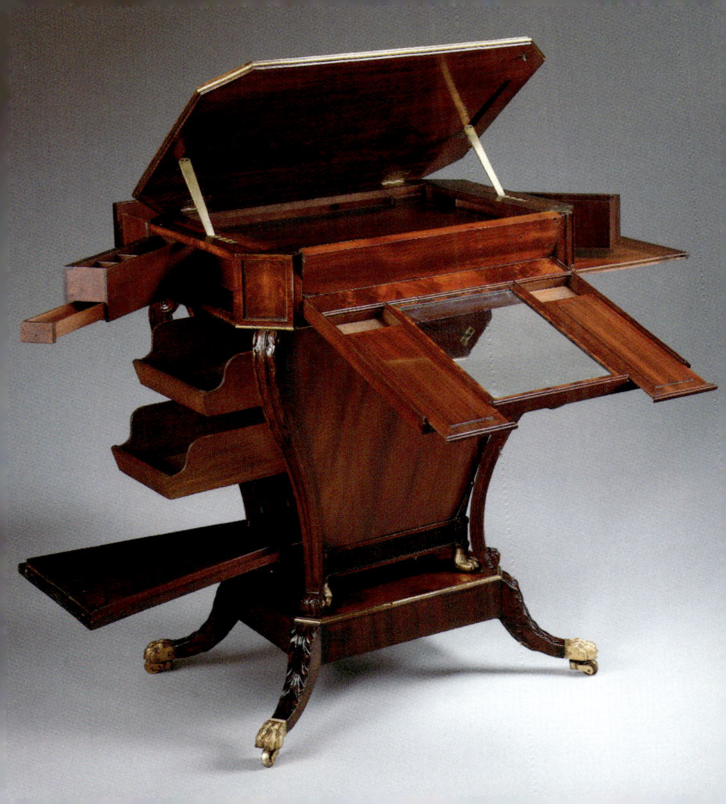

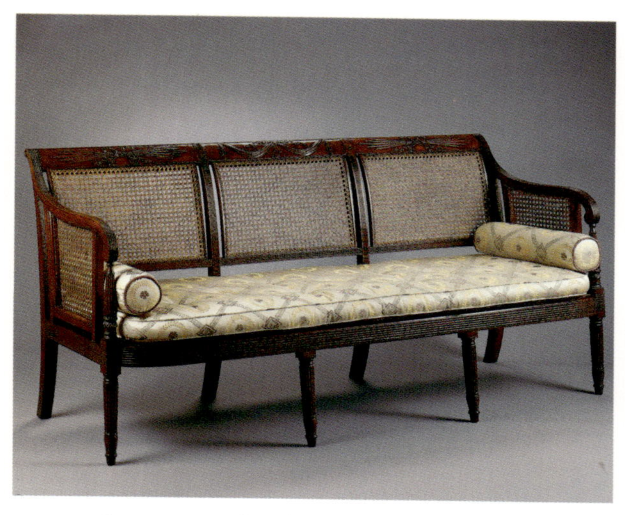

SOFA · *Duncan Phyfe (1768–1854) · New York, c. 1810*
Mahogany, 35 1/2 x 72 x 22 1/2 in. (90.2 x 182.9 x 57.2 cm)

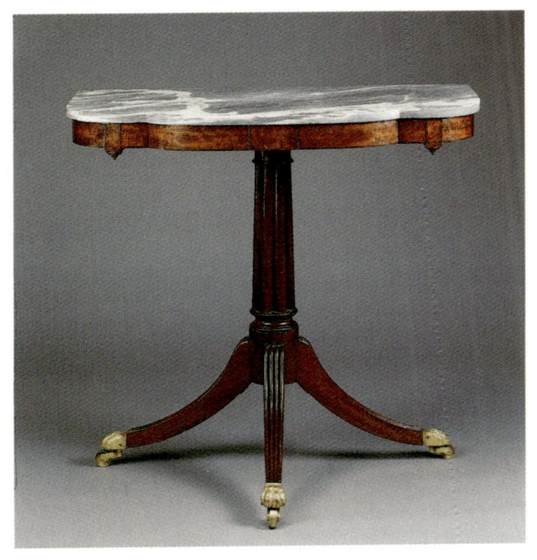

PIER TABLE · *Attributed to Duncan Phyfe (1768–1854)* · *New York, c. 1815*
Mahogany, marble, 34 5/8 x 35 1/4 x 18 in. (88 x 89.5 x 45.7 cm)

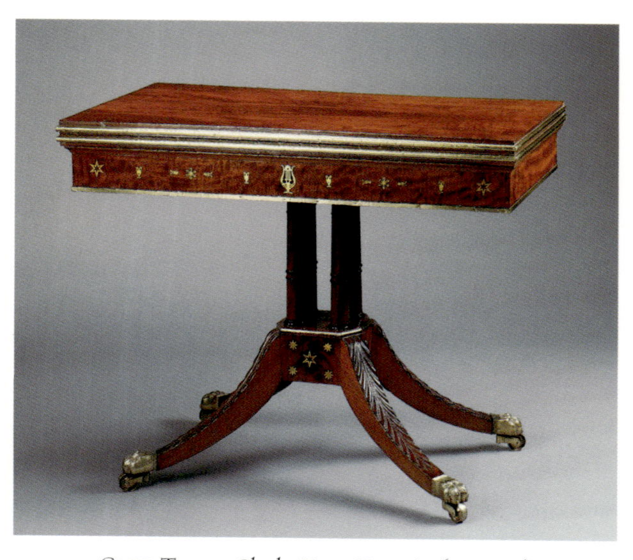

CARD TABLE · *Charles-Honoré Lannuier (1779–1819)*
*New York, c. 1810–15* · Mahogany
$29\frac{1}{2} \times 36\frac{1}{8} \times 18\frac{1}{8}$ in. (74.9 x 91.7 x 46 cm)

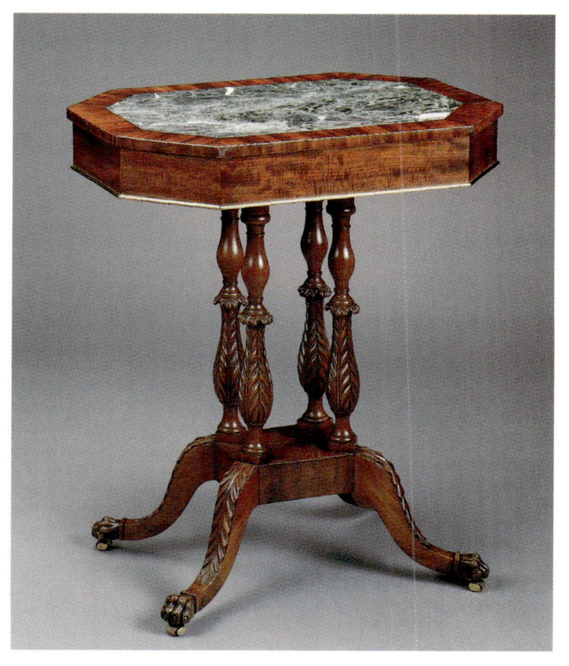

MIXING TABLE/STAND · *Charles-Honoré Lannuier (1779–1819)*
*New York, c. 1810–15* · Mahogany, marble
$28^{1}/4$ x $23^{3}/4$ x $16^{1}/4$ in. (71.7 x 60.3 x 41.2 cm)

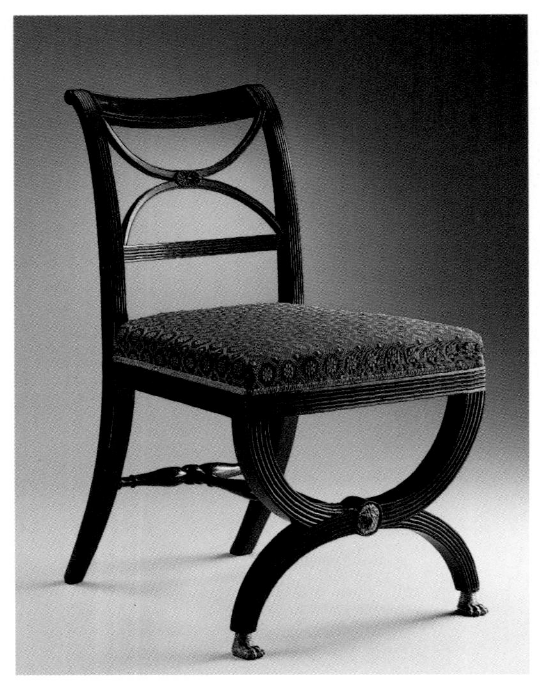

SIDE CHAIR · *Attributed to Duncan Phyfe (1768–1854)* · *New York*
*c. 1810–20* · Mahogany, 33 x 20 x 20 in. (83.8 x 50.8 x 50.8 cm)

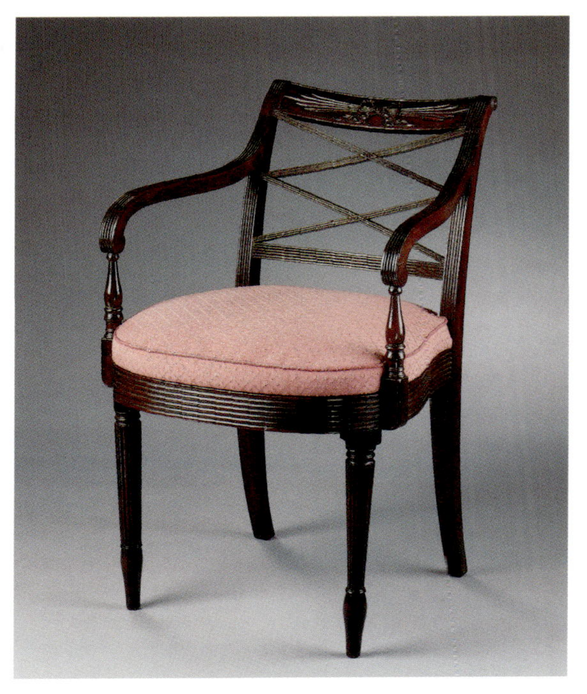

ARMCHAIR · *Duncan Phyfe (1768–1854)* · *New York, c. 1810*
Mahogany, 35 1/2 x 72 x 22 1/2 in. (90.2 x 182.9 x 57.2 cm)

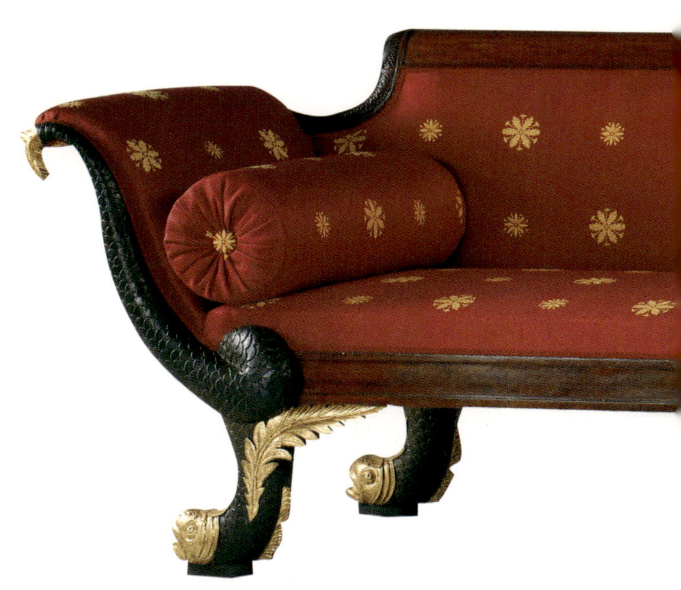

Sofa · *New York, c. 1810–25* · Mahogany, gilded and painted pine
34 x 84½ x 24 in. (86.4 x 214.6 x 61 cm)

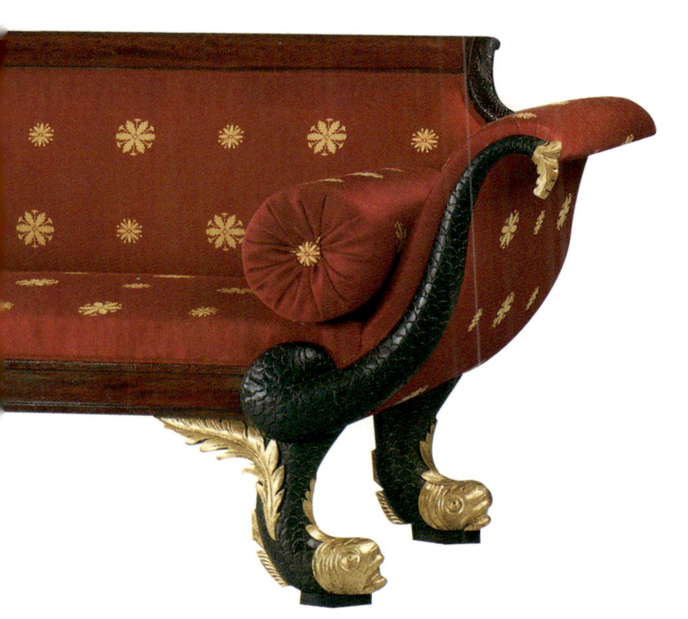

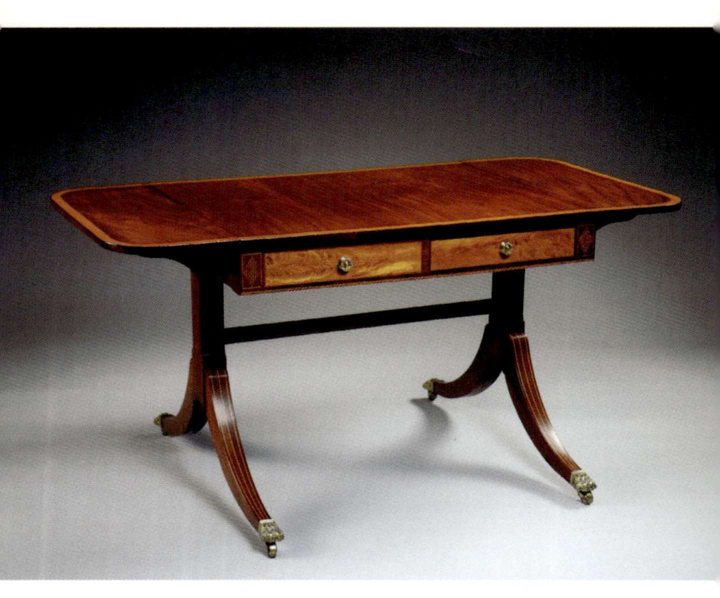

SOFA TABLE · *John Seymour (c. 1738–1818) and/or Thomas Seymour (1771–1848)* · *Boston, c. 1805–10*

 Mahogany, birch, 27 1/2 x 53 3/4 (open) x 33 in. (69.8 x 136.5 x 83.8 cm)

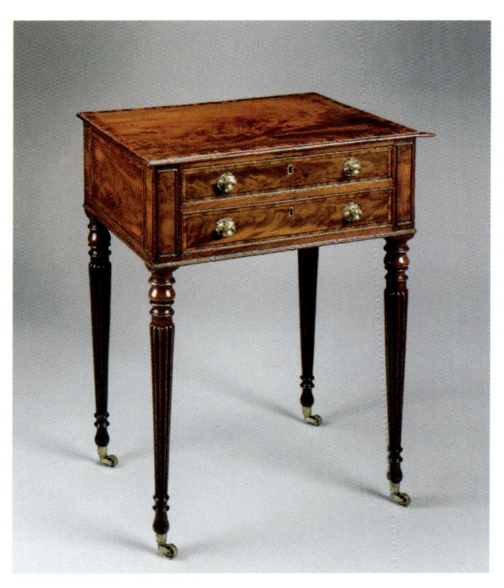

WORK TABLE · *Attributed to Thomas Seymour (1771–1848)*
*Boston, 1814* · Mahogany, 30 1/2 x 21 3/4 x 16 3/4 in. (77.5 x 55.2 x 42.6 cm)

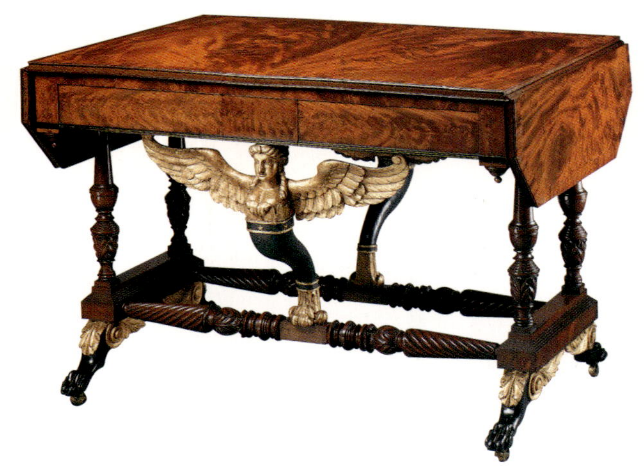

SOFA TABLE · *In the manner of Charles-Honoré Lannuier*
*New York, c. 1815–20* · Mahogany, gilded and painted wood
28 1/2 x 55 3/4 x 28 in. (72.4 x 141.6 x 71.1 cm)

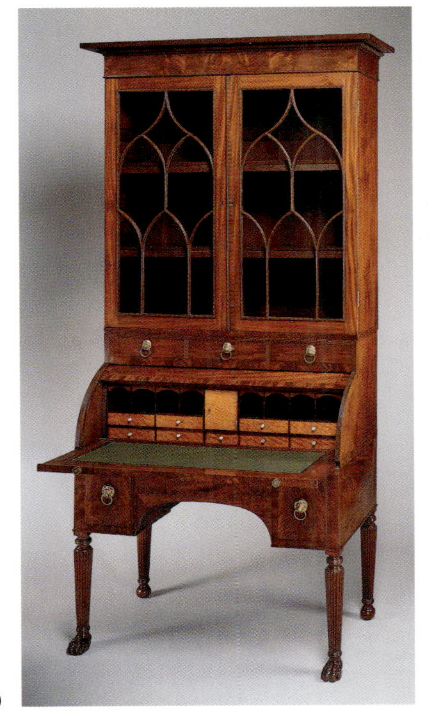

BOOKCASE-DESK
*Attributed to*
*Duncan Phyfe,*
*(1768–1854)*
*New York, c. 1815–20*
Mahogany,
96 1/4 x 41 1/2 x 21 1/2 in.
(244.5 x 105.4 x 54.6 cm)

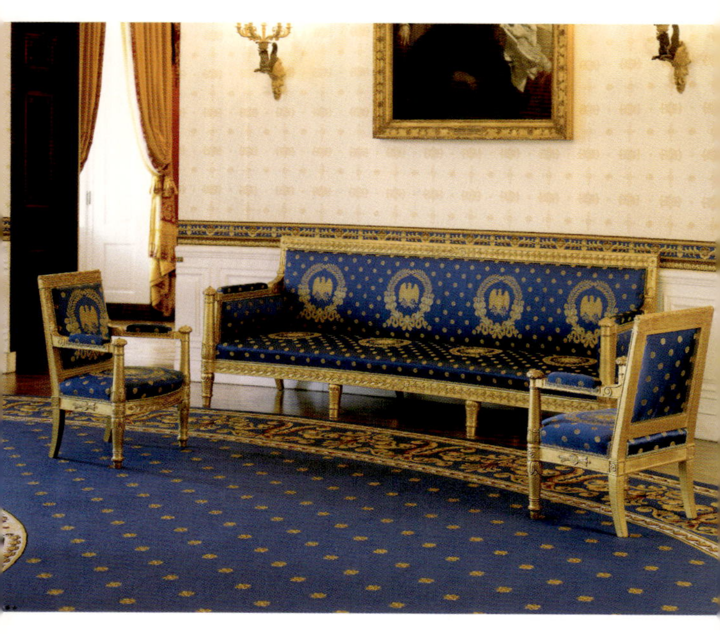

SOFA AND ARMCHAIRS · *Pierre-Antoine Bellangé (1758–1827)*
*Paris, c. 1817* · Gilded beechwood; Sofa- 42½ x 110¾ x 31¼ in.
(108 x 281.3 x 79.4 cm) · *James Monroe Administration*

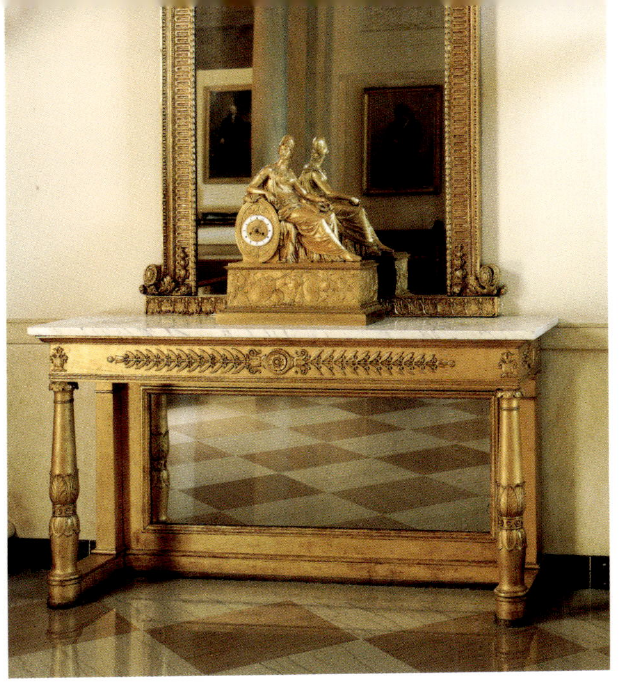

PIER TABLE · *Pierre-Antoine Bellangé (1758–1827)* · *Paris, c. 1817*
Gilded beechwood, marble, mirror, 43¼ x 75 x 20¾ in.
(109.9 x 190.5 x 52.7 cm) · *James Monroe Administration*

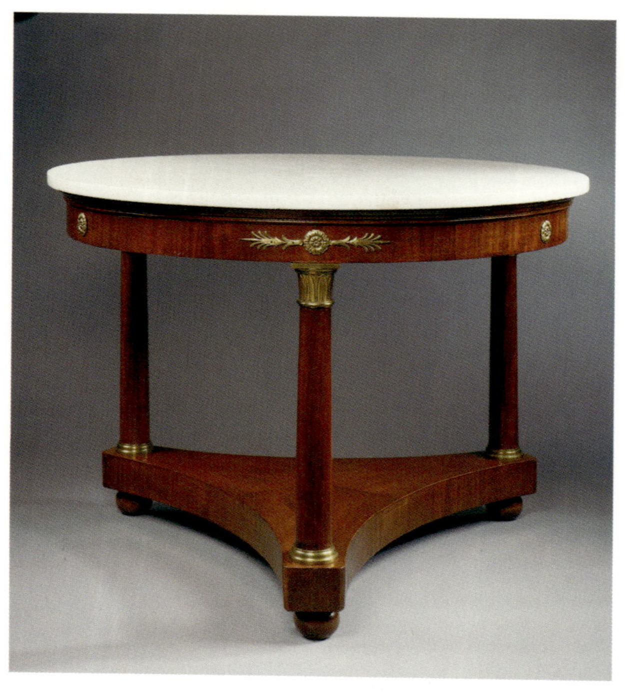

CENTER TABLE · *France, c. 1817* · Mahogany, marble
$33\frac{3}{4}$ x 45 in. (85.7 x 114.3 cm) · *James Monroe Administration*

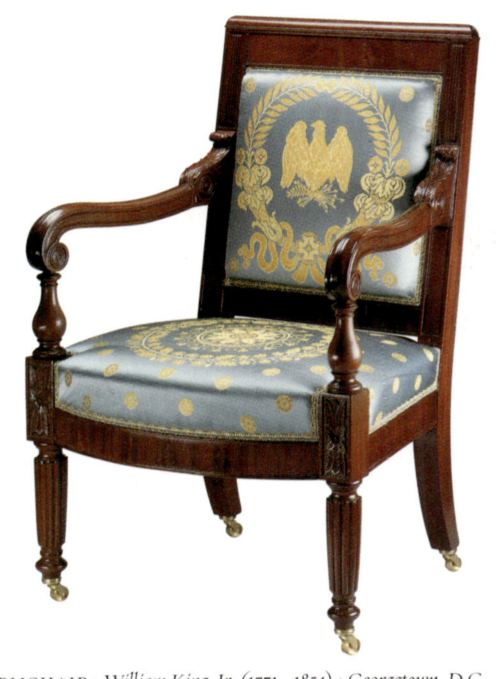

ARMCHAIR · *William King, Jr. (1771–1854) · Georgetown, D.C., 1818*
Mahogany, 41 1/4 x 25 1/2 x 25 3/8 in. (104.8 x 64.8 x 64.4 cm)
*James Monroe Administration*

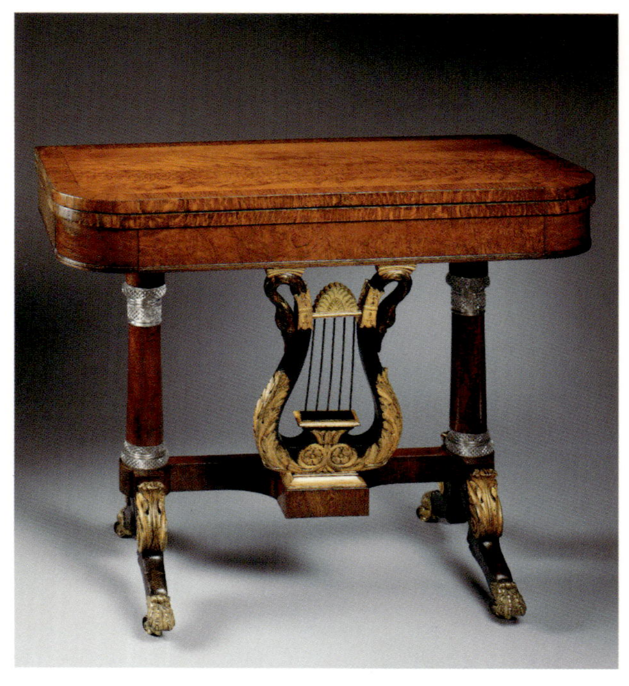

CARD TABLE · *Probably New York, c. 1825*
Mahogany, oak, 29½ x 36 x 18 in. (74.9 x 91.4 x 45.7 cm)

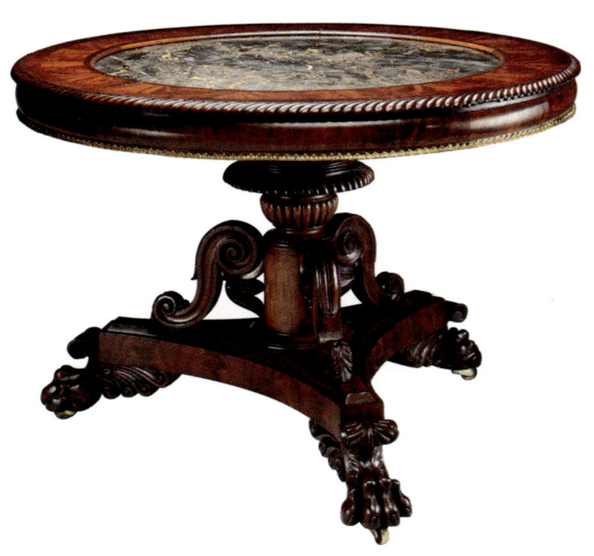

CENTER TABLE · *Anthony Gabriel Quervelle (1789–1856)*
*Philadelphia, c. 1829* · Mahogany, marble
29½ x 40½ in. (74.9 x 102.9 cm) · *Andrew Jackson Administration*

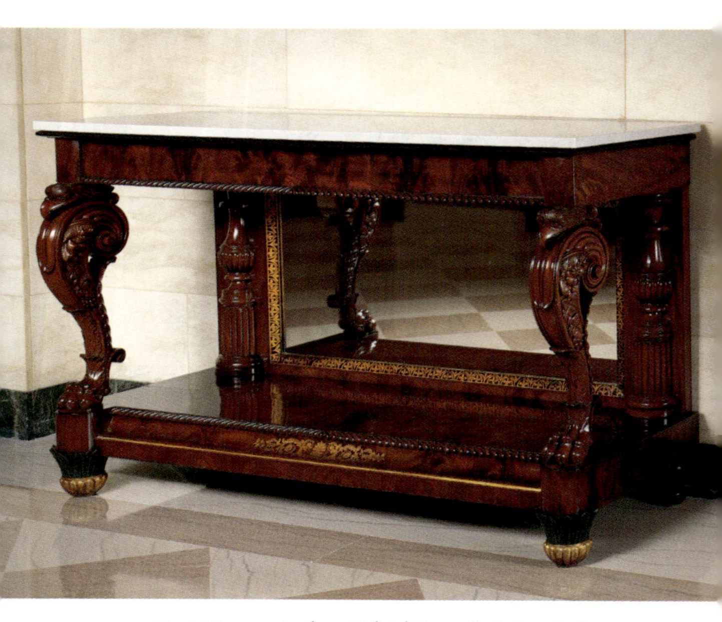

PIER TABLE · *Anthony Gabriel Quervelle (1789–1856)*
*Philadelphia, c. 1829* · Mahogany, marble, mirror, $43\frac{1}{8}$ x 66 x $25\frac{15}{16}$ in.
(109.5 x 167.6 x 65.9 cm) · *Andrew Jackson Administration*

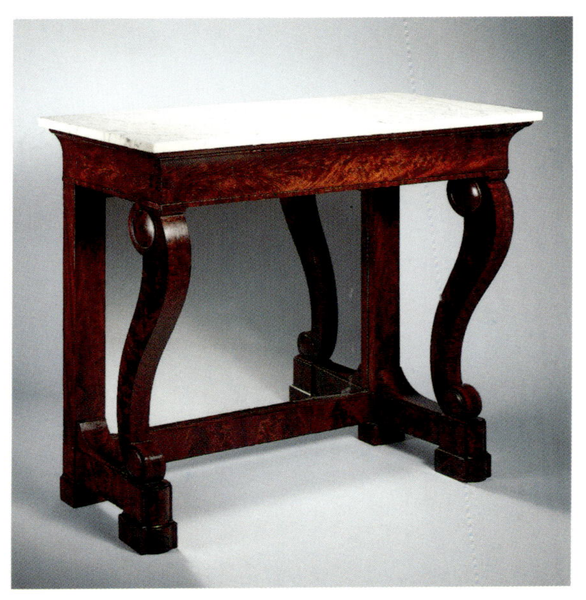

PIER TABLE · *Duncan Phyfe (1768–1854)* · *New York, c. 1834*
Mahogany, marble, mirror, $35\frac{1}{2} \times 42\frac{3}{4} \times 18\frac{1}{8}$ in.
(90.2 x 108.6 x 46 cm)

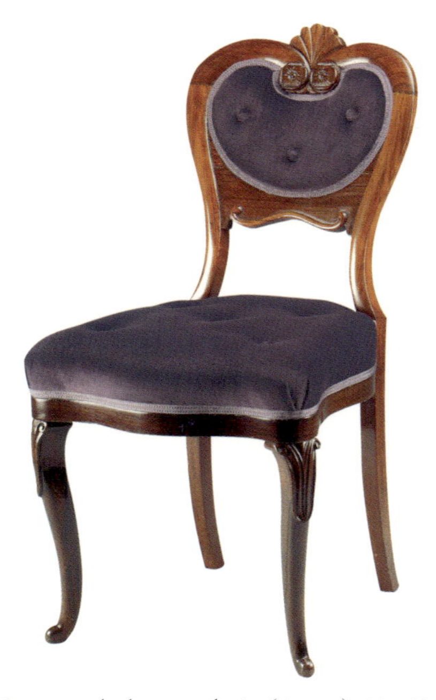

SIDE CHAIR · *Charles A. Baudouine (1808–95)* · *New York, c. 1845*
Rosewood, 35 1/8 x 18 x 21 1/4 in. (89.5 x 45.7 x 54 cm)
*James K. Polk Administration*

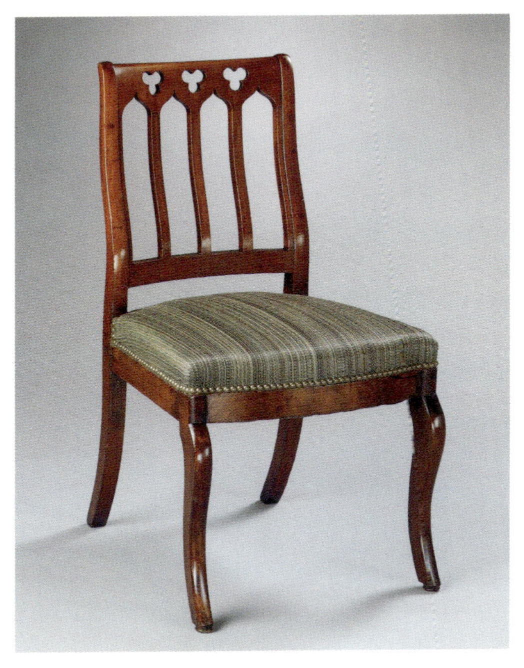

SIDE CHAIR · *J. & J. W. Meeks · New York, c. 1846*
Walnut, $34\frac{1}{8}$ x $18\frac{1}{8}$ x $21\frac{1}{8}$ in. (86.7 x 46 x 53.7 cm)
*James K. Polk Administration*

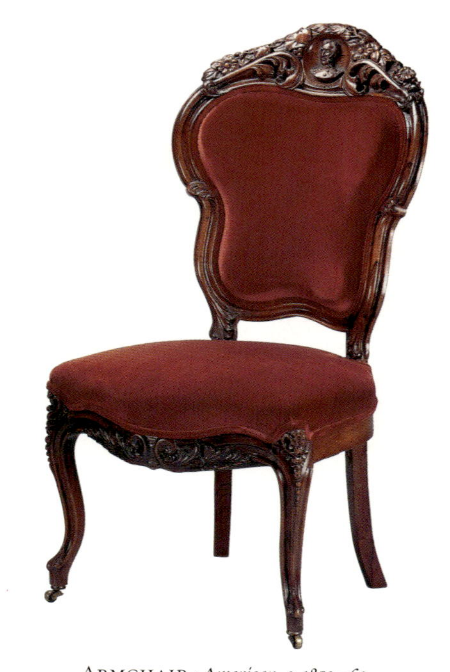

ARMCHAIR · *American, c. 1850–60*
Mahogany, 36¼ x 18½ x 18 ½ in. (92.1 x 47 x 47 cm)

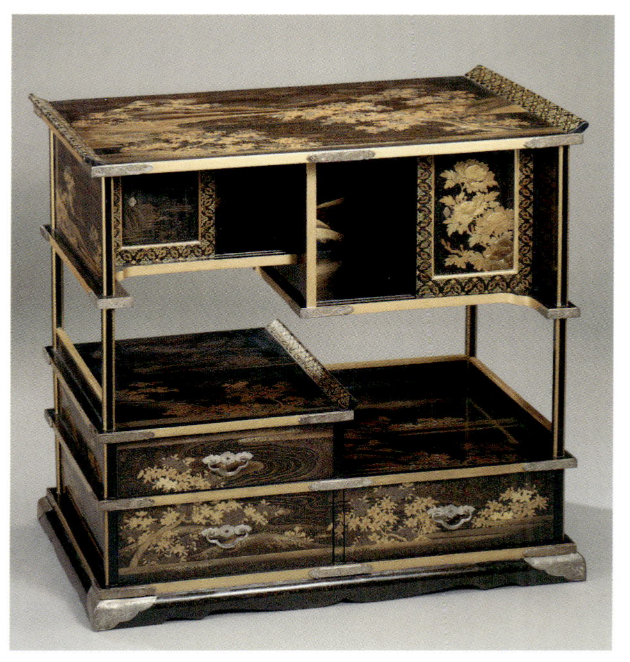

CHIGAI-DANA · *Japan, c. 1850–60* · Lacquered and gilded wood
25 7/8 x 26 3/4 x 14 7/8 in. (65.7 x 68 x 37.8 cm)
*Franklin Pierce or James Buchanan Administration*

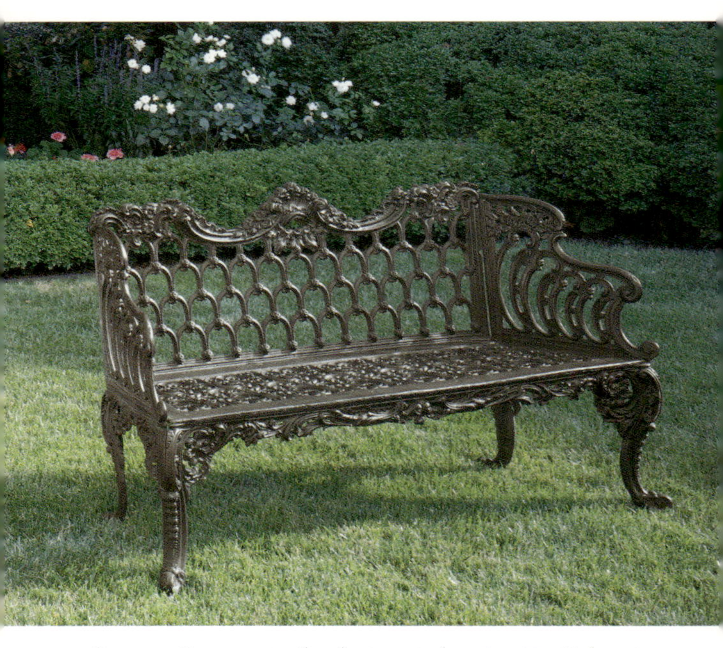

GARDEN SETTEE · *Attributed to Janes, Beebe & Co.* · *New York, c. 1852*
Painted cast iron, 37 1/2 x 64 x 19 1/2 in. (95.3 x 162.6 x 49.1 cm)
*Millard Fillmore Administration*

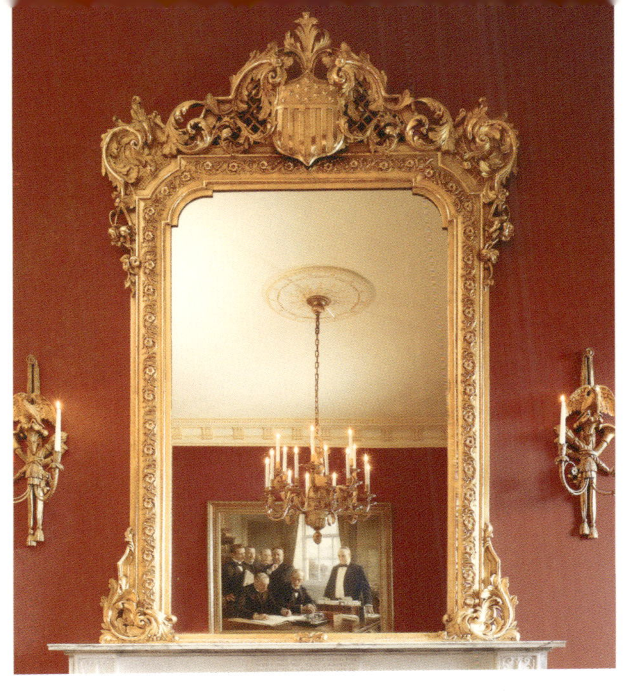

OVERMANTEL MIRROR · *L. R. Menger · New York, 1853*
Gilded wood, mirror, 102 x 72 x 6 3/4 in. (259.1 x 182 9 x 17.2 cm)
*Franklin Pierce Administration*

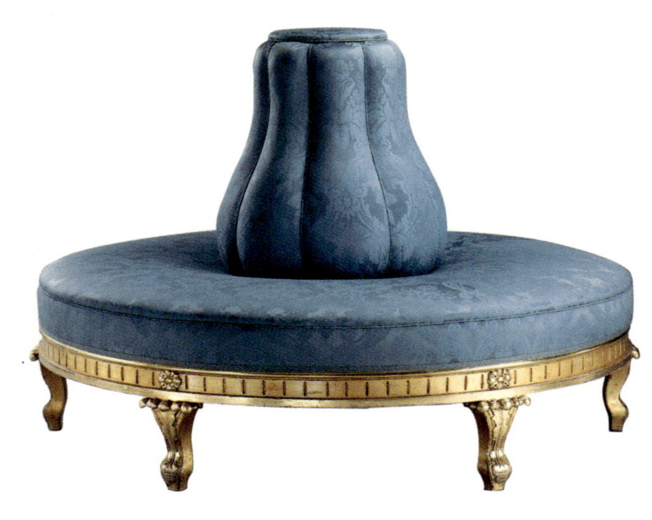

CENTER DIVAN · *Gottlieb Vollmer (1816–83) · Philadelphia, 1859*
Gilded ash, 43 x $60^{1}/4$ in. (109.2 x 153 cm)
*James Buchanan Administration*

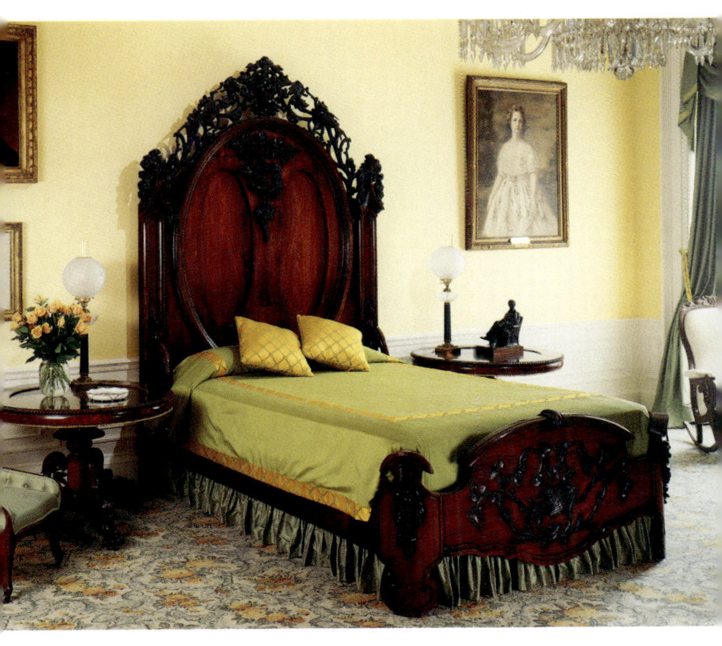

BED · *American, c. 1861* · Rosewood, grained walnut, 112¼ x 73¼ x 102¾ in. (285.1 x 186.1 x 261 cm) · *Abraham Lincoln Administration*

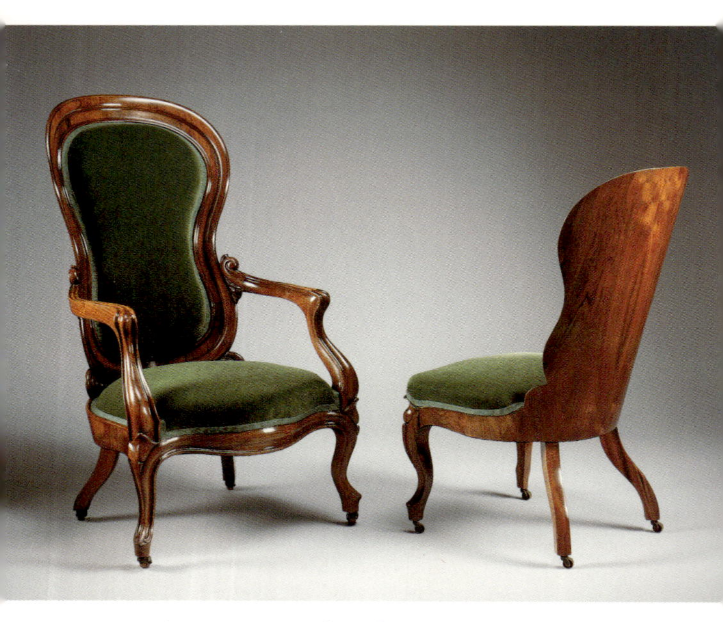

ARMCHAIR AND SIDE CHAIR · *American, c. 1861*
Rosewood; Armchair-$42\frac{1}{2} \times 23\frac{7}{8} \times 28\frac{1}{2}$ in. (108 x 60.6 x 73.4 cm)
*Abraham Lincoln Administration*

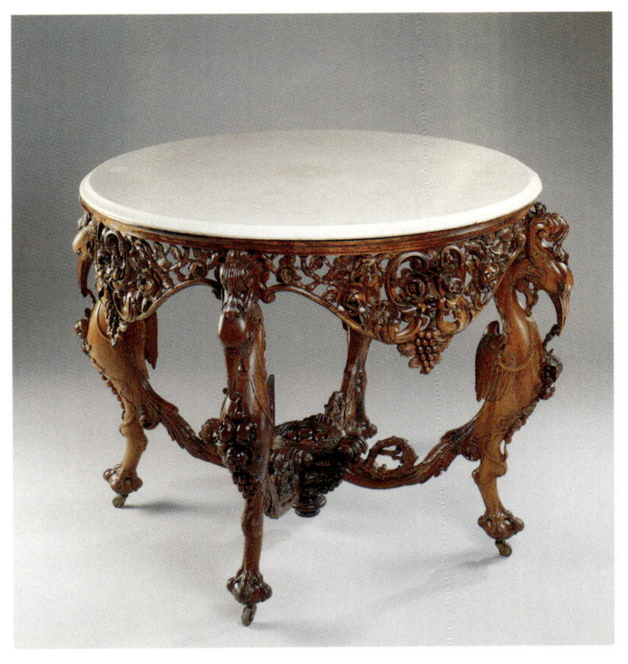

CENTER TABLE · *Attributed to John Henry Belter (1804–63)*
*New York, c. 1861* · Rosewood, marble
30 1/8 x 40 5/8 in. (76.8 x 103.2 cm) · *Abraham Lincoln Administration*

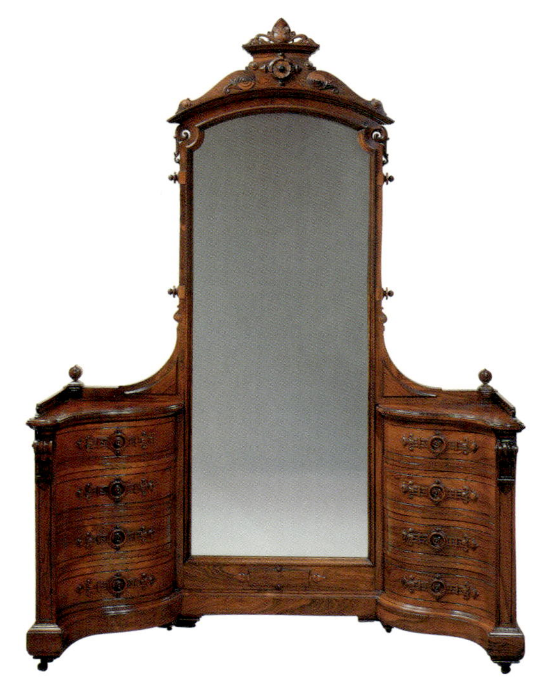

DRESSING CHEST OF DRAWERS · *American, c. 1865–70*
Rosewood, mirror, 98 3/8 x 69 1/2 x 23 1/8 in. (249.9 x 176.5 x 58.7 cm)

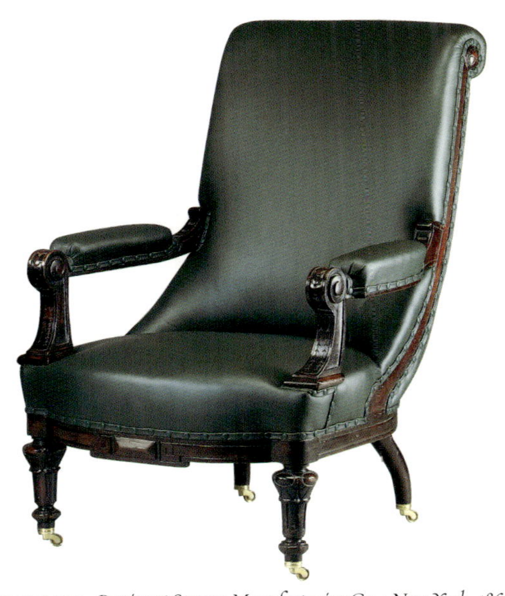

ARMCHAIR · *Pottier & Stymus Manufacturing Co. · New York, 1869*
Black walnut, 38 x 28½ x 25½ in. (96.5 x 72.4 x 64.8 cm)
*Ulysses S. Grant Administration*

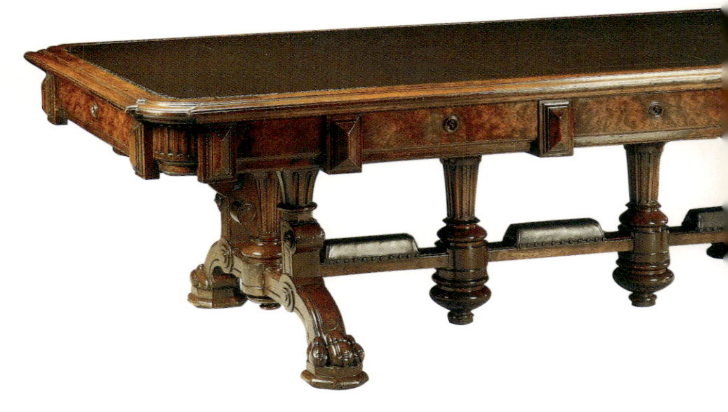

CONFERENCE TABLE · *Pottier & Stymus Manufacturing Co.*
*New York, 1869* · Walnut, 28 3/4 x 96 1/2 x 48 in. (73 x 245.1 x 121.9 cm)
*Ulysses S. Grant Administration*

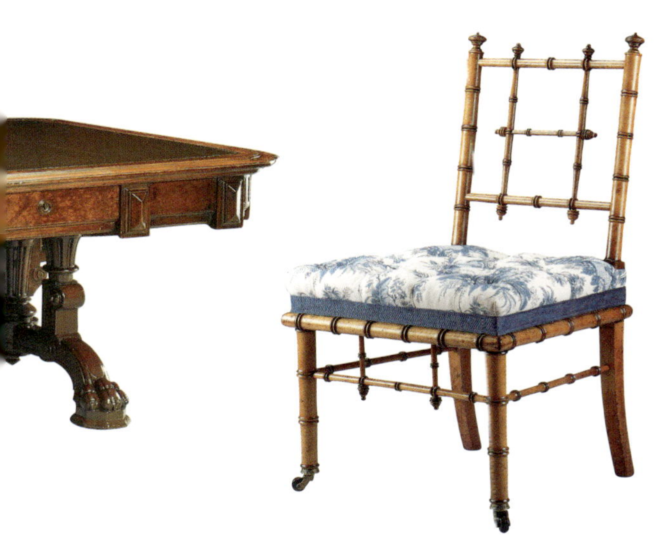

SIDE CHAIR · *Probably New York, c. 1873–81*
Maple, $33^{1}/16 \times 19^{1}/2 \times 20^{1}/4$ in. (84 x 49.5 x 51.4 cm)
*Ulysses S. Grant or Rutherford B. Hayes Administration*

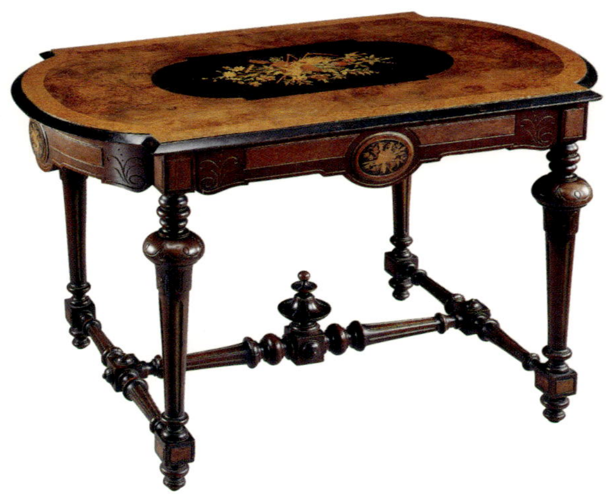

CENTER TABLE · *American, c. 1875–85*
Black walnut, marquetry, 28½ x 47 x 28½ in. (72.4 x 119.4 x 72.4 cm)

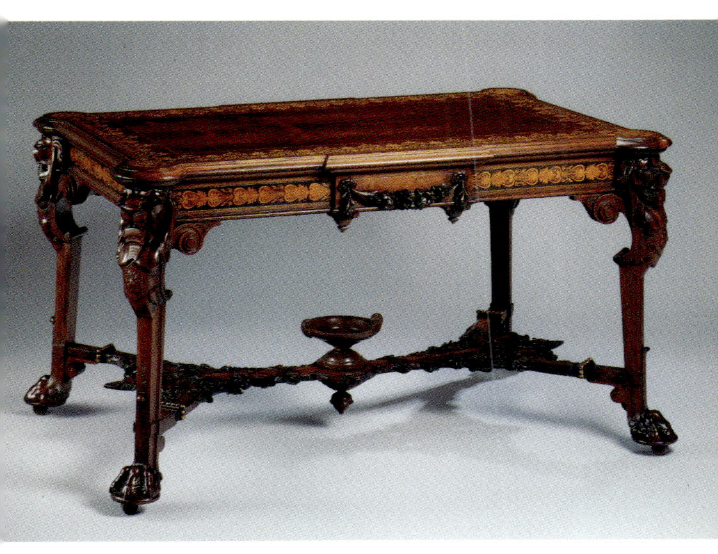

CENTER TABLE · *Herter Brothers* · *New York, c. 1875*
Rosewood, 30½ x 53 x 32¾ in. (77.5 x 134.6 x 83.2 cm)
*Ulysses S. Grant Administration*

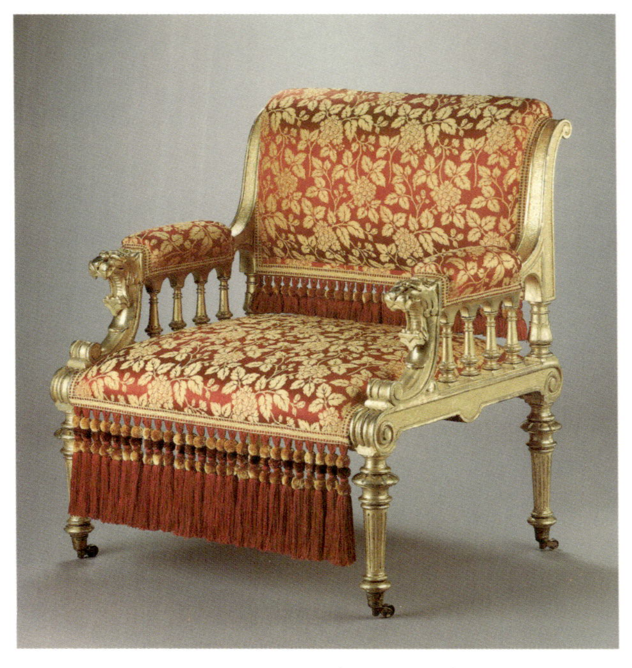

ARMCHAIR · *Herter Brothers · New York, c. 1875*
Gilded ash, 30½ x 26⅛ x 23¼ in. (77.5 x 66.4 x 59.1 cm)
*Ulysses S. Grant Administration*

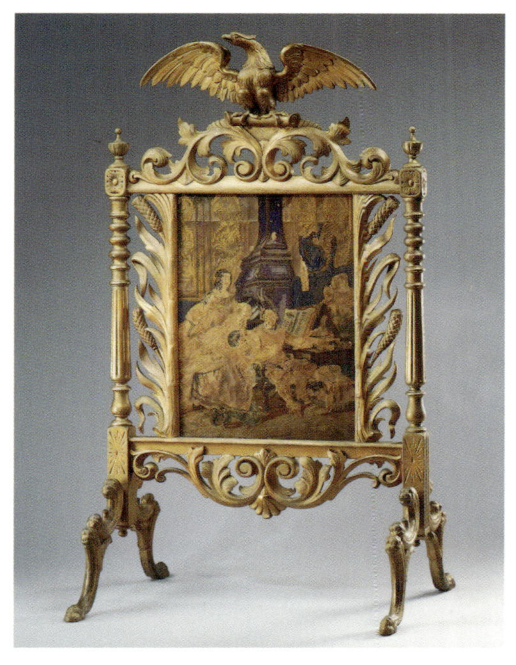

FIRE SCREEN · *Edward A. Richter · Vienna, c. 1876* · Gilded wood, embroidery, 56 1/2 x 31 1/4 x 23 5/16 in. (143.5 x 79.4 x 59.2 cm)
*Ulysses S. Grant Administration*

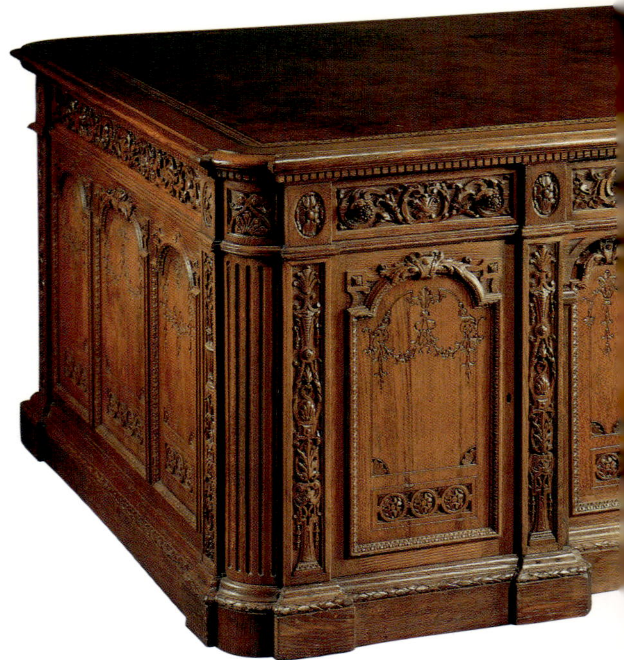

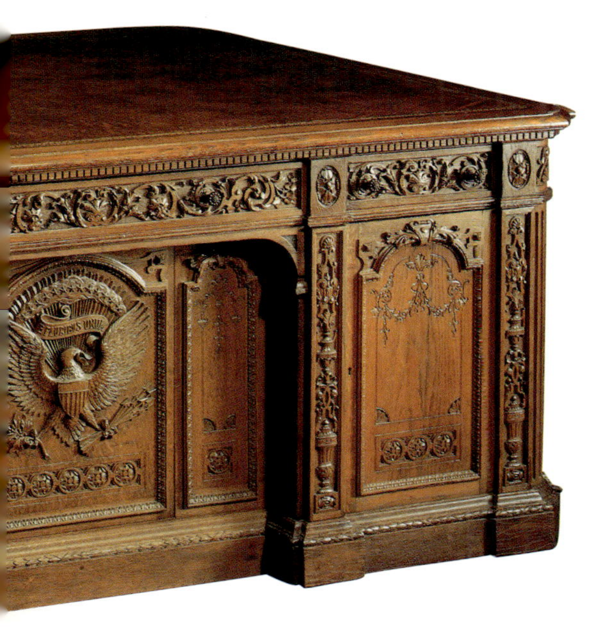

PARTNER'S DESK · *William Evenden · Chatham, England, 1880*
White oak, mahogany, 29 x 72 x 48 in. (73.7 x 182.9 x 121.9 cm)
*Rutherford B. Hayes Administration*

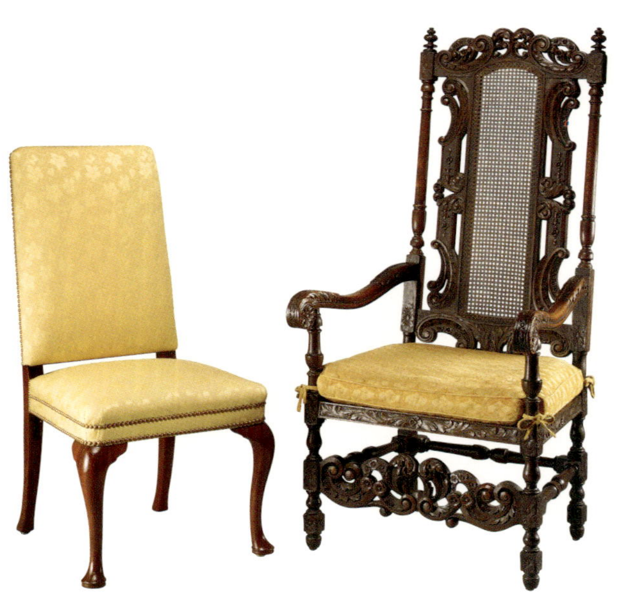

SIDE CHAIR AND ARMCHAIR · *A. H. Davenport · Boston, 1902*
Armchair, oak- 56 7/8 x 27 x 27 3/4 in. (144.5 x 68.6 x 70.5 cm)
Side chair, mahogany · *Theodore Roosevelt Administration*

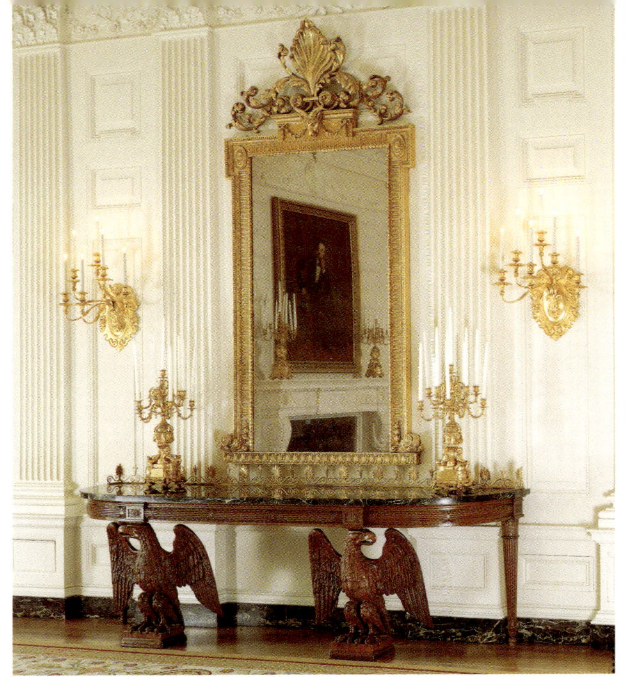

CONSOLE TABLE · *A. H. Davenport* · *Boston, 1902*
Mahogany, marble, 44 1/8 x 120 1/8 x 31 in. (112.1 x 355.1 x 78.7 cm)
*Theodore Roosevelt Administration*

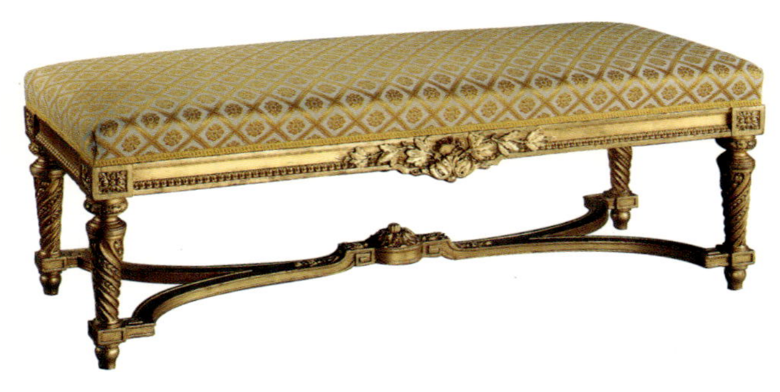

BENCH · *L. Marcotte & Co.* · *New York, 1902*
Gilded cherry, 20 x 54 x 18½ in. (50.8 x 137.2 x 47 cm)
*Theodore Roosevelt Administration*

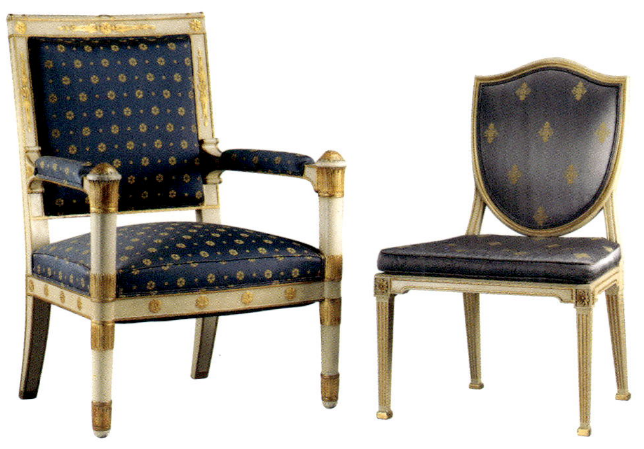

ARMCHAIR AND SIDE CHAIR · *L. Marcotte & Co.* · *New York, 1902*
Armchair, painted cherry–42 1/8 x 29 1/4 x 28 in. (107 x 74.3 x 71.1 cm)
Side chair, painted birch · *Theodore Roosevelt Administration*

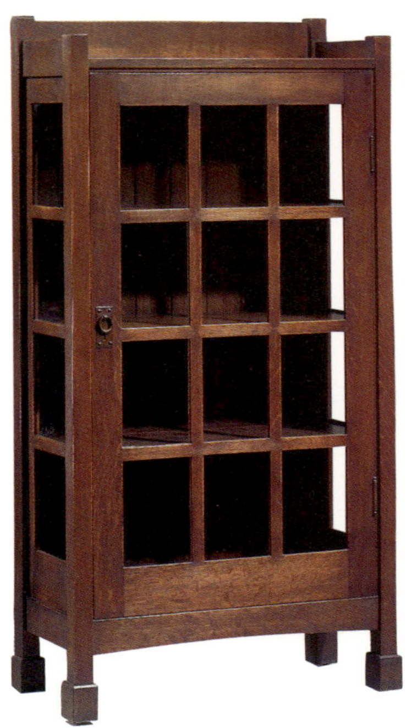

CABINET · *Gustav Stickley · Eastwood, New York, c. 1904*
White oak, $69^{1}/8$ x $36^{1}/8$ x 14 in. (175.6 x 91.8 x 35.6 cm)
*Theodore Roosevelt Administration*

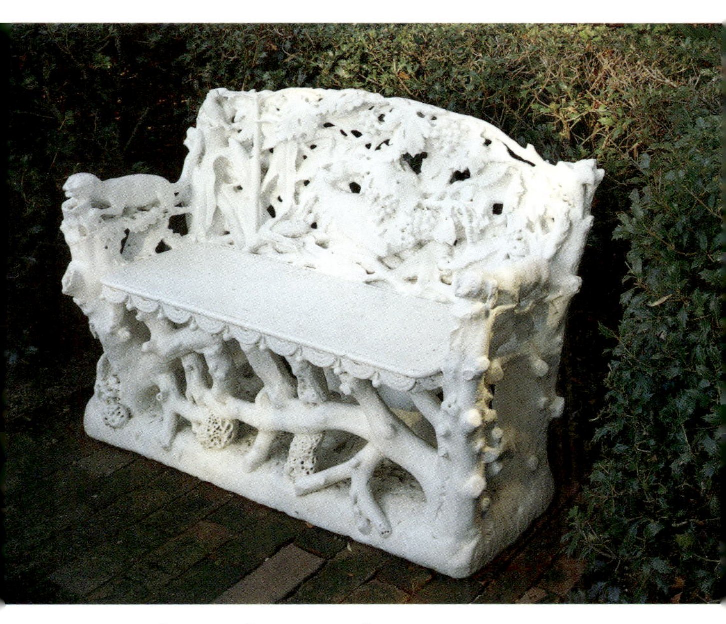

GARDEN SETTEE · *Northern Europe, c. 1902–09*
Painted limestone, 30¾ x 54½ x 18 in. (78.1 x 138.4 x 45.7 cm)
*Theodore Roosevelt Administration*

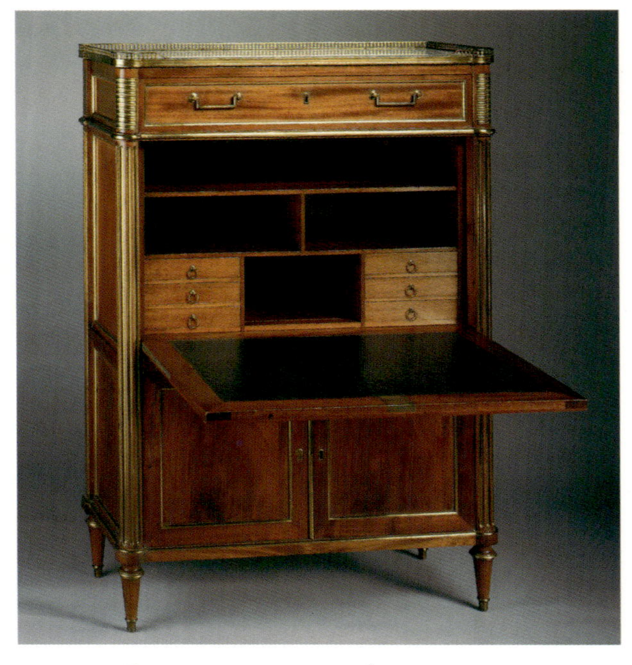

DESK · *Morris W. Dove · Washington, D.C., 1932*
Mahogany, marble, 57 5/8 x 38 x 34 (open) in. (148.9 x 96.5 x 86.4 cm)
*Herbert Hoover Administration*

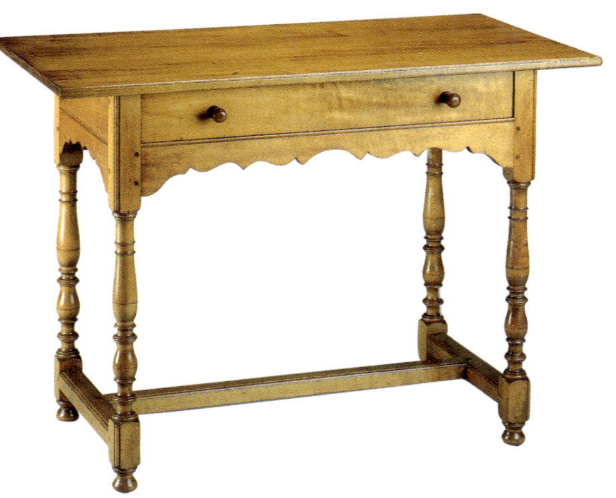

DRESSING TABLE · *Otto Berge, The Val-Kill Furniture Shop Hyde Park, New York, c. 1933* · Maple, 29$^{1}/_{8}$ x 38 x 19$^{3}/_{4}$ in. (74 x 96.5 x 50.2 cm) · *Franklin D. Roosevelt Administration*

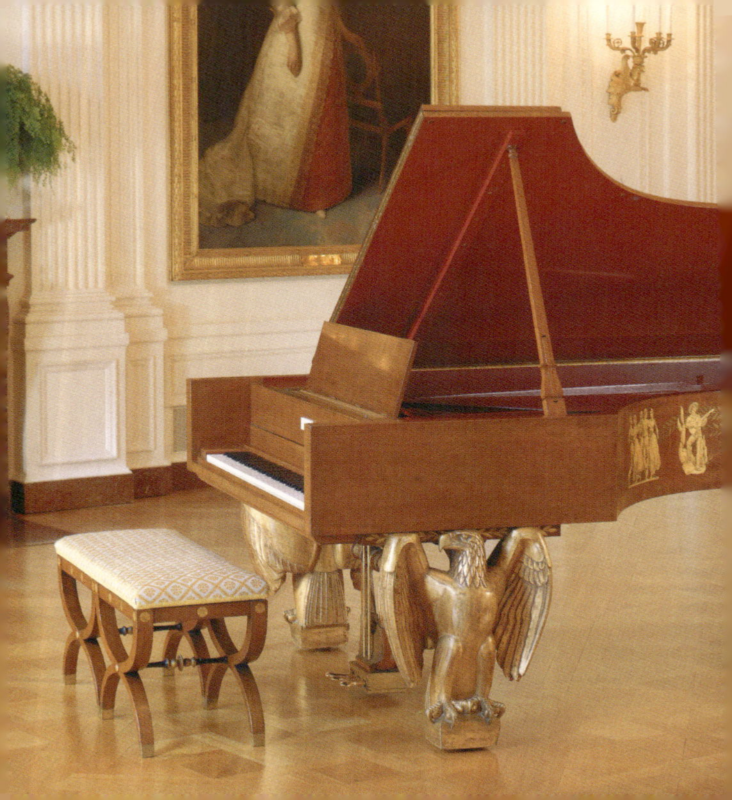

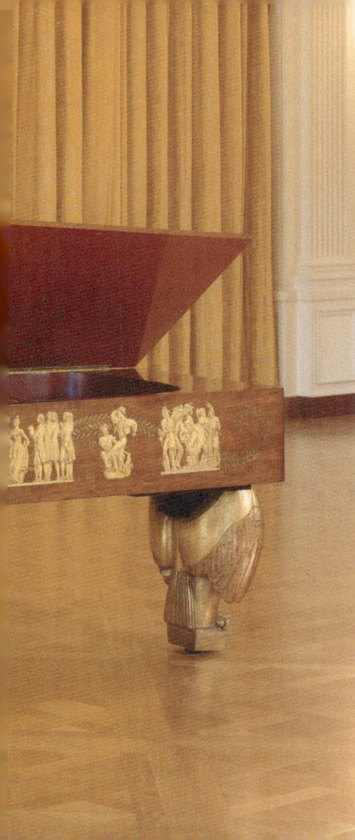

Piano and Bench
*Steinway & Sons*
*Long Island City, New York, 1938*
Mahogany, gilded wood
$38\frac{3}{8}$ x 115 x $59\frac{3}{4}$ in.
(97.5 x 292.1 x 151.8 cm)
*Franklin D. Roosevelt Administration*

Overleaf: The State Floor:
The Green Room, 1999

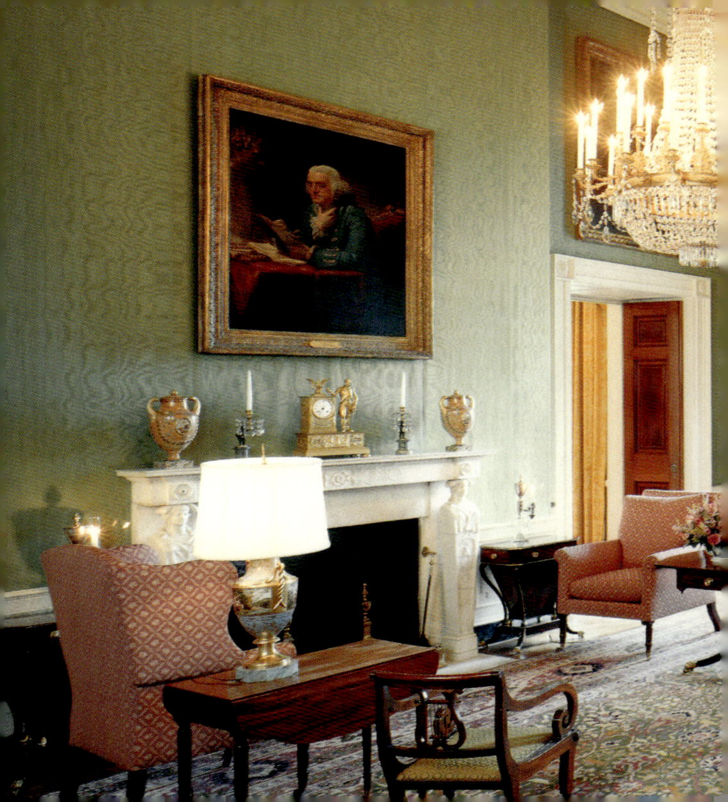

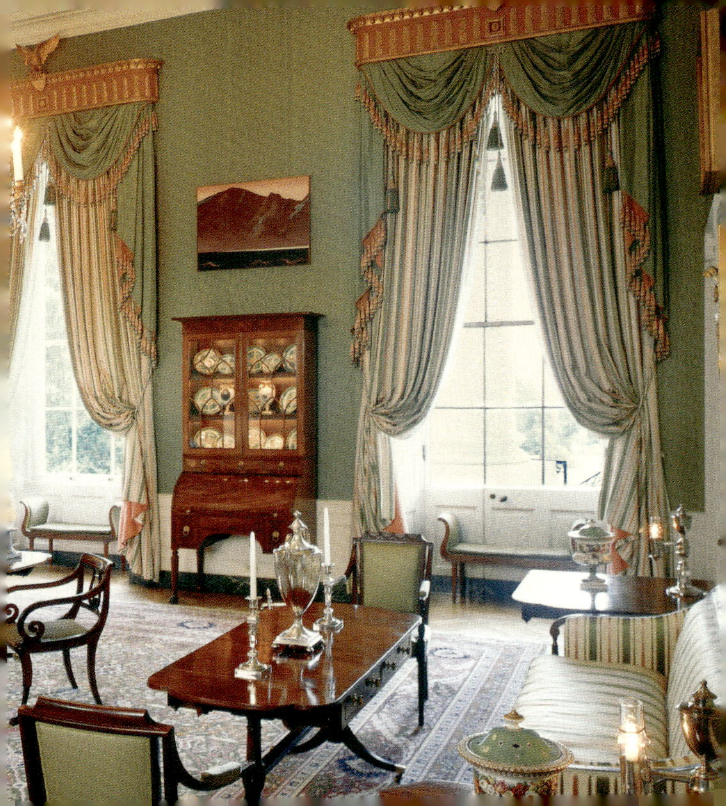

# Silver and Other Metalware

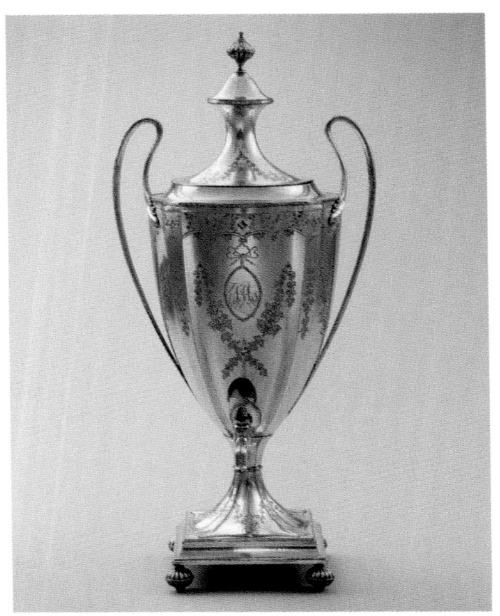

Tea or Coffee Urn · *Sheffield, England, c. 1785–88*
Sheffield silverplate, 22 7/8 x 10 3/4 x 11 1/4 in. (58.1 x 27.3 x 28.6 cm)
*Belonged to John Adams*

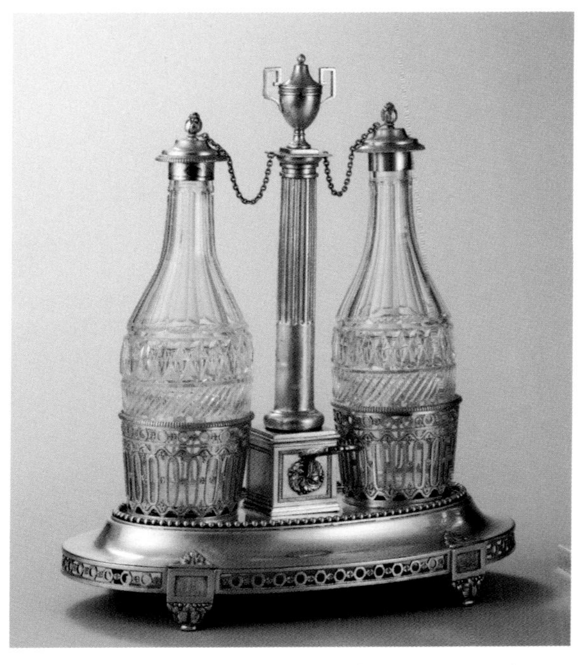

CRUET STAND · *Roch-Louis Dany (working c.1779–1820)*
*Paris, 1789* · Silver, 12 7/8 x 10 11/16 x 6 3/8 in. (32.7 x 27.2 x 16.2 cm)
*Belonged to James Monroe and James Madison*

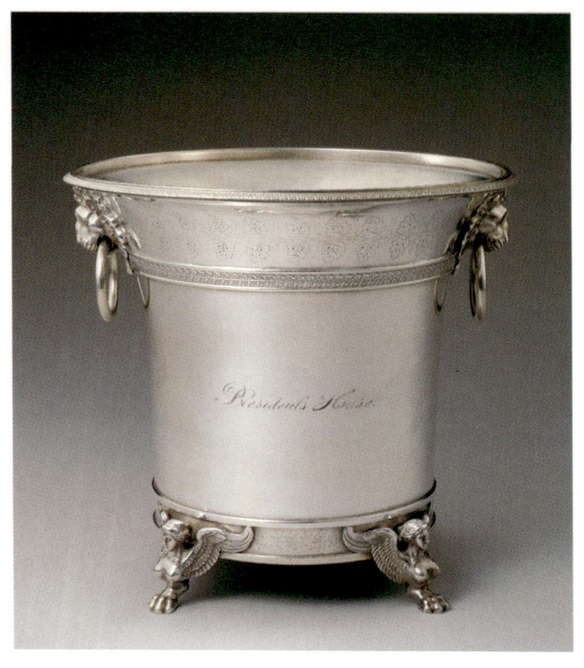


WINE COOLER · *Jean-Baptiste-Claude Odiot (1763–1850)*
*Paris, 1798–1809* · Silver, 17 3/4 x 8 1/2 in. (45.1 x 21.6 cm)
*James Monroe Administration*

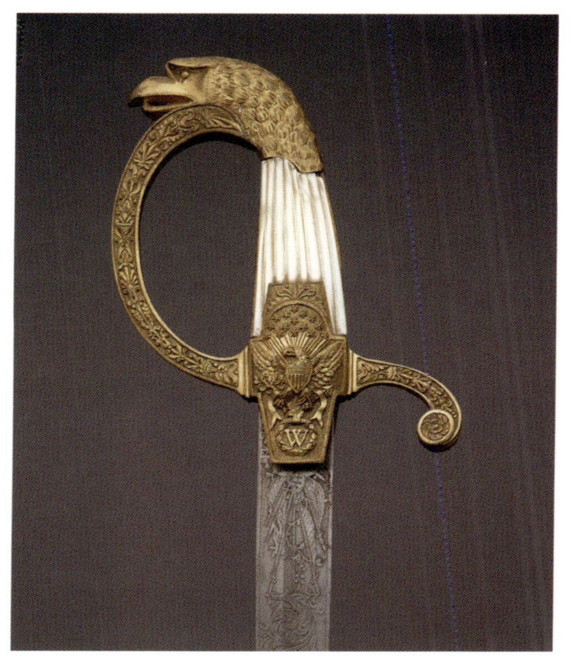

PRESENTATION SABER · *Klingenthal Armory, Alsace, France, c. 1799–1800*
Gilded brass, mother-of-pearl, steel, 40 11/16 x 5 3/8 x 1 1/8 in.
(103.4 x 9.2 x 2.9 cm) · *Made for George Washington*

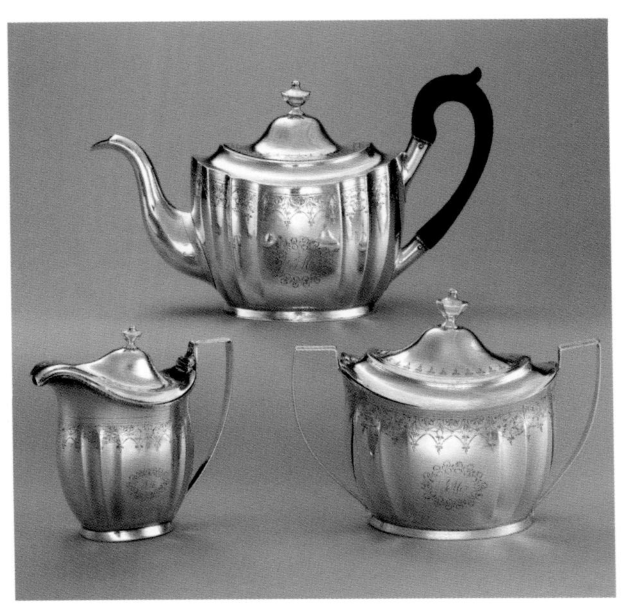

TEA SERVICE · *Sayre and Richards* · *New York, c. 1803–13*
Silver; Teapot-7 3/4 x 12 3/8 x 4 7/8 in. (19.7 x 31.4 x 12.4 cm)
*Belonged to James Madison*

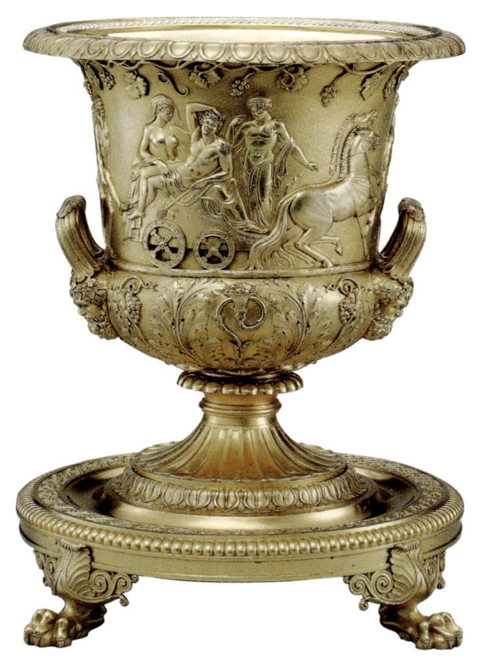

WINE COOLER · *Paul Storr (1771–1844)* · *London, 1809–10*
Gilded silver, 13 7/8 x 13 1/4 in. (35.2 x 33.7 cm)

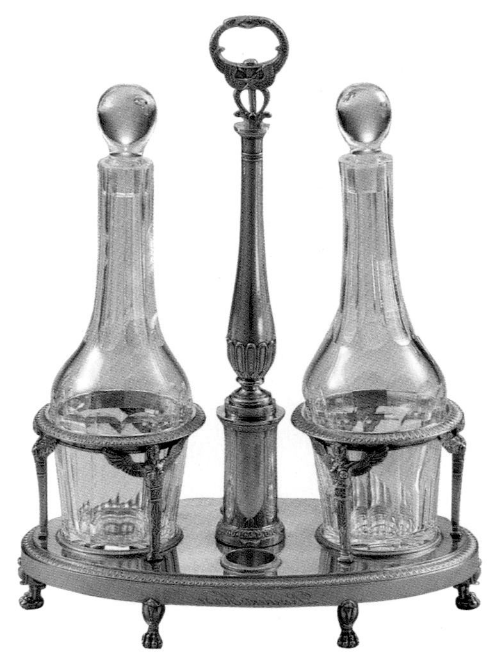

CRUET STAND · *Martin-Guillaume Biennais (1764–1843)*
*Paris, 1809–19* · Silver, 12 3/4 x 9 1/4 x 4 7/8 in. (32.4 x 23.5 x 12.4 cm)
*Andrew Jackson Administration*

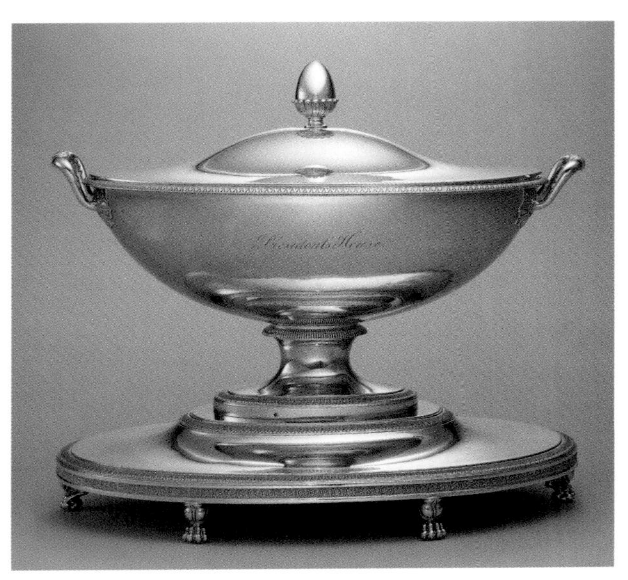

SOUP TUREEN · *Martin-Guillaume Biennais (1764–1843)*
*Paris, 1809–19* · Silver, 14¾ x 16¼ x 11⅛ in. (37.5 x 41.3 x 28.3 cm)
*Andrew Jackson Administration*

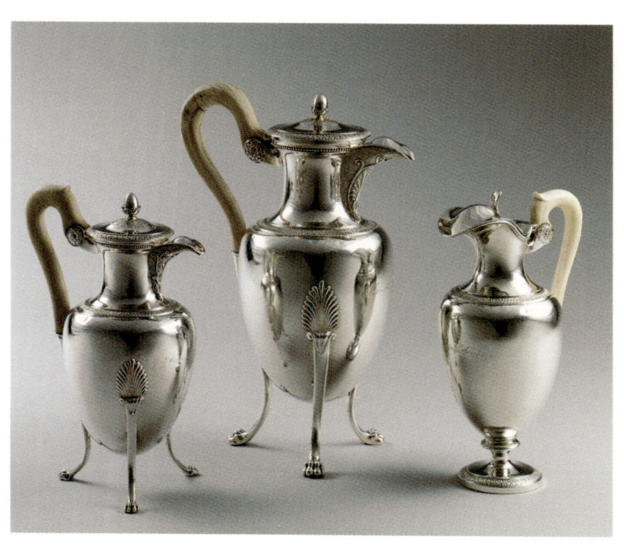

COFFEE SERVICE · *Martin-Guillaume Biennais (1764–1843)*
*Paris, 1809–19* · Silver; Coffeepot-13 3/8 x 8 3/4 x 5 1/4 in.
(34 x 22.2 x 13.3 cm) · *Andrew Jackson Administration*

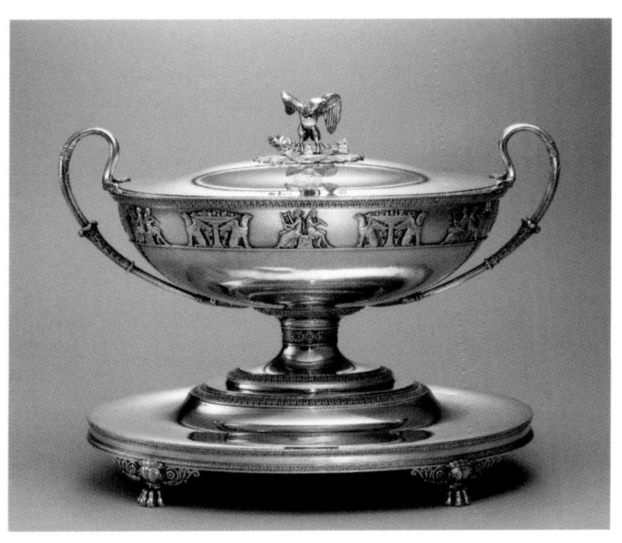

Soup Tureen · *Jacques-Henri Fauconnier (1779–1839) · Paris, c. 1817*
Silver, 14 5/8 x 18 1/4 x 11 5/8 in. (37.2 x 46.4 x 29.5 cm)
*James Monroe Administration*

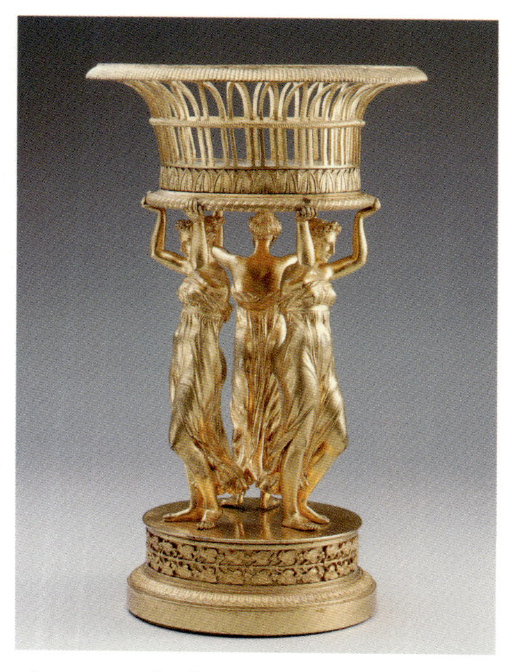

BASKET · *Attributed to Denière et Matelin · Paris, c. 1817*
Gilded bronze, 15 3/4 x 9 3/8 in. (40 x 23.8 cm)
*James Monroe Administration*

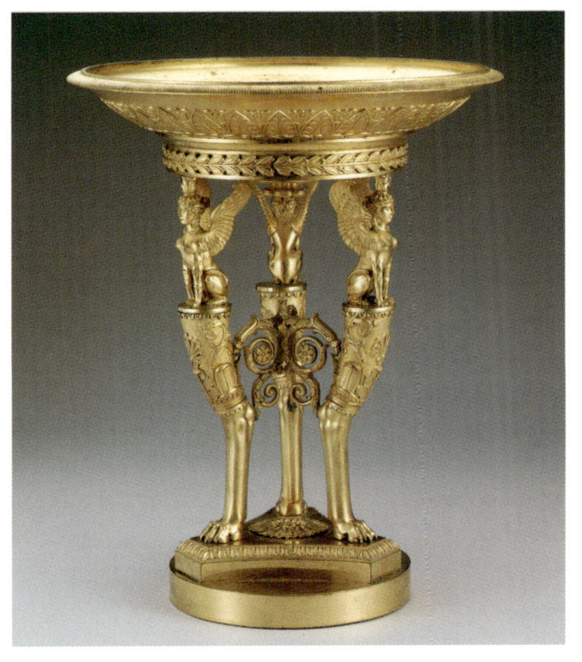

STAND · *Possibly by Denière et Matelin · Paris, c. 1817*
Gilded bronze, 15 1/8 x 11 7/8 in. (38.4 x 30.2 cm)
*James Monroe Administration*

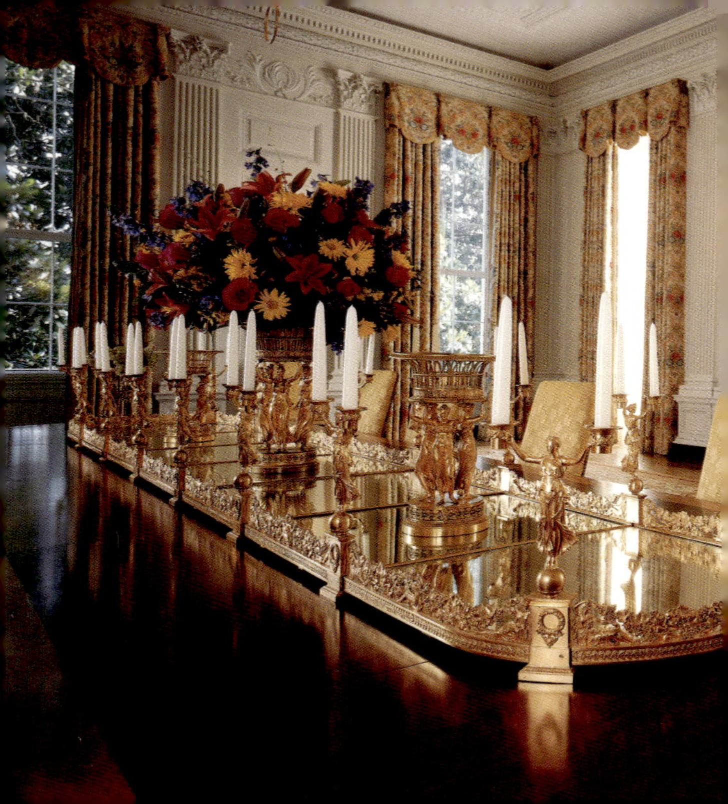

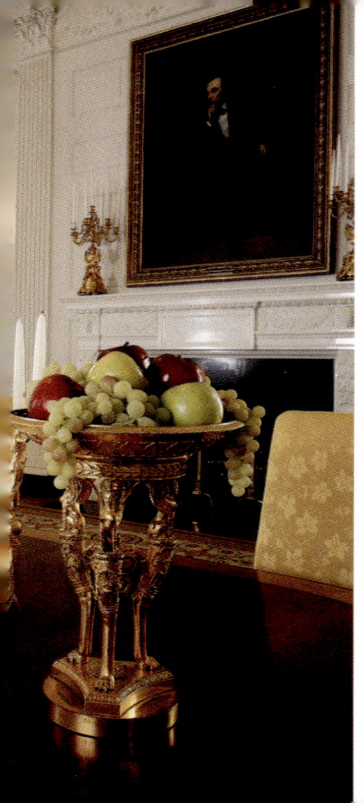

PLATEAU · *Denière et Matelin*
*Paris, c. 1817*
Gilded bronze, mirror
$13\frac{5}{8}$ x 174 x $25\frac{5}{8}$ in.
(34.6 x 442 x 65.1 cm)
*James Monroe Administration*

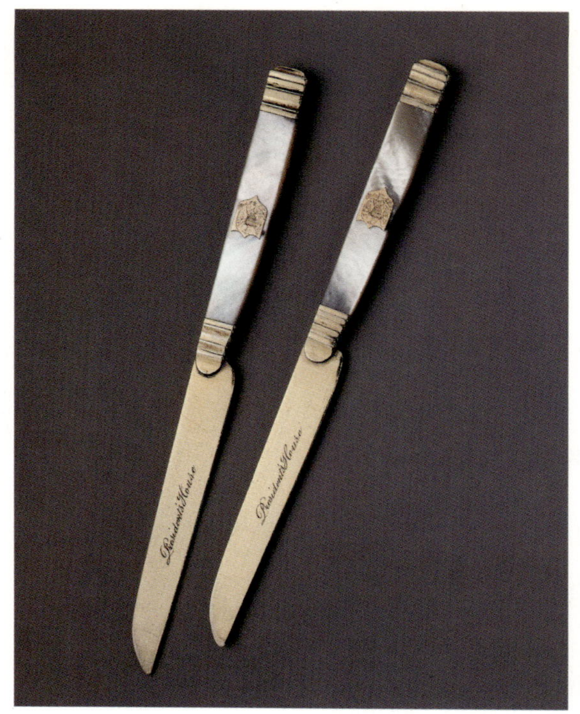
President's House
President's House

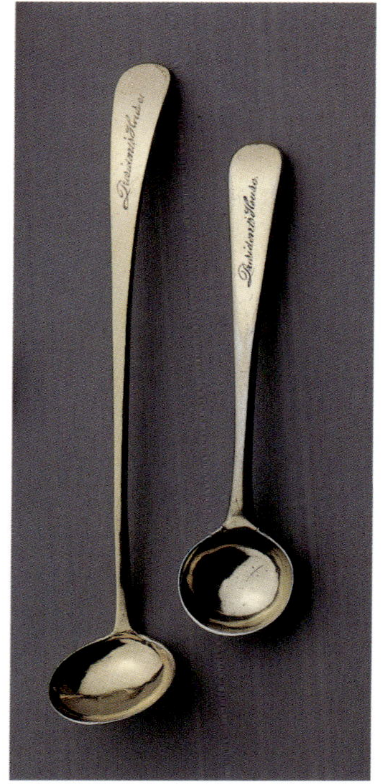

OPPOSITE:
FRUIT KNIVES
*J. B. Boitin · Paris, c. 1817*
Gilded silver, mother-of-pearl,
8 in. (20.3 cm)
*James Monroe Administration*
RIGHT:
MUSTARD SPOON
AND SALT SPOON
*Charles Alexander Burnett,*
*(1769–1848)*
*Georgetown, D.C., c. 1817–30*
Gilded silver; Mustard-
5½ in. (14 cm)
*James Monroe Administration*

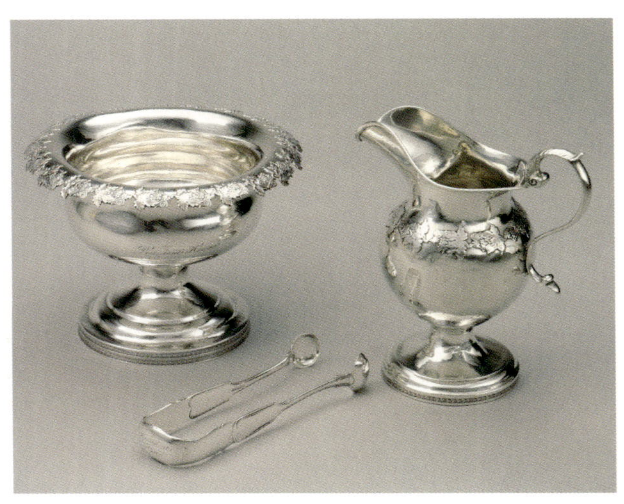

ABOVE: PARTIAL TEA SERVICE · *Robert Keyworth (1795–1856)*
*Washington, D.C., c. 1835–51* · Silver; Bowl-6 x 4½ in. (15.2 x 11.4 cm)
OPPOSITE: WATER PITCHER · *G. C. Allen (working c.1844–58)*
*New York, 1858* · Silver, 12½ x 8½ x 4½ in. (31.8 x 21.6 x 11.4 cm)
*Belonged to Martin Van Buren*

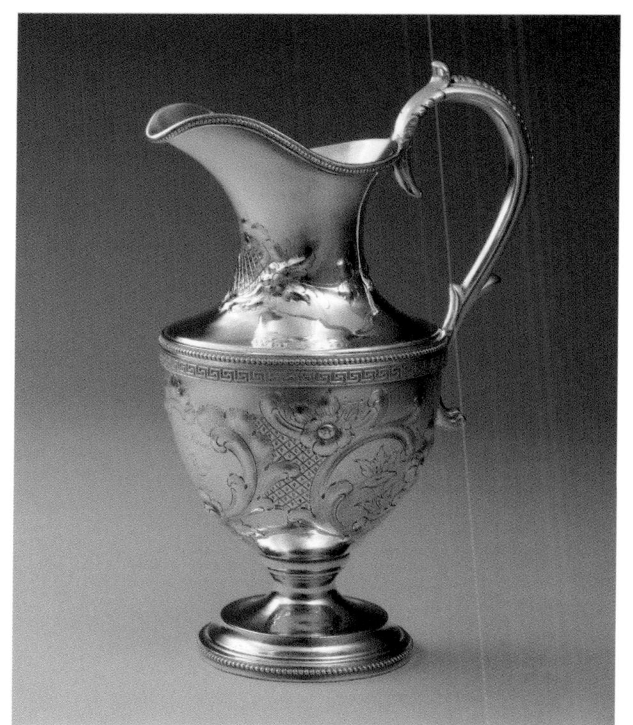

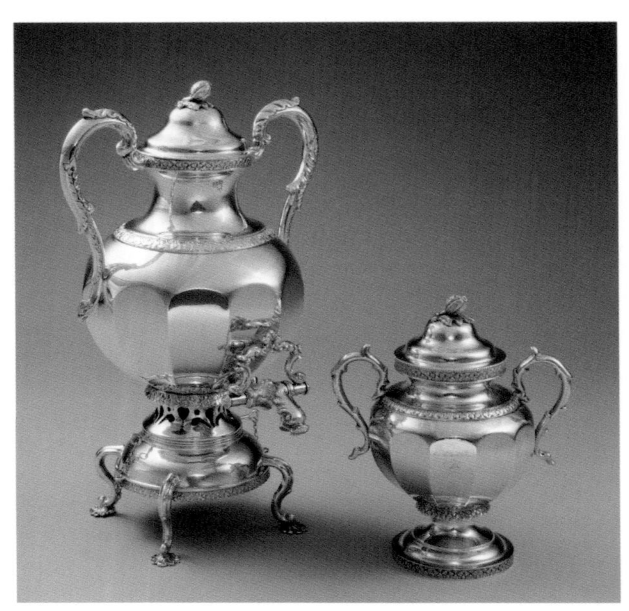

HOT WATER URN AND SUGAR BOWL · *Wood & Hughes*
*New York, c. 1858* · Silver; Urn-17 x 10¾ x 10¾ in.
(43.2 x 27.3 x 27.3 cm) · *Belonged to Millard Fillmore*

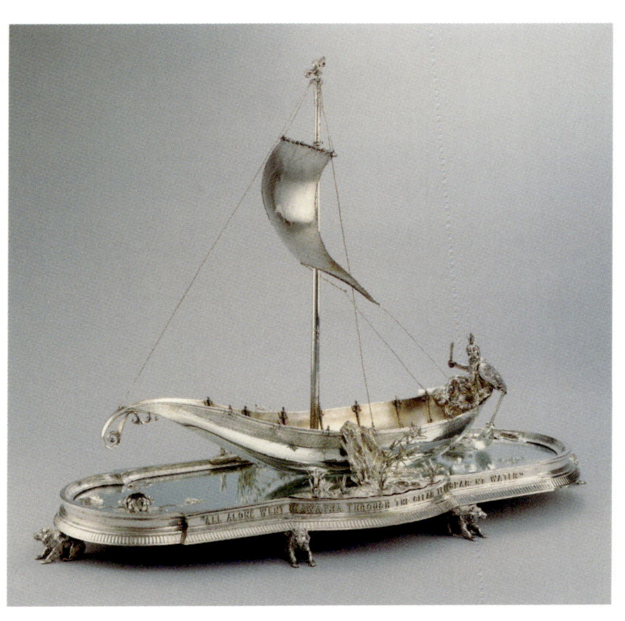


CENTERPIECE · *Gorham Mfg. Co.* · *Providence, Rhode Island, 1871*
Silver, mirror-34 x 44½ x 19 in. (86.4 x 113 x 48.3 cm)
*Ulysses S. Grant Administration*

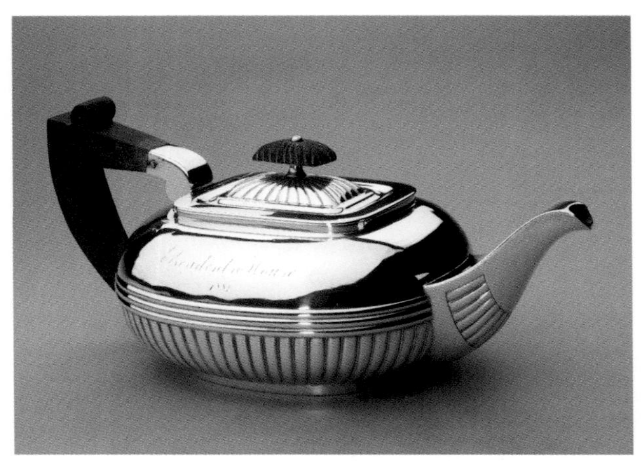

TEAPOT · *Dominick & Haff* · *New York, 1881*
Silver, $4^{5}/8$ x $11^{3}/8$ x $5^{1}/4$ in. (11.8 x 28.9 x 13.3 cm)
*James A. Garfield Administration*

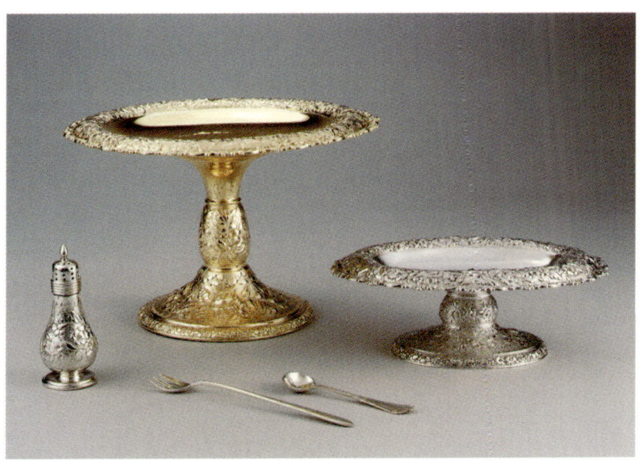

PEPPER SHAKER, COMPOTE, OLIVE DISH, OYSTER FORK AND SALT SPOON · *Tiffany & Co.* · *New York, c. 1882*
Silver and silver electroplate; Compote-6 x 9 7/8 in. (15.2 x 25.1 cm)
*Chester A. Arthur Administration*

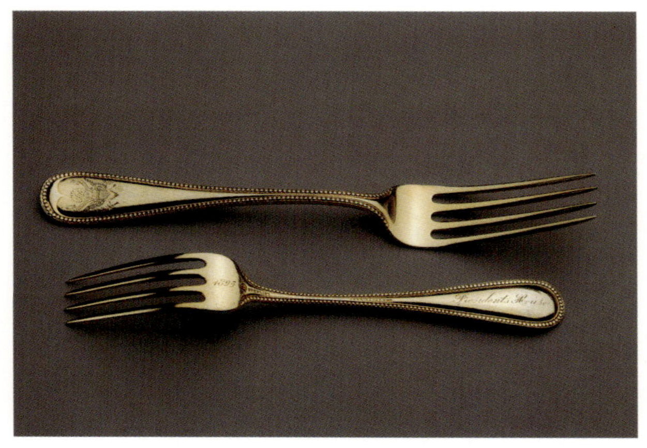

ABOVE: DINNER FORK AND BREAKFAST FORK · *Wm. B. Durgin Co. Concord, New Hampshire, 1894* · Gilded silver; Dinner Fork-
7 7/8 in. (20 cm) · *Grover Cleveland Administration*
OPPOSITE: PRESENTATION CUP · *Tiffany & Co.* · *New York, 1899*
Silver, 13 3/4 x 12 1/8 in. (34.9 x 30.7 cm) · *William McKinley Administration*

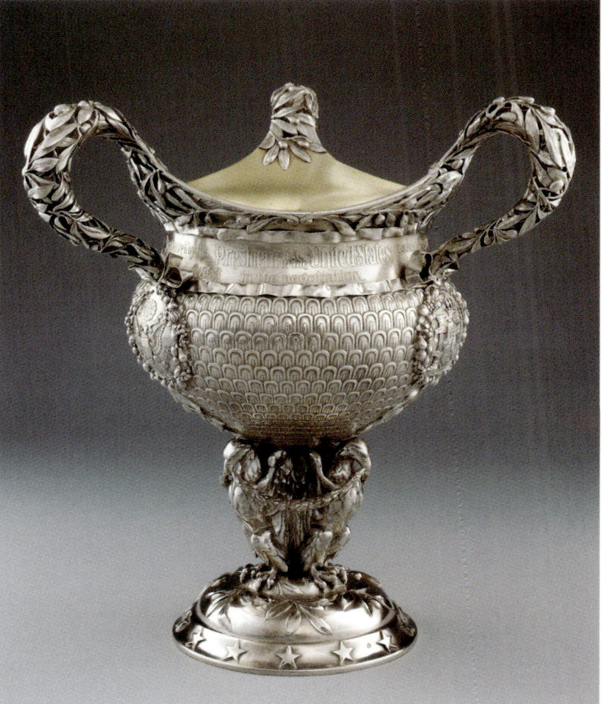
United States

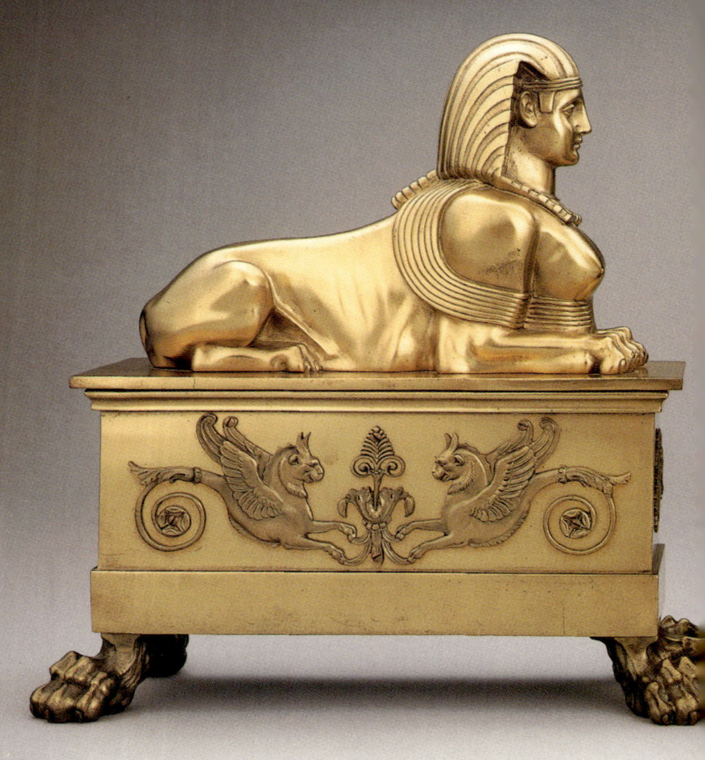

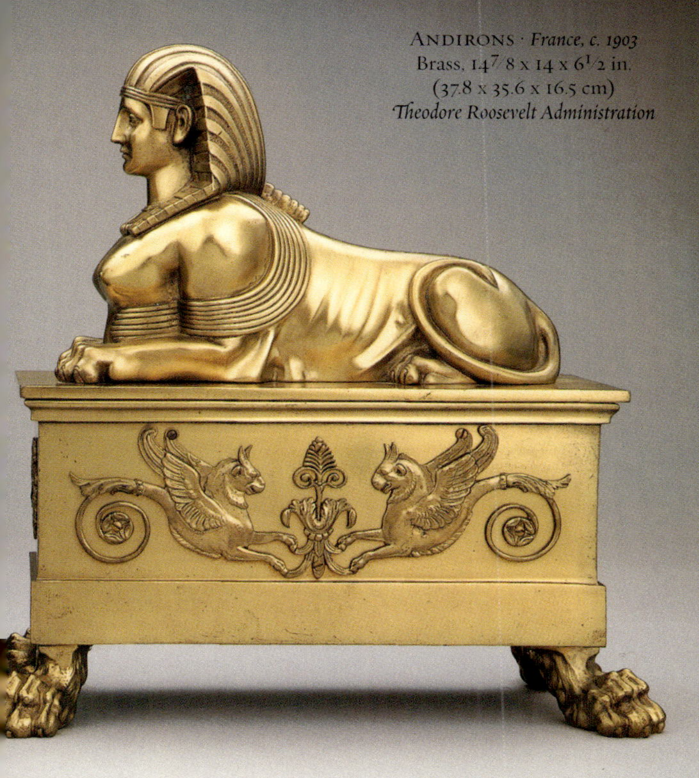

ANDIRONS · *France, c. 1903*
Brass, $14^{7}/8 \times 14 \times 6^{1}/2$ in.
(37.8 x 35.6 x 16.5 cm)
*Theodore Roosevelt Administration*

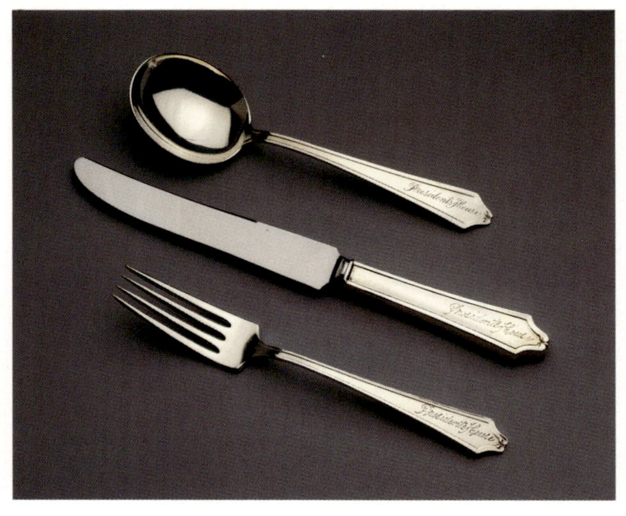

ABOVE: SOUP SPOON, DINNER KNIFE, AND DINNER FORK
*International Silver Co. · Wallingford, Connecticut, c. 1926–60*
Silver, stainless steel, Dinner Knife-$9\frac{5}{8}$ in. (24.6 cm)
*Calvin Coolidge Administration*
OPPOSITE: SILVER GILT SELECTION
*Europe and America, 18th and 19th centuries*
Gilded silver; Wine Ewer-$16\frac{5}{8}$ x $8\frac{3}{4}$ x 7 in. (42.6 x 22.2 x 17.8 cm)

 PAGES 190–191: THE STATE FLOOR: THE EAST ROOM, 2000

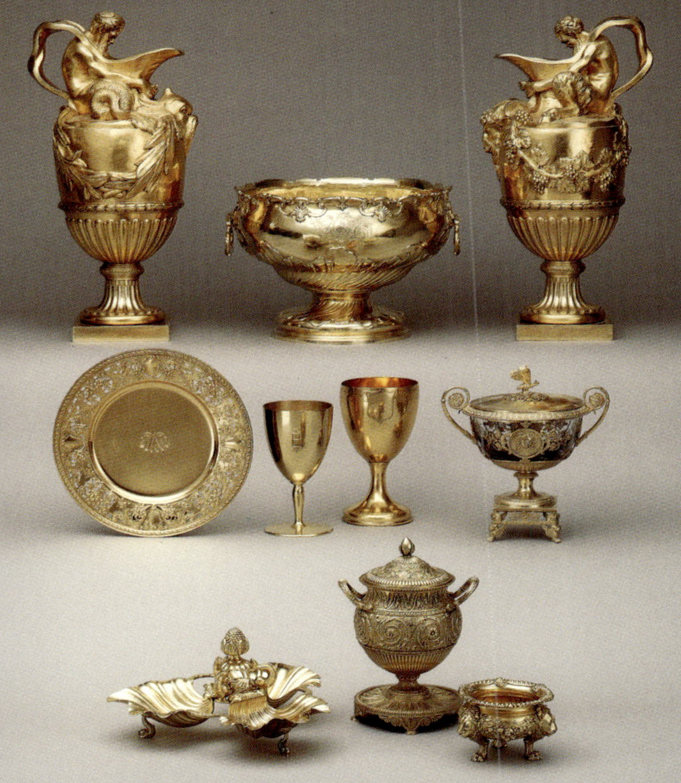

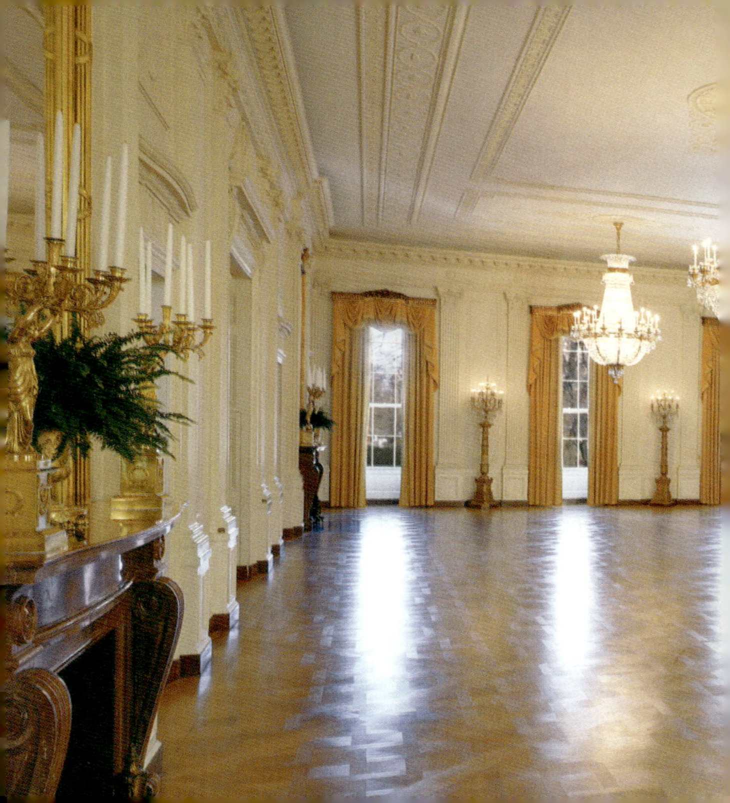

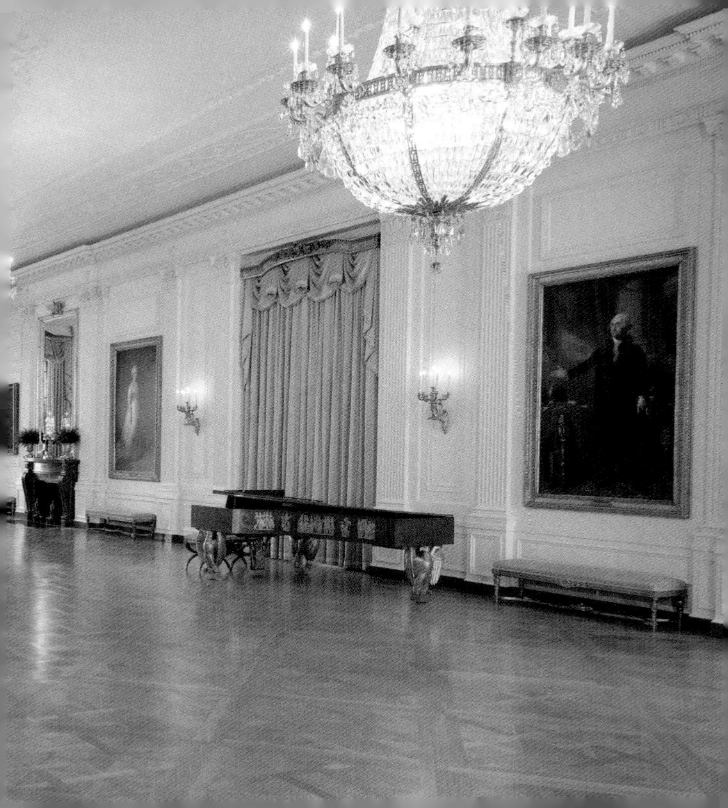

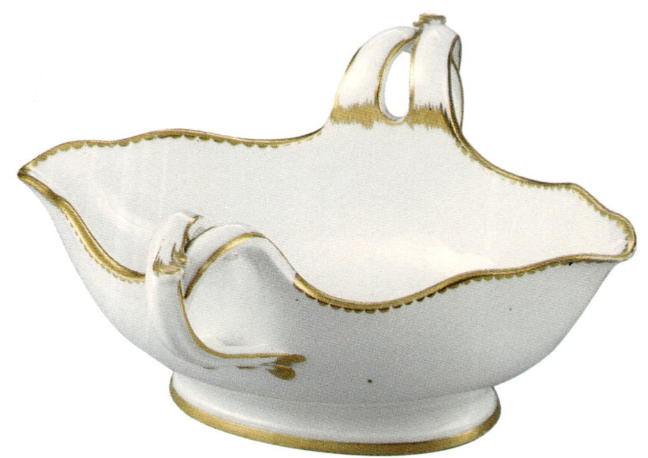

SAUCE BOAT · *Royal Porcelain Manufactory of Sèvres · France, c. 1778*
Porcelain, 4 x 8⅝ x 7¾ in. (10.2 x 21.9 x 19.7 cm)
*Belonged to George Washington*

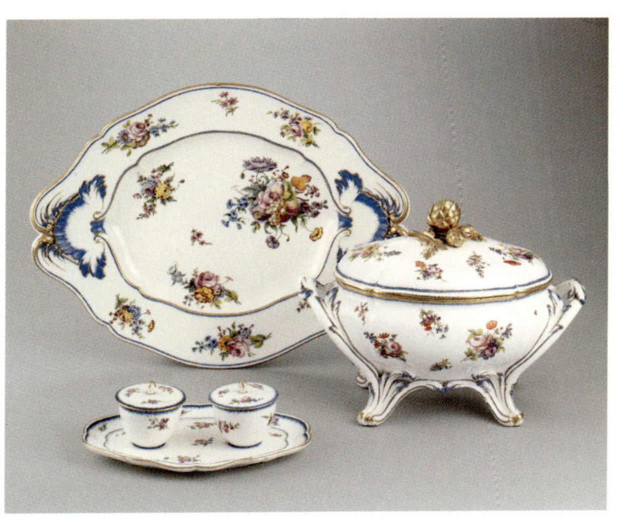

Soup Tureen and Stand and Preserves Stand
*Royal Porcelain Manufactory of Sèvres* · *France, 1782* · Porcelain; Tureen-13 x 7 3/8 x 6 1/2 in. (33 x 18.7 x 16.5 cm) · *Belonged to John Adams*

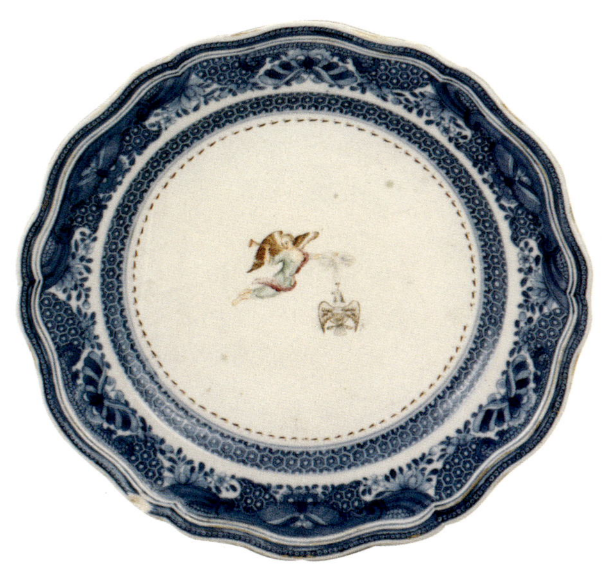

Dinner Plate · *China, 1784–85*
Porcelain, 9½ in. (24.1 cm)
*Belonged to George Washington*

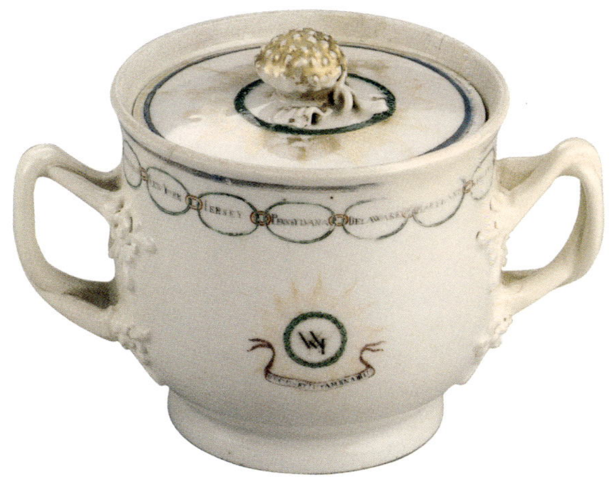

SUGAR BOWL AND TEAPOT COVER · *China, 1795*
Porcelain, Bowl - 3¾ x 6 x 4⅛ in. (9.5 x 15.2 x 10.5 cm)
*Belonged to George Washington*

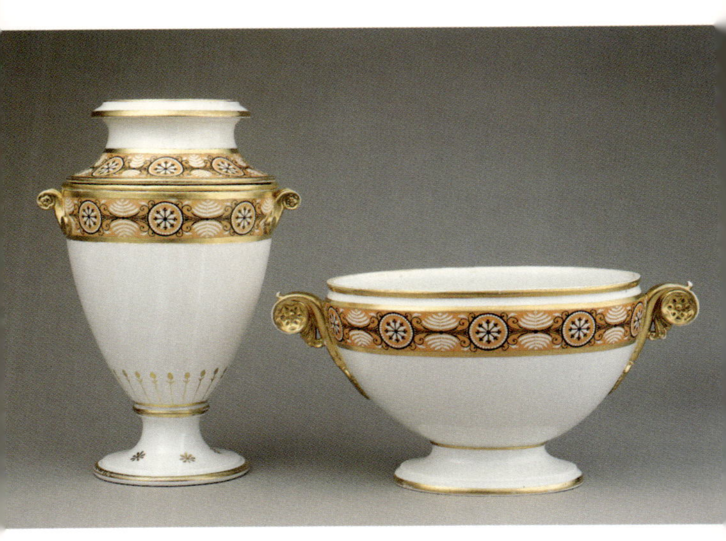

DESSERT COOLER AND SOUP TUREEN

*Nast Manufactory* · *Paris, c. 1806* · Porcelain; Cooler - 12 1/2 x 8 1/2 x 6 7/8 in. (31.8 x 21.6 x 17.5 cm) · *Belonged to James Madison*

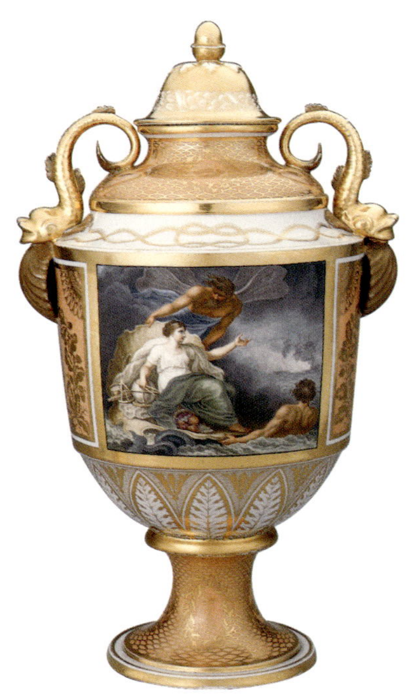

URN · *Barr, Flight & Barr · Worcester, England, c. 1807*
Porcelain, $16\,3/8 \times 9\,1/4 \times 7\,1/2$ in. (41.6 x 23.5 x 19.1 cm)

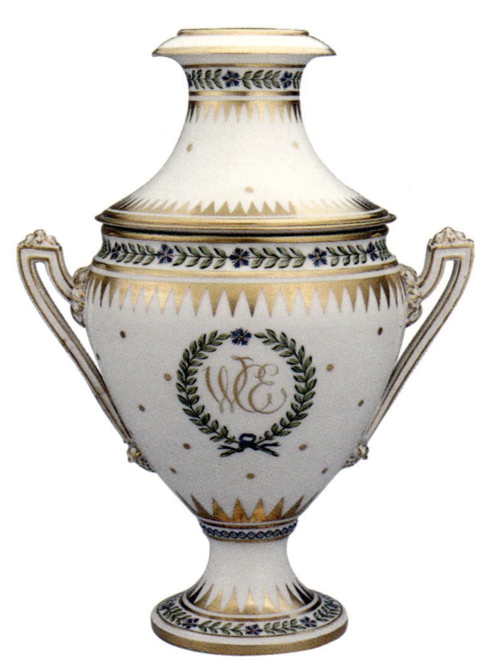

DESSERT COOLER · *France, c. 1815–25*
Porcelain, 15 3/4 x 11 1/2 x 8 1/2 in. (40 x 29.2 x 21 cm)

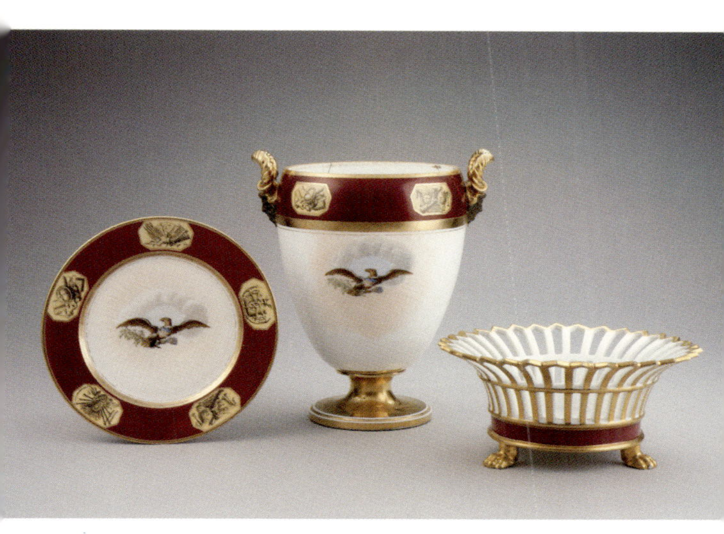

Dessert Plate, Dessert Cooler, and Basket
*Pierre-Louis Dagoty (1771–1840) and Edouard Honoré (?–1850)*
*Paris, c. 1817* · Porcelain; Cooler - 11 x 9 1/2 x 7 3/8 in.
(27.9 x 24.1 x 18.7 cm) · *James Monroe Administration*

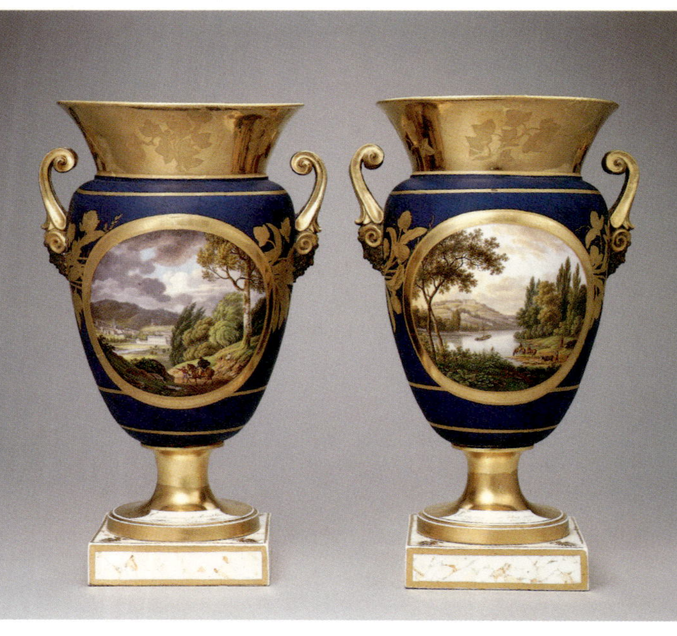

VASES · *Paris, c. 1817* · Porcelain, 16 x 9½ x 8¼ in.
(40.6 x 24.1 x 21 cm) · *James Monroe Administration*

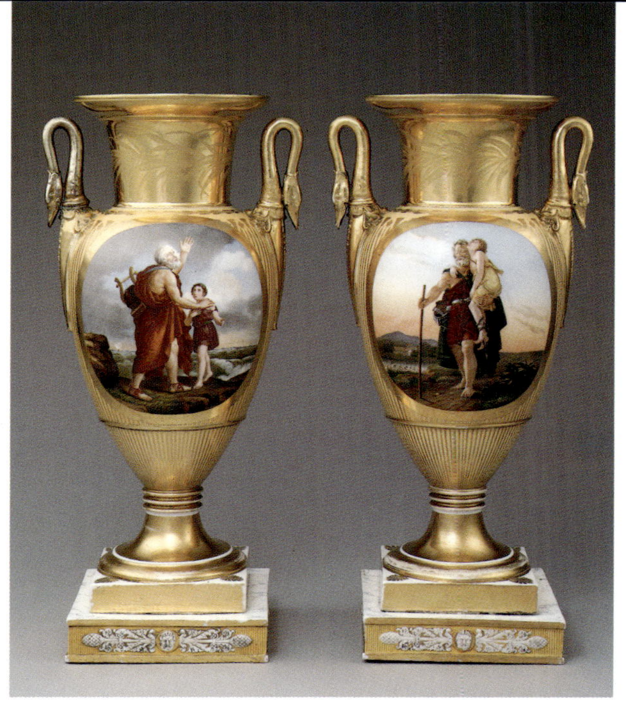

VASES · *Paris, c. 1817* · Porcelain, 15¾ x 8¾ x 6⅞ in. (40 x 22.2 x 17.5 cm) · *James Monroe Administration*

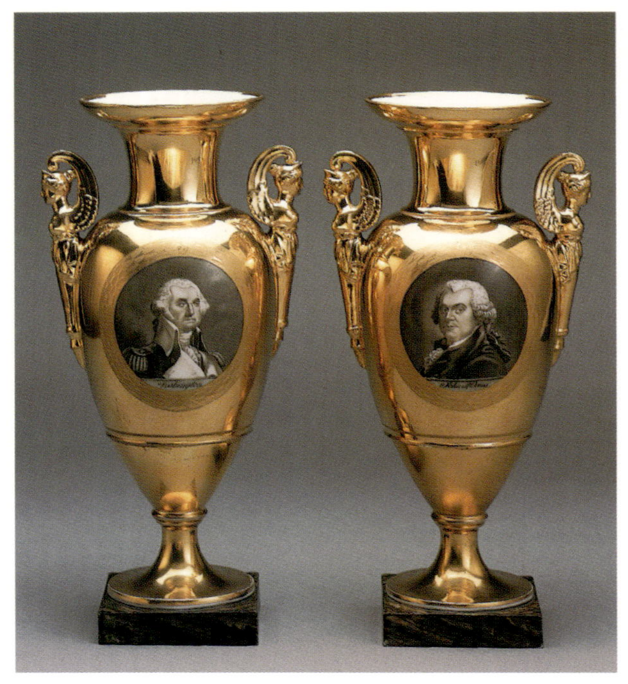

VASES · *Paris, c. 1820*
Porcelain, $12^{3}/_{4}$ x 6 x $4^{1}/_{4}$ in. (32.4 x 15.2 x 10.8 cm)

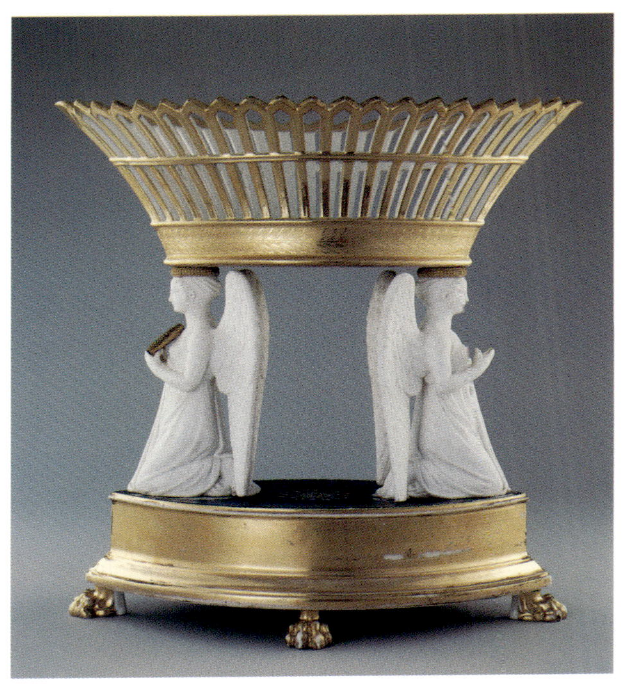

FRUIT BASKET · *France, c. 1820–30* · Glazed and biscuit porcelain
16 3/8 x 16 1/4 x 8 1/2 in. (41.6 x 41.3 x 21.6 cm) · *Belonged to John Tyler*

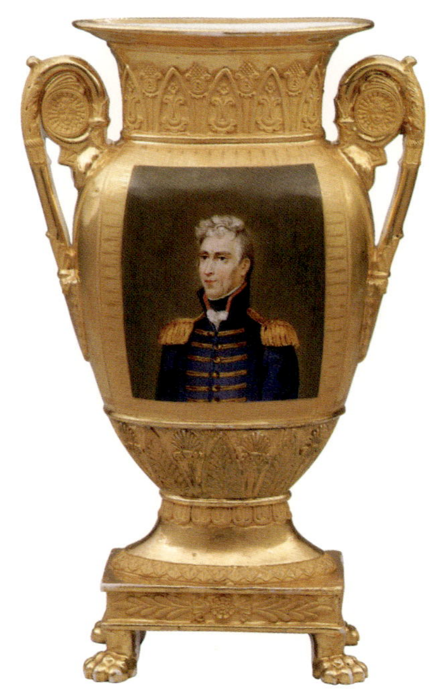

VASE · *France, c. 1825–30*
Porcelain, 12 13/16 x 7 3/4 x 3 1/4 in. (32.5 x 19.7 x 8.3 cm)

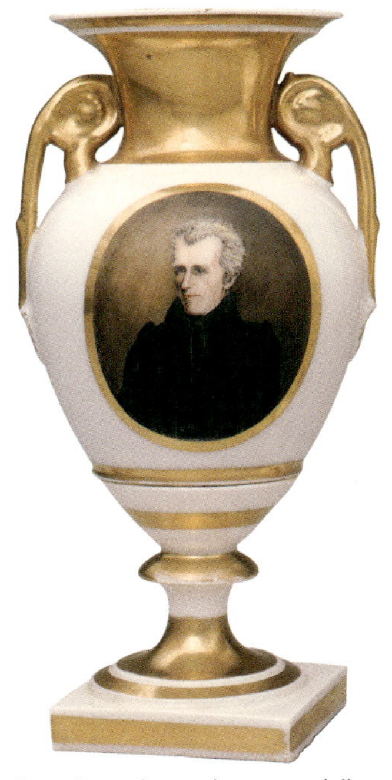

VASE · *William Ellis Tucker, Tucker & Hemphill, or Joseph Hemphill*
*Philadelphia, c. 1830–38* · Porcelain
11 5/8 x 5 3/4 x 5 1/8 in. (29.5 x 14.6 x 13 cm)

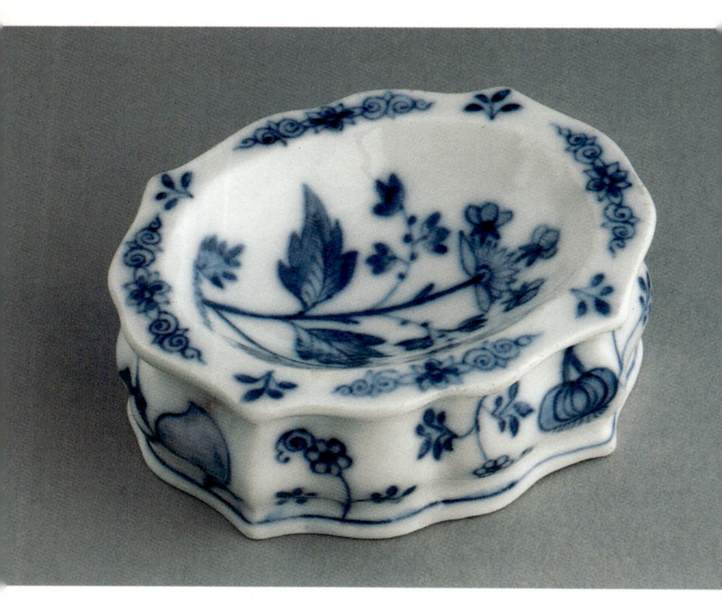

SALT CELLAR · *Meissen* · *Saxony, Early 19th century*
Porcelain, 3¼ x 2½ x 1⅜ in. (8.3 x 5.4 x 3.5 cm)
*Belonged to John Quincy Adams*

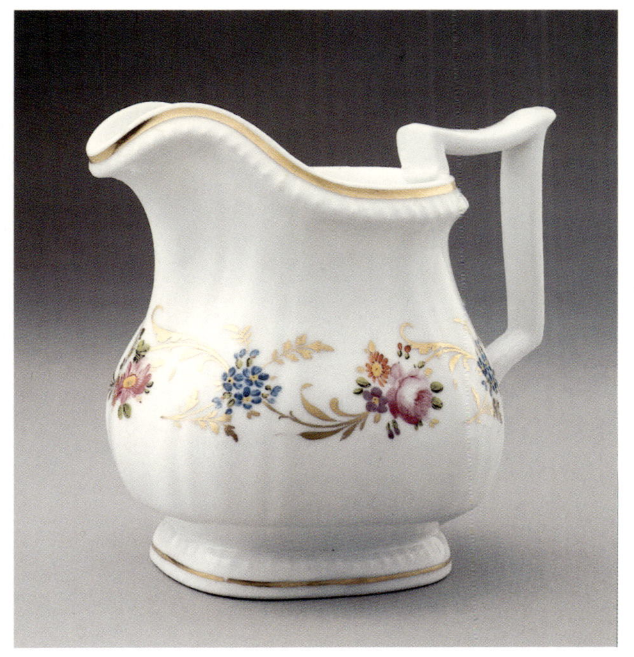

PITCHER · *Tucker and Hulme · Philadelphia, 1828*
Porcelain, 7 1/2 x 4 1/2 x 3 3/4 in. (19.1 x 11.4 x 9.5 cm)

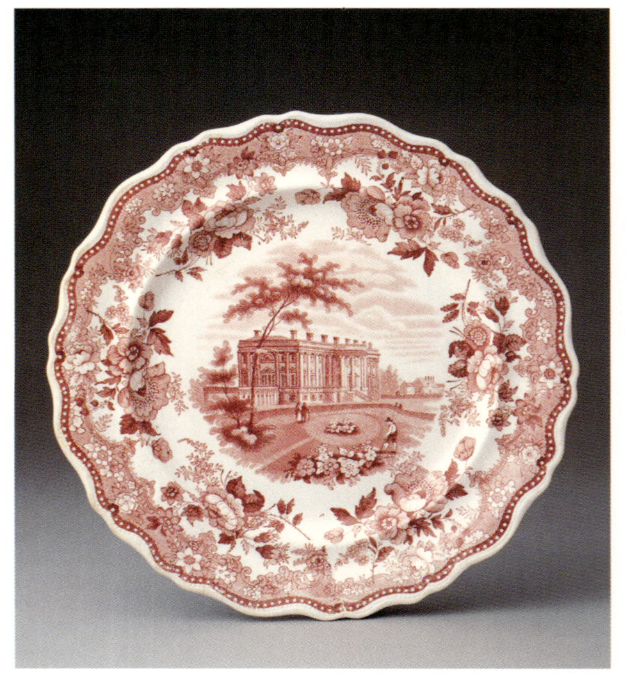

PLATE · *Job & John Jackson · Burslem, England, 1831–43 (?)*
Transfer-printed earthenware, 10 1/4 in. (26 cm)

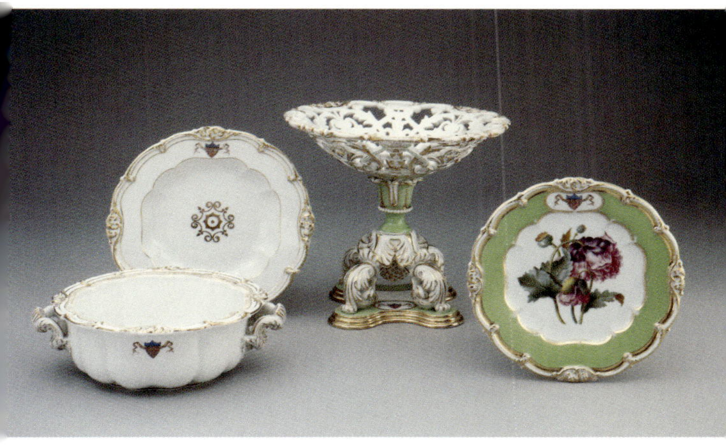

Vegetable Dish, Soup Plate, Fruit Basket, Dessert Plate
*Edouard Honoré (?–1850) · Champroux, France, 1846*
Porcelain; Basket - 10 x 10 7/8 in. (25.4 x 27.6 cm)
*James K. Polk Administration*

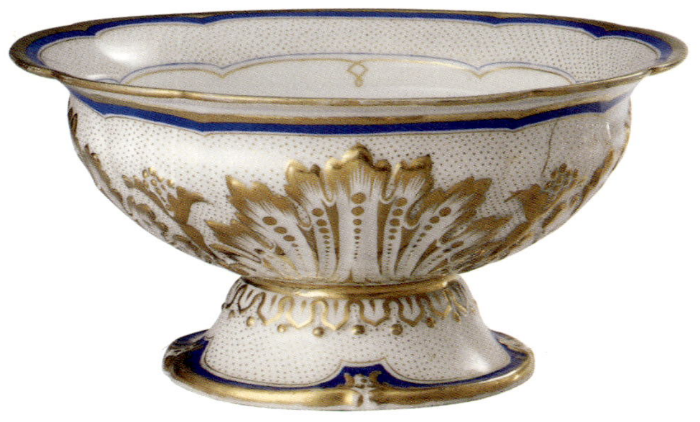

COMPOTE · *France* · *Decorated by Haughwout & Dailey* · *New York, 1853*
Porcelain, 5 1/2 x 11 1/8 in. (14 x 28.3 cm)
*Franklin Pierce Administration*

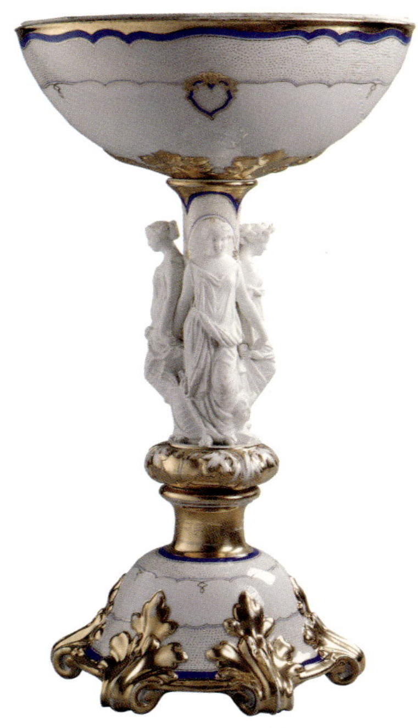

CENTERPIECE · *France* · *Decorated by Haughwout & Dailey*
*New York, 1853* · Porcelain and Parian ware
25 1/2 x 14 1/2 in. (64.8 x 36.8 cm) · *Franklin Pierce Administration*

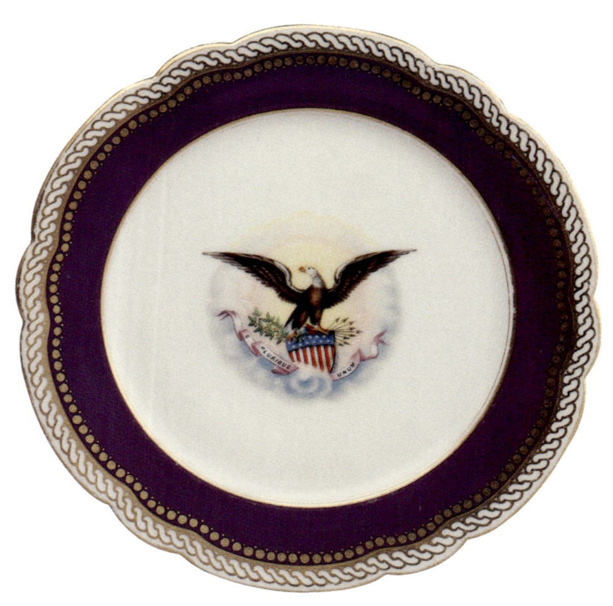


DINNER PLATE · *Haviland & Co., Limoges, France*
*Decorated by E. V. Haughwout, New York, 1861*
Porcelain, 9¼ in. (23.5 cm)
*Abraham Lincoln Administration*

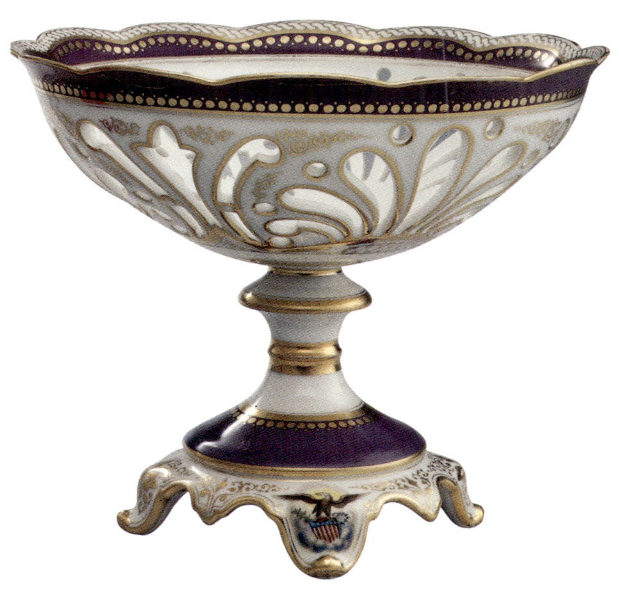

FRUIT BASKET · *Haviland & Co., Limoges, France*
*Decorated by E. V. Haughwout, New York, 1861 or 1866*
Porcelain, 7 7/8 x 9 1/2 in. (20.1 x 24.1 cm)
*Abraham Lincoln Administration*

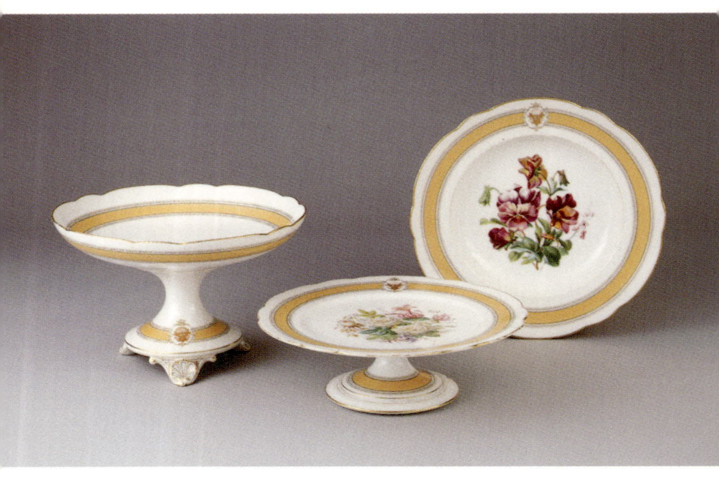

COMPOTE, CAKE STAND, AND DINNER PLATE
*Haviland & Co. · Limoges, France, 1869–70 and 1874*
Porcelain; Compote - 5 3/4 x 8 7/8 in. (14.6 x 22.5 cm)
*Ulysses S. Grant Administration*

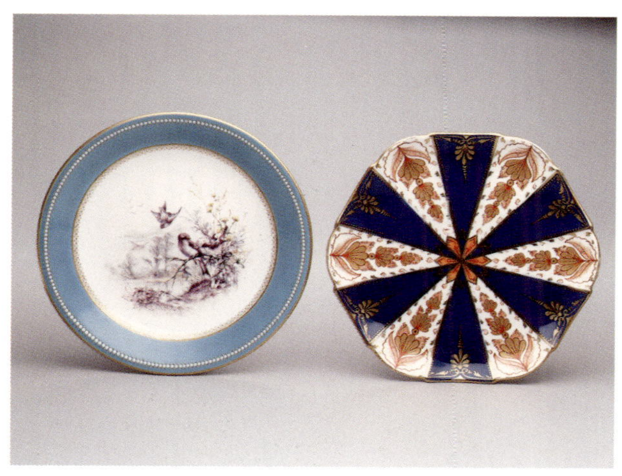

PLATES · *Left: Royal Worcester Porcelain Co., England, c.1881*
*Right: Probably England, c. 1881*
Porcelain; Left-9 1/4 in. (23.5 cm)
*Chester A. Arthur Administration*

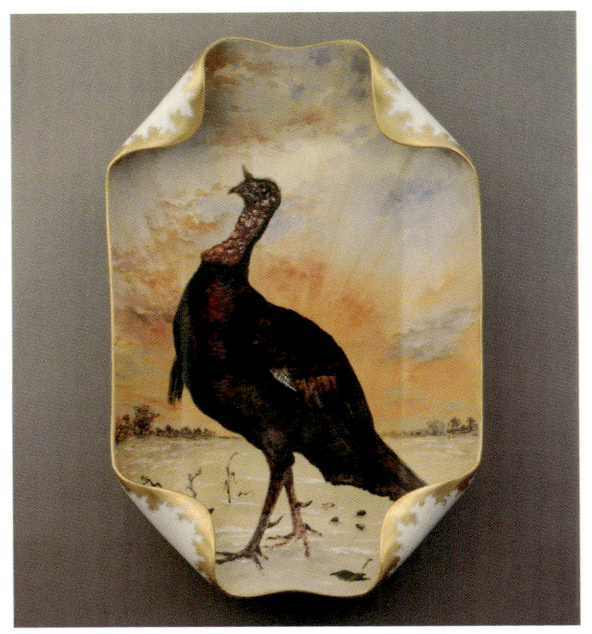

ABOVE: PLATTER AND OPPOSITE: STATE SERVICE
*Haviland & Co. · Limoges, France, 1880* · Porcelain, 20 x 12 7/8 in. (50.8 x 32.7 cm) · Porcelain; Dinner Plate - 10 1/8 in. (25.7 cm)
*Rutherford B. Hayes Administration*

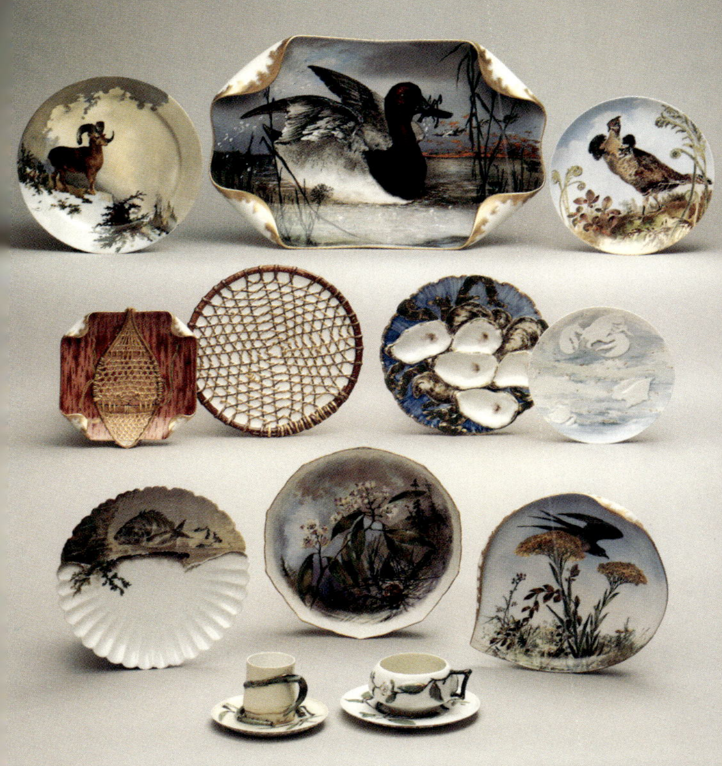

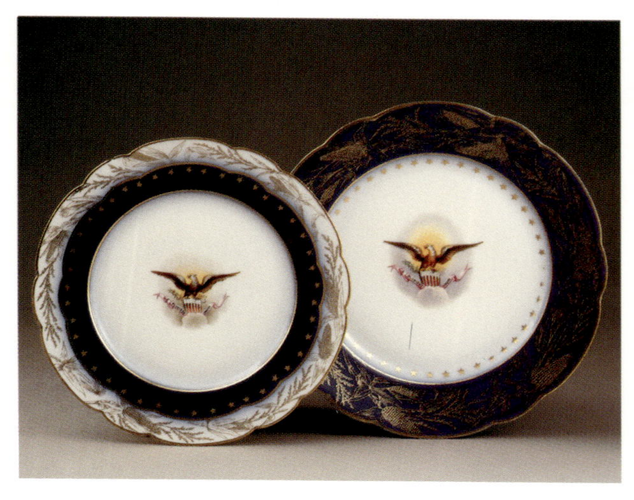

Breakfast Plate and Dinner Plate
*Tressemannes & Vogt · Limoges, France, 1891*
Porcelain; Dinner Plate - 9½ in. (24.1 cm)
*Benjamin Harrison Administration*

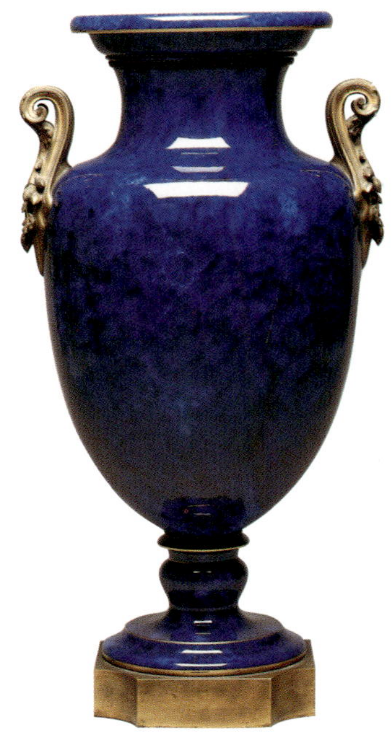

VASE · *National Porcelain Manufactory of Sèvres · France, 1898*
Porcelain, gilded metal, 34 x 17 1/2 x 15 5/8 in. (86.4 x 44.4 x 39.7 cm)
*William McKinley Administration*

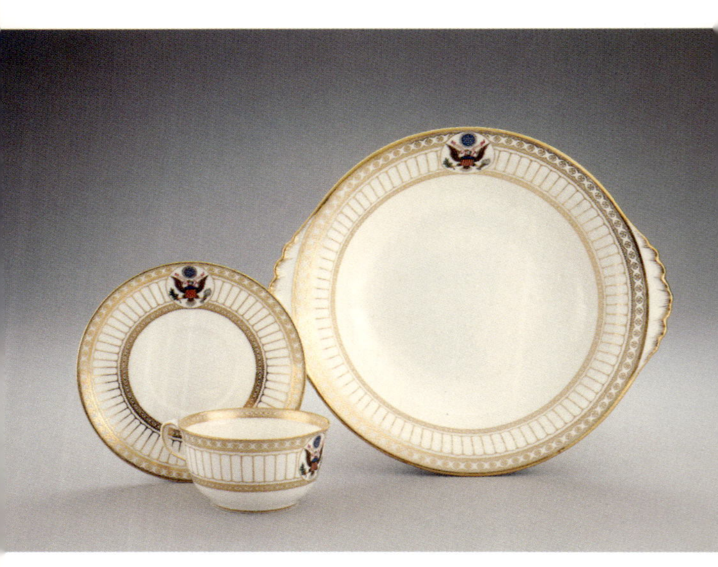

Tea Cup and Saucer and Oyster Plate
*Josiah Wedgwood & Sons, Ltd. · Etruria, England, 1903*
Porcelain; Plate - $10^{1}/8$ x 9 in. (25.7 x 22.9 cm)
*Theodore Roosevelt Administration*

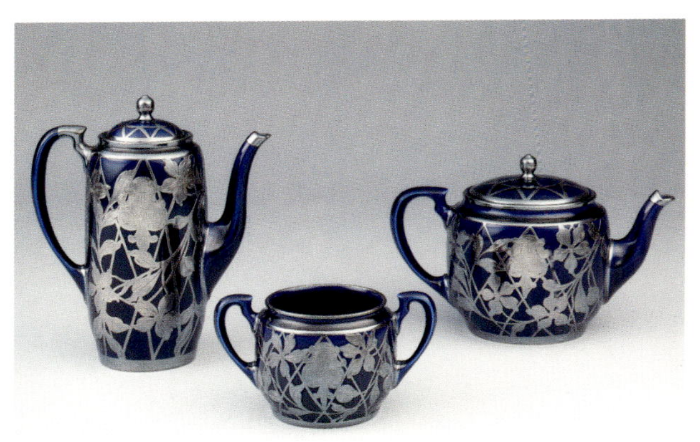

TEA AND COFFEE SET · *Lenox, Inc.* · *Trenton, New Jersey, 1911*
Silver-overlaid china; Coffeepot-
6 5/8 x 5 5/8 x 2 3/4 in. (16.8 x 14.3 x 7 cm)
*Belonged to William H. Taft*

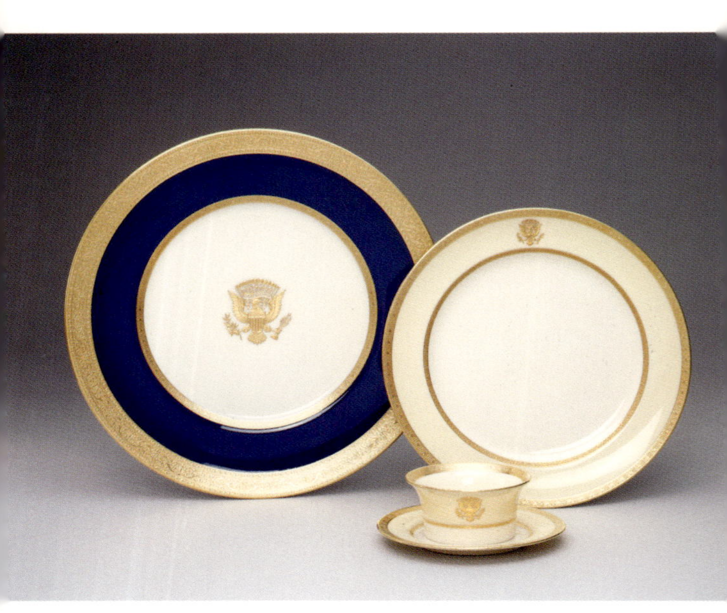

Service Plate, Entrée/Fish Plate, and Ramekin and Plate · *Lenox, Inc. · Trenton, New Jersey, 1918*
China; Service Plate - 11 1/8 in. (28.3 cm) · *Woodrow Wilson Administration*

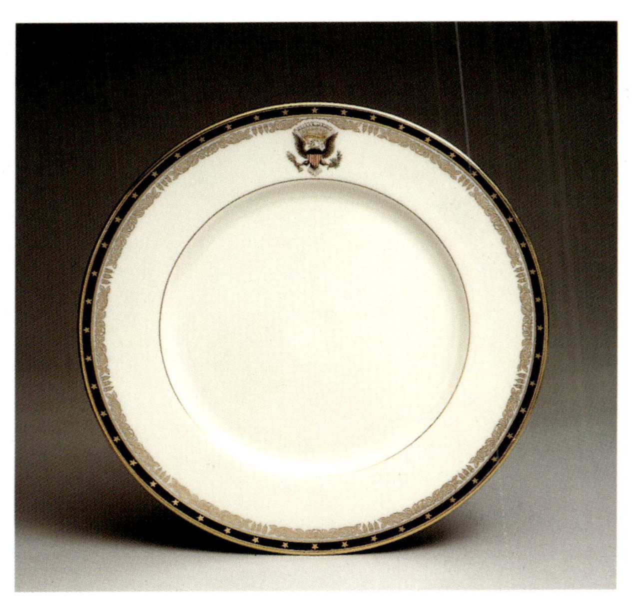

SALAD PLATE · *Lenox, Inc.*
*Trenton, New Jersey, 1934* · China, $7^{1}/_{4}$ in. (18.4 cm)
*Franklin D. Roosevelt Administration*

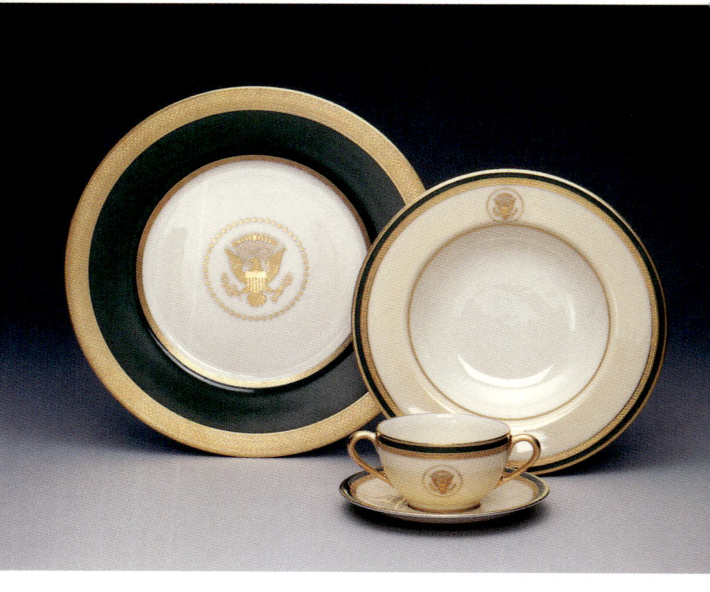

Service Plate, Soup Plate, and Bouillon Cup and Saucer · *Lenox, Inc. · Trenton, New Jersey, 1951*
China; Service Plate-11 3/8 in. (28.9 cm)
*Harry S. Truman Administration*

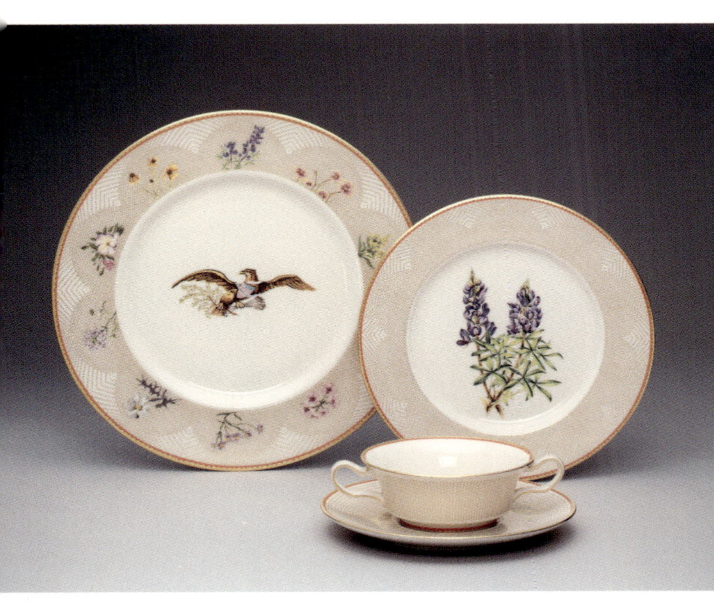

SERVICE PLATE, DESSERT PLATE, AND CREAM SOUP CUP AND SAUCER · *Castleton China, Inc.* · *New Castle, Pennsylvania, 1968–72*
Porcelain; Service Plate-11 5/8 in. (29.5 cm)
*Lyndon B. Johnson Administration*

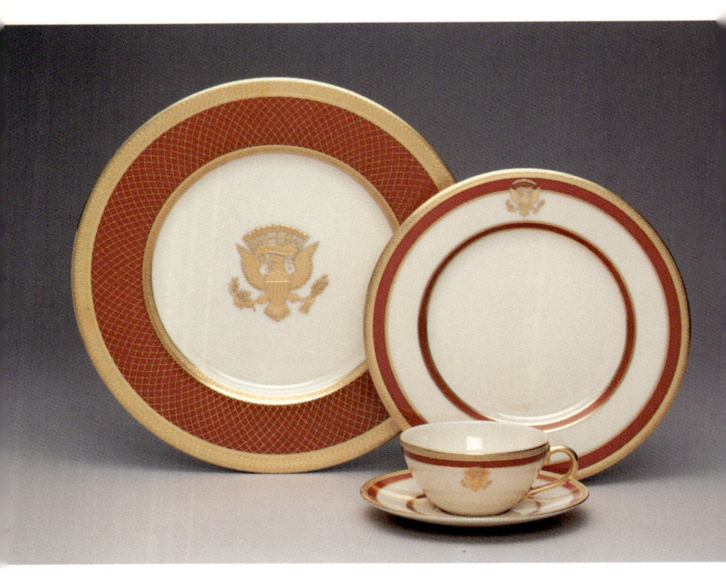

SERVICE PLATE, FISH/LUNCH PLATE, AND TEA CUP AND SAUCER · *Lenox, Inc. · Trenton, New Jersey, 1981–82*
China; Service Plate-11 5/8 in. (29.5 cm)
*Ronald W. Reagan Administration*

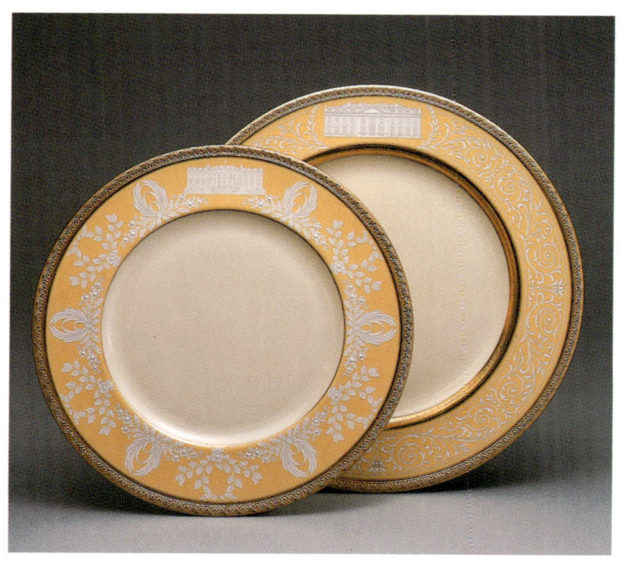

DESSERT AND DINNER PLATES · *Lenox, Inc. · Trenton, New Jersey, 2000*
China; Dinner Plate-10 5/8 in. (27.1 cm) · *William J. Clinton Administration*

OVERLEAF: THE STATE FLOOR: THE STATE DINING ROOM, 2000

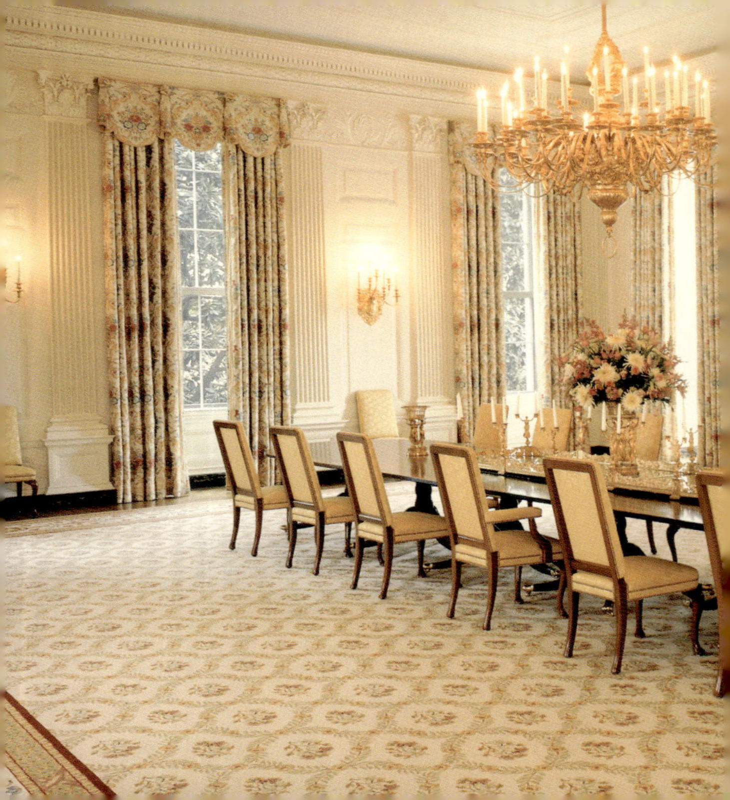

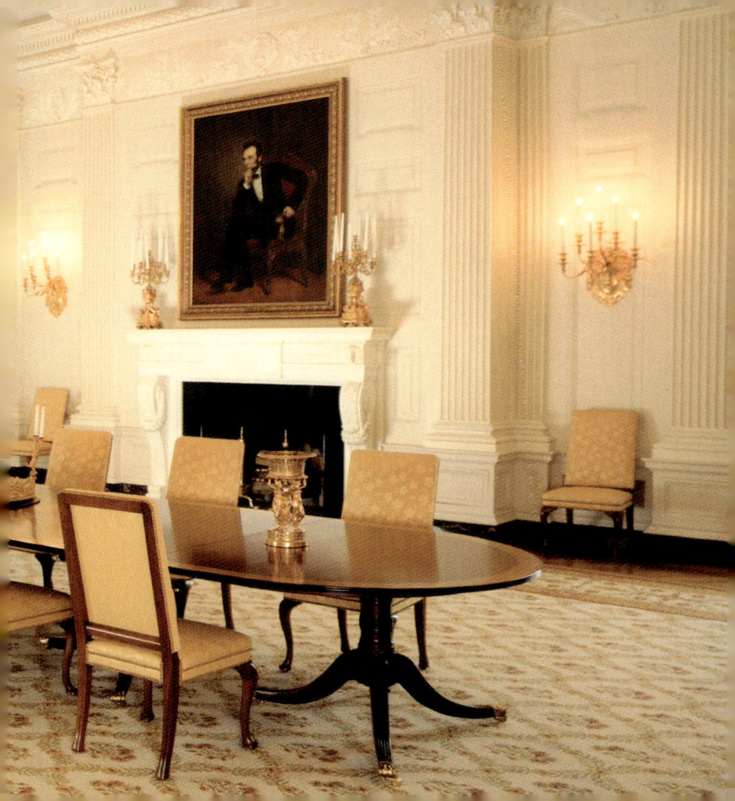

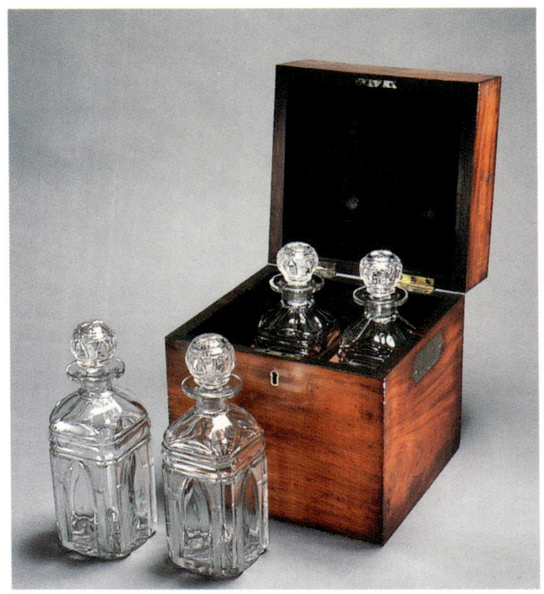

TRAVELING LIQUOR SET · *Probably Bakewell, Page & Bakewell Pittsburgh, c. 1815–35* · Cut glass; mahogany, Decanters-10 x 3½ x 3½ in. (25.4 x 8.9 x 8.9 cm) · *Belonged to Andrew Jackson*

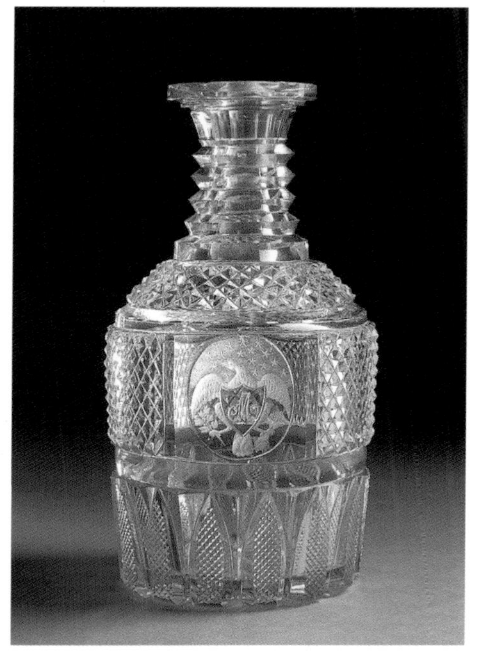

DECANTER · *Bakewell, Page & Bakewell · Pittsburgh, 1816*
Cut and engraved glass, 8 11/16 x 4 1/2 in. (22.1 x 11.4 cm)
*Belonged to James Madison*

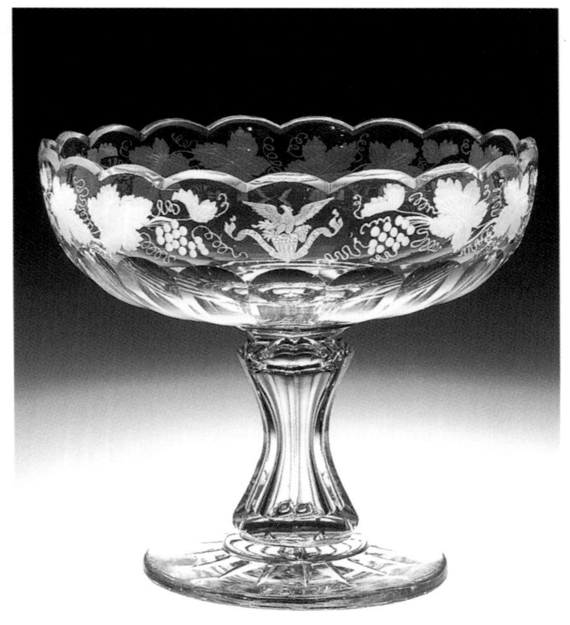

Compote or Center Dish

*Bakewell, Page & Bakewell · Pittsburgh, 1829*

Cut and engraved glass, 11 1/8 x 11 3/4 in. (28.3 x 29.8 cm)

*Andrew Jackson Administration*

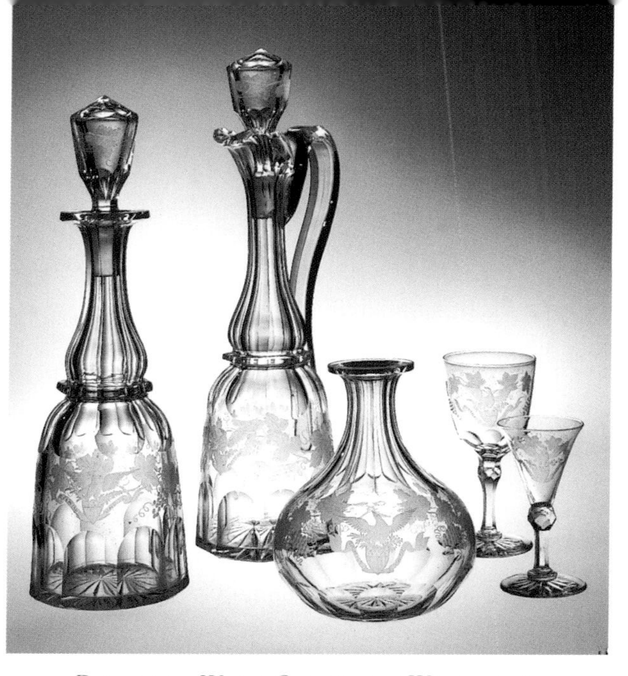

DECANTERS, WATER CARAFE, AND WINEGLASSES
*Bakewell, Page & Bakewell · Pittsburgh, 1829–33*
Cut and engraved glass; Water Carafe-6¾ x 5¼ in. (17.2 x 13.3 cm)
*Andrew Jackson Administration*

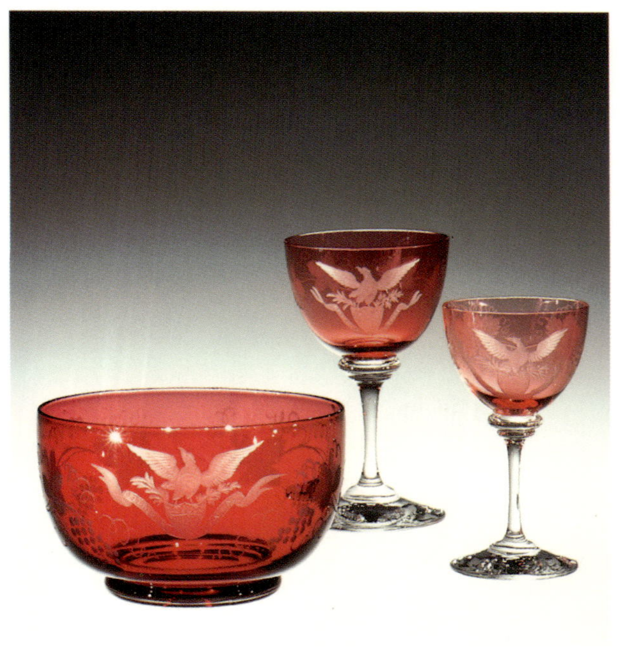

FINGER BOWL, CLARET GLASS, AND DESSERT-WINE GLASS
*American, 1849–53* · Engraved ruby-stained glass; Finger Bowl - 2⁷⁄8 x 4½ in. (7.3 x 11.4 cm) · *Zachary Taylor and Millard Fillmore Administrations*

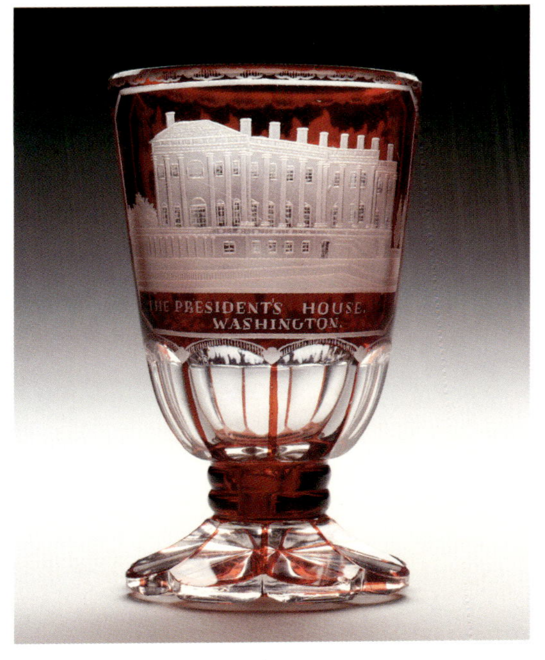


GOBLET · *Bohemia, c. 1840–60*
Engraved ruby-stained glass, $4^{15}/16$ x $2^{15}/16$ in. (12.5 x 7.5 cm.)

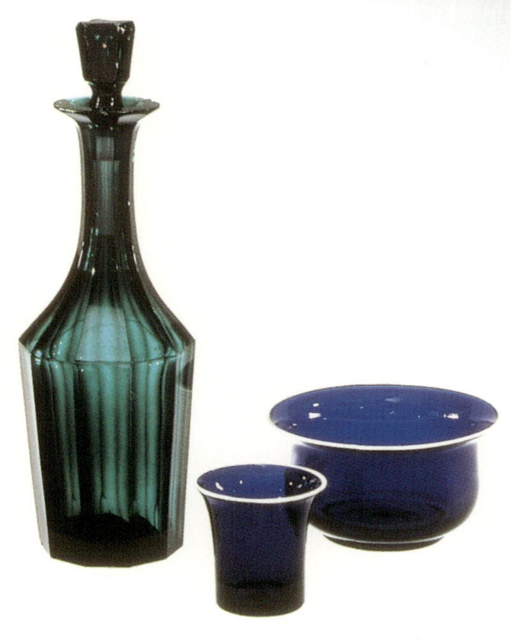

Decanter, Glass, and Finger Bowl
*Probably England, 1820–40*
Colored glass; Decanter-12 x 3 in. (30.5 x 7.6 cm)
*Glass and bowl belonged to James K. Polk*

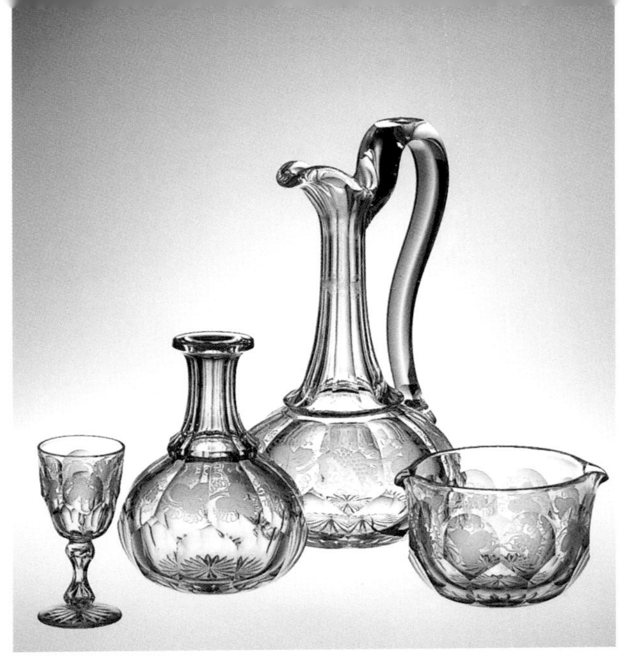

WINE GLASS, WATER CARAFE, CLARET DECANTER AND WINE-GLASS COOLER · *Probably Haughwout & Dailey · New York, 1853*
Cut and engraved glass; Water Carafe-6 7/8 x 5 1/4 in. (17.5 x 13.3 cm)
*Franklin Pierce Administration*

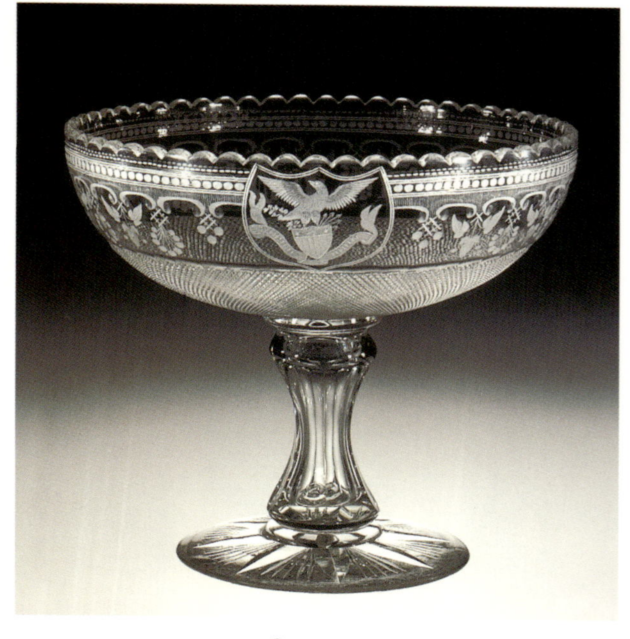

COMPOTE
*Greenpoint Glass Works of Christian Dorflinger · Brooklyn, New York, 1861*
Cut and engraved glass, 8¼ x 9¼ in. (21 x 23.5 cm)
*Abraham Lincoln Administration*

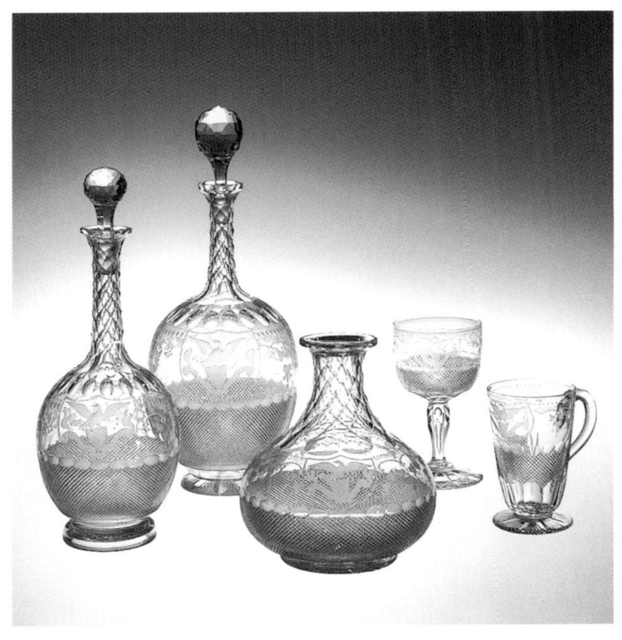

DECANTERS, WATER CARAFE, GOBLET, AND PUNCH GLASS
*Greenpoint Glass Works of Christian Dorflinger · Brooklyn, New York, 1861*
Cut and engraved glass; Water Carafe-6 x 5 in. (15.2 x 12.7 cm.)
*Abraham Lincoln Administration*

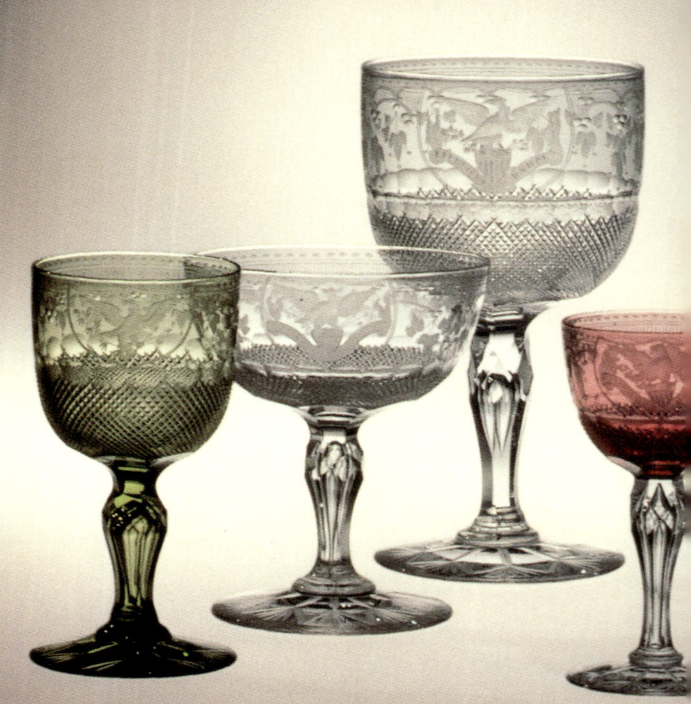

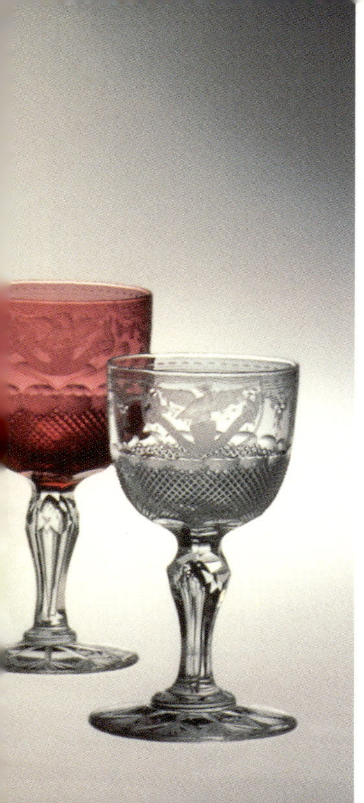

GOBLET, CHAMPAGNE GLASS, AND WINEGLASSES
*Greenpoint Glass Works of Christian Dorflinger*
*Brooklyn, New York, 1861*
Cut and engraved glass; Goblet-
$6^{1}/_{2}$ x $3^{1}/_{2}$ in. (16.5 x 8.9 cm)
*Abraham Lincoln Administration*

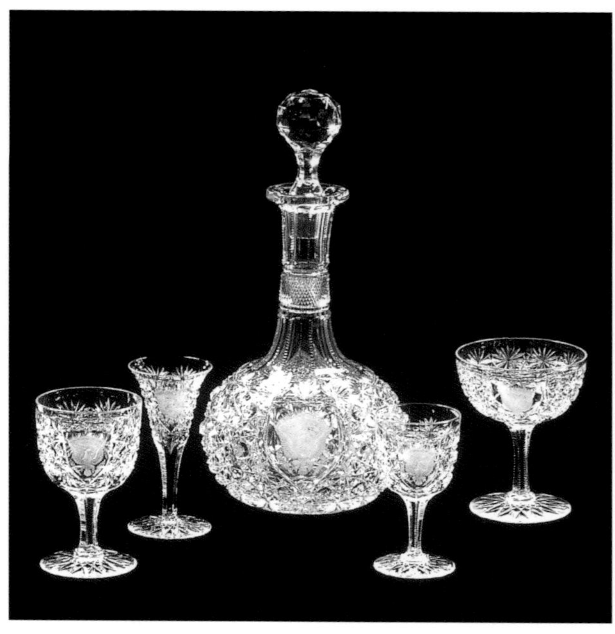

CLARET GLASS, SHERRY GLASS, DECANTER, WINEGLASS, AND CHAMPAGNE GLASS · *C. Dorflinger & Sons*
*White Mills, Pennsylvania, 1891* · Cut and engraved glass; Champagne- $4\frac{1}{2}$ x $3\frac{1}{2}$ in. (11.4 x 8.9 cm) · *Benjamin Harrison Administration*

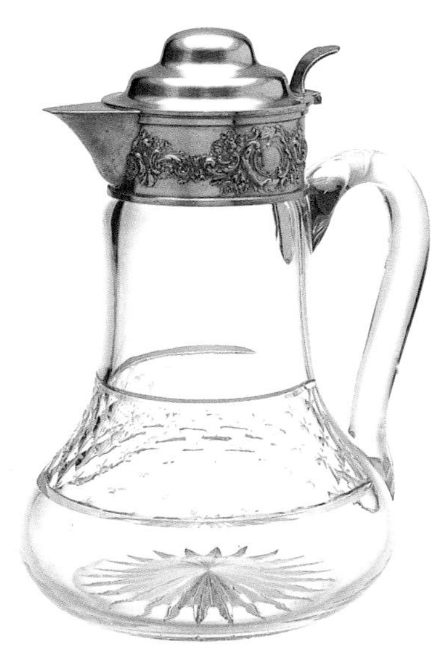

WATER JUG · *R. Wallace & Sons*
*Wallingford, Connecticut, 1894* · Cut glass and silver
9 1/2 x 6 1/2 x 5 1/2 in. (24.1 x 16.5 x 14 cm.)
*Grover Cleveland Administration*

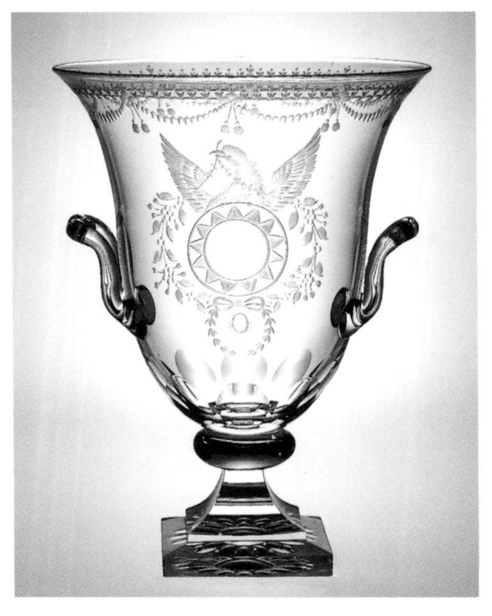

Urn

*Steuben Glass · Corning, New York, 1939*

Cut and engraved glass, 12½ x 9½ in. (31.8 x 24.1 cm)

*Franklin D. Roosevelt Administration*

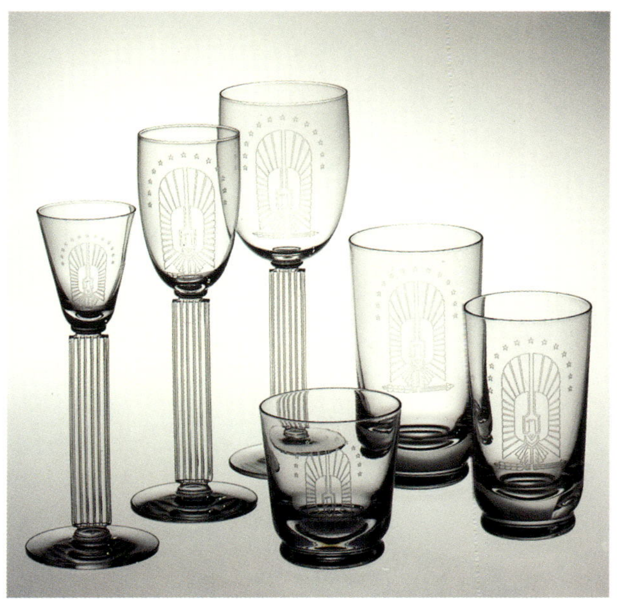

Sherry Glass; Delmonico Glass; Goblet; and
Old Fashioned, Highball, and Tom Collins Tumblers
*Libbey Glass Company · Toledo, Ohio, 1939*
Engraved glass; Goblet - $8\frac{3}{4}$ x $2\frac{3}{4}$ in. (22.2 x 7 cm)
*Franklin D. Roosevelt Administration*

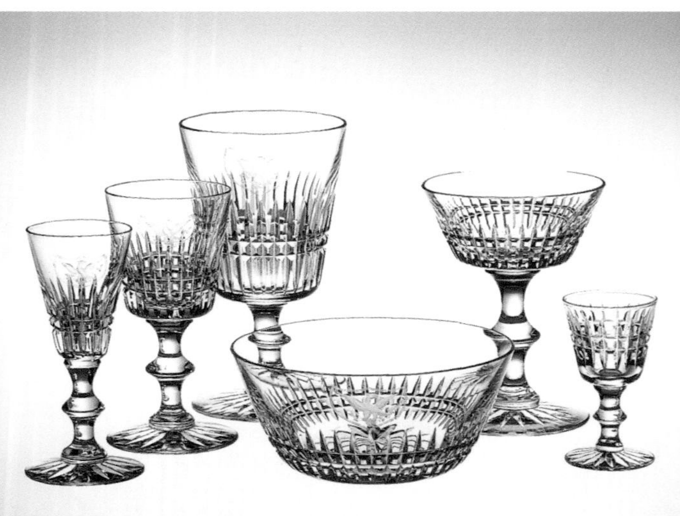

Sherry Glass, Wineglass, Goblet, Finger Bowl,
Champagne Glass and Cordial Glass
*T. G. Hawkes & Co. · Corning, New York, 1937*
Cut and engraved glass; Goblet - 6 x 3 3/8 in. (16.2 x 8.6 cm)
*Franklin D. Roosevelt Administration*

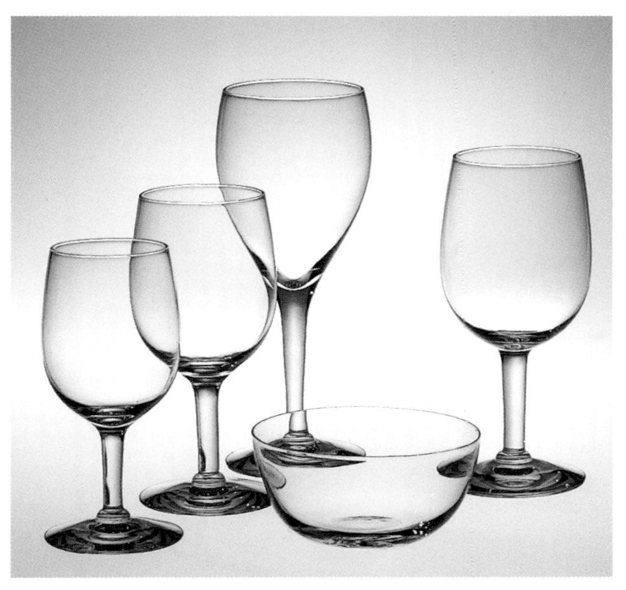

WINEGLASSES, TULIP CHAMPAGNE GLASS, FINGER BOWL, AND GOBLET · *Morgantown Glass Guild · Morgantown, West Virginia, 1961*
Glass; Goblet - 6¾ x 2⅞ in. (17.2 x 7.3 cm)
*John F. Kennedy Administration*

OVERLEAF: THE GROUND FLOOR: THE LIBRARY, 1980

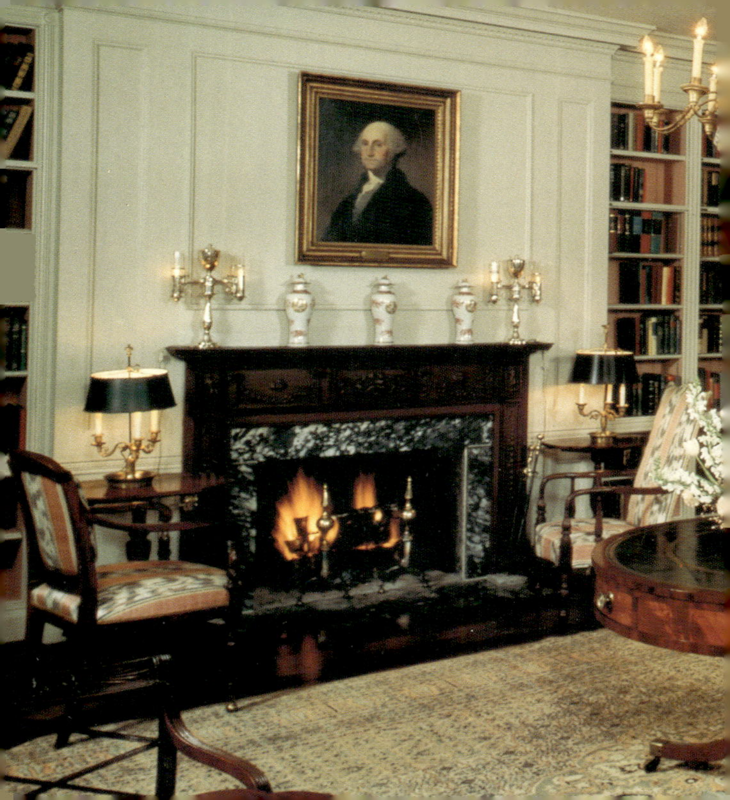

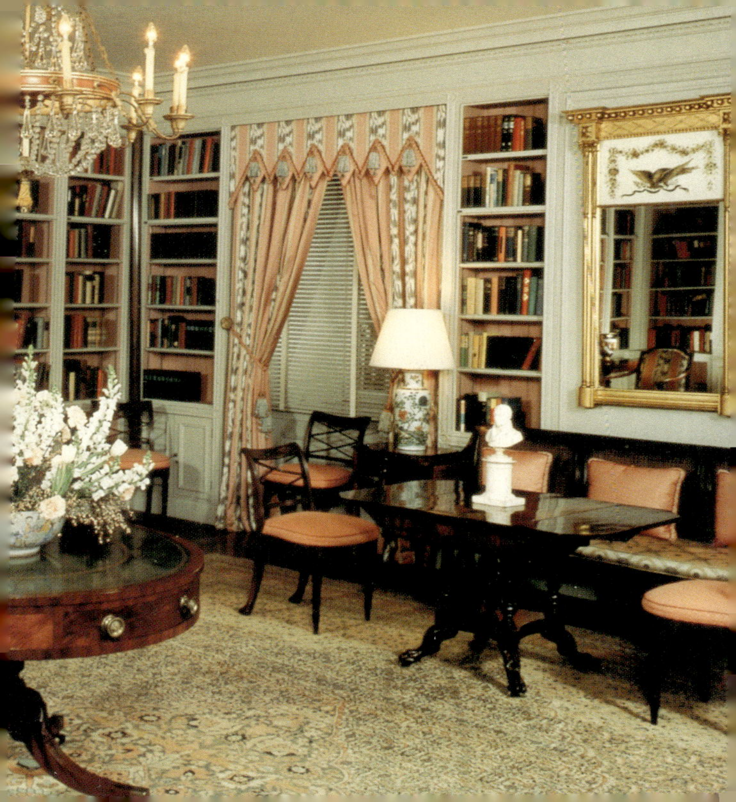

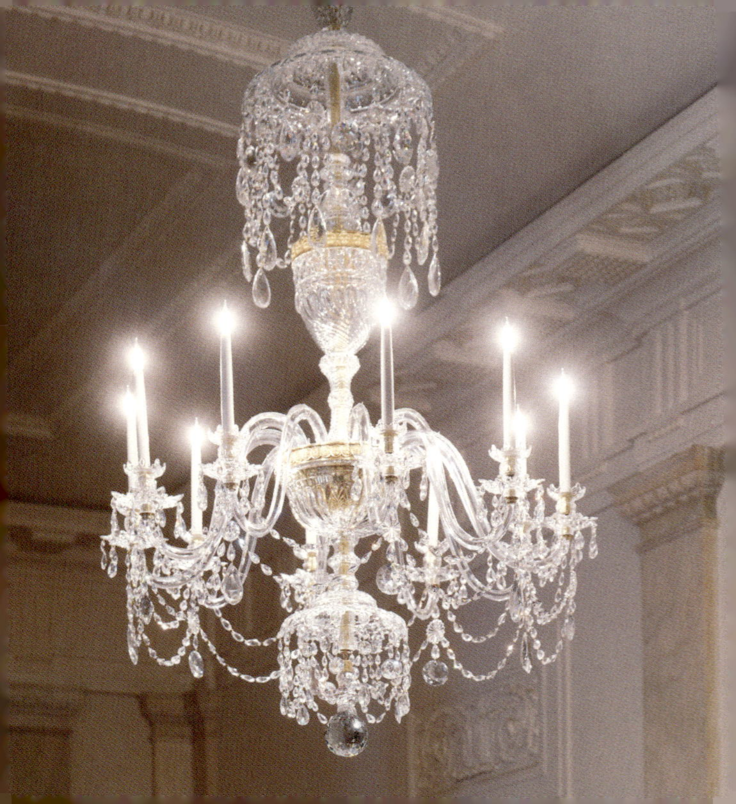

# LIGHTING

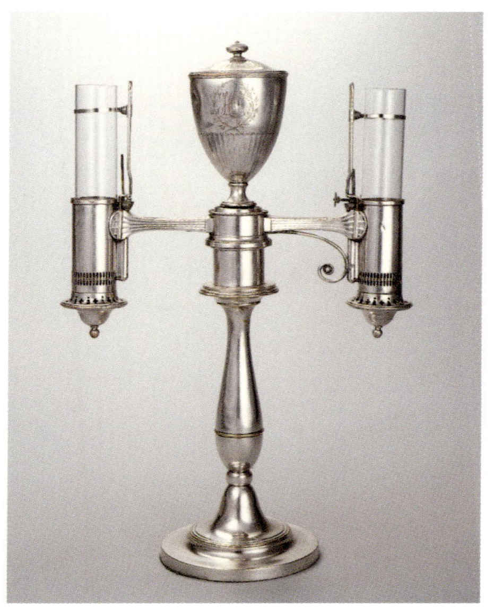

OPPOSITE: CHANDELIER · *William Parker · London, c. 1774*
Cut glass, gilded metal, 72 x 42 in. (182.9 x 106.9 cm)
ABOVE: ARGAND LAMP · *Matthew Boulton · Soho, England, 1784*
Sheffield silverplate, 19 3/8 x 12 7/8 x 5 7/8 in. (49.2 x 32.7 x 14.9 cm)

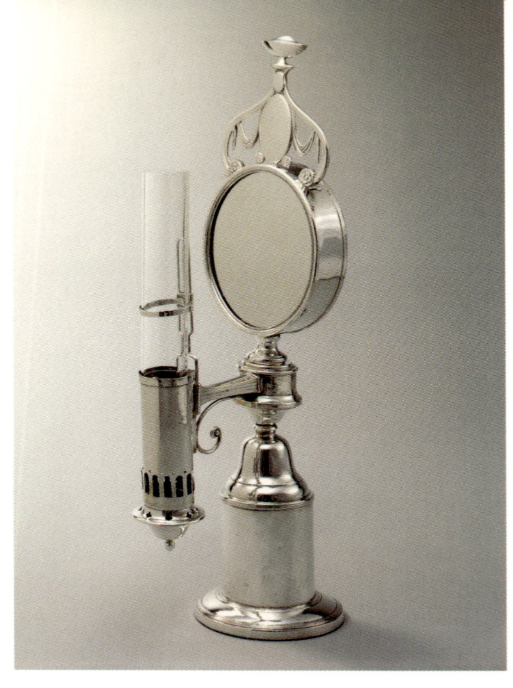

ARGAND LAMP · *Matthew Boulton · Soho, England, c. 1786*
Sheffield silverplate, 20½ x 5 x 5 in. (52.1 x 12.7 x 12.7 cm)

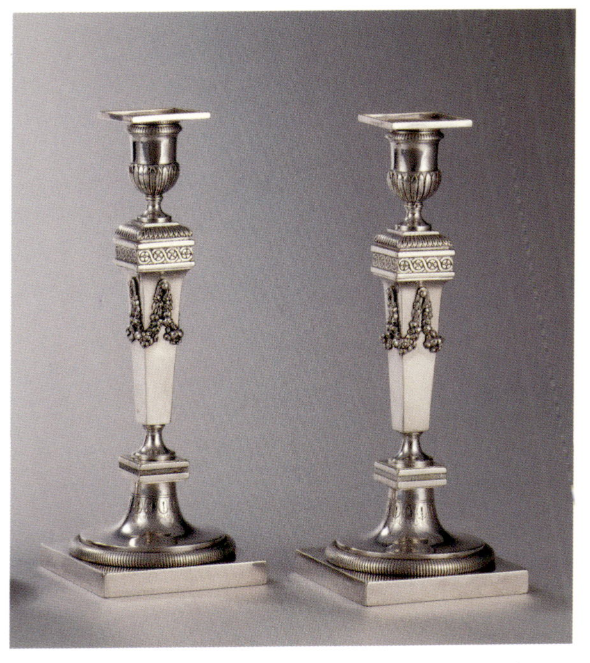

CANDLESTICKS · *Roch-Louis Dany (working c. 1779–1820)*
*Paris, 1789* · Silver, 11 x 4 x 4 in. (27.9 x 10.2 x 10.2 cm)
*Belonged to James Monroe and James Madison*

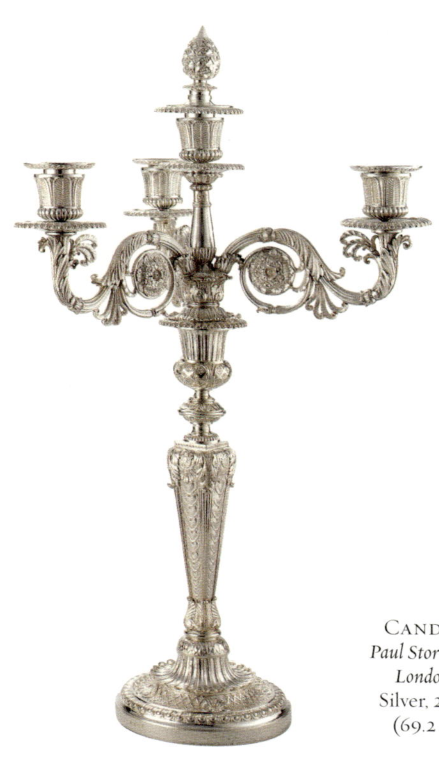

CANDELABRUM
*Paul Storr (1771–1844)*
*London, 1810–11*
Silver, $27\frac{1}{4}$ x 18 in.
(69.2 x 45.7 cm)

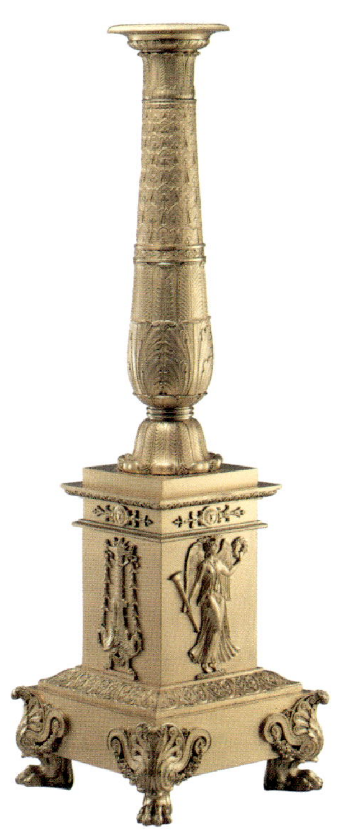

CANDLESTICK · *France, c. 1817*
Gilded bronze
$27^{3}/8 \times 8^{1}/8 \times 8^{1}/8$ in.
(69.5 x 20.6 x 20.6 cm)
*James Monroe Administration*

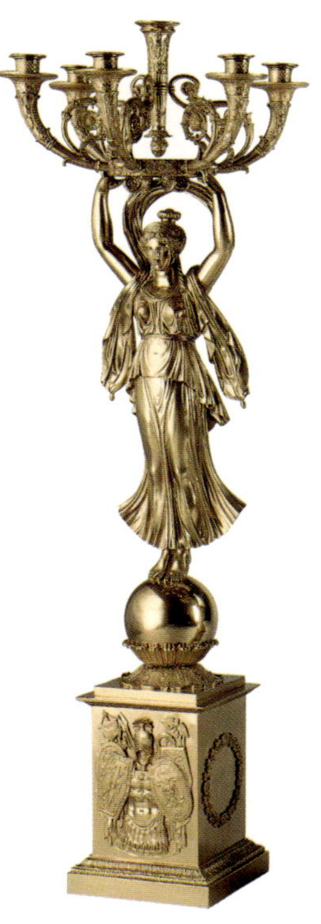

CANDELABRUM · *Paris, c. 1817*
Gilded bronze, 42 x 13½ x 12¼ in.
(106.7 x 34.3 x 31 cm)
*James Monroe Administration*

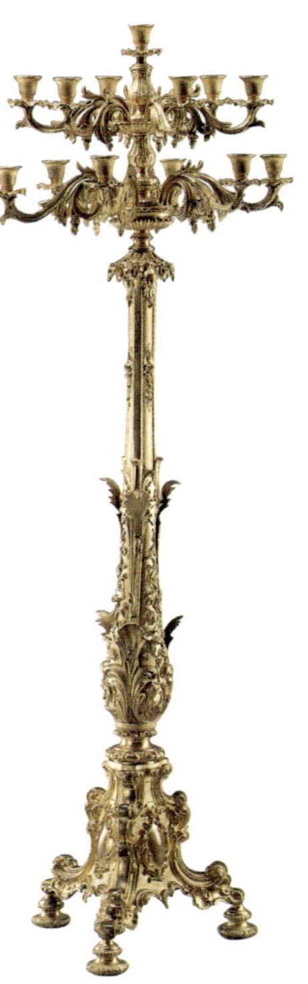

TORCHÈRE · *France, c. 1830–37*
Gilded bronze, 64½ x 22½ in.
(163.8 x 57.2 cm)
*Andrew Jackson Administration*

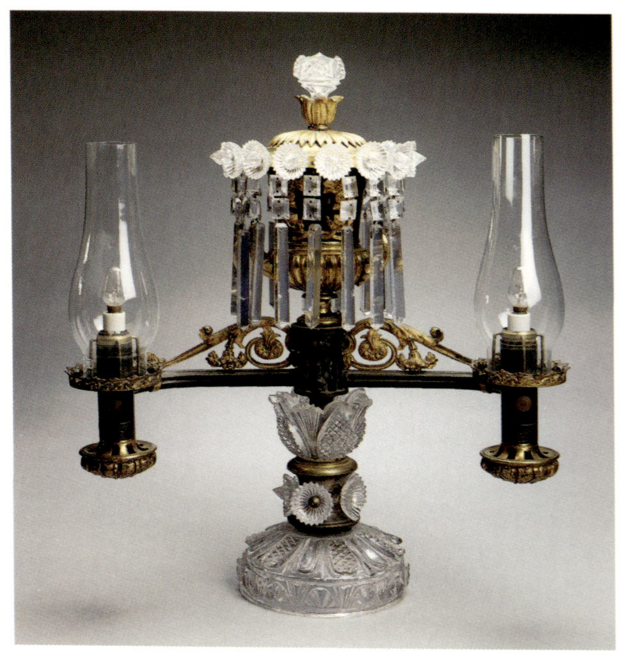

ARGAND LAMP · *Possibly Messinger & Son, Birmingham, England, c. 1830*
Parcel-gilt bronze, cut glass, 19¾ x 16½ x 7⅞ in. (50.2 x 41.9 x 20 cm)
*Belonged to Dolley Madison*

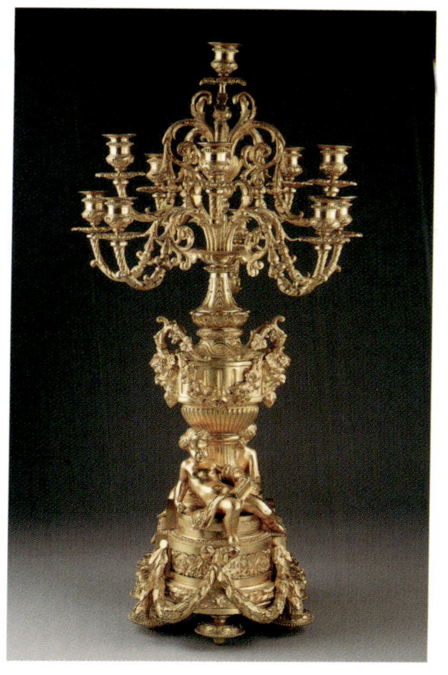

CANDELABRUM · *Probably European, c. 1880*
Gilded brass, $30^{15}/16$ x 16 in. (78.6 x 40.6 cm)
*Rutherford B. Hayes Administration*

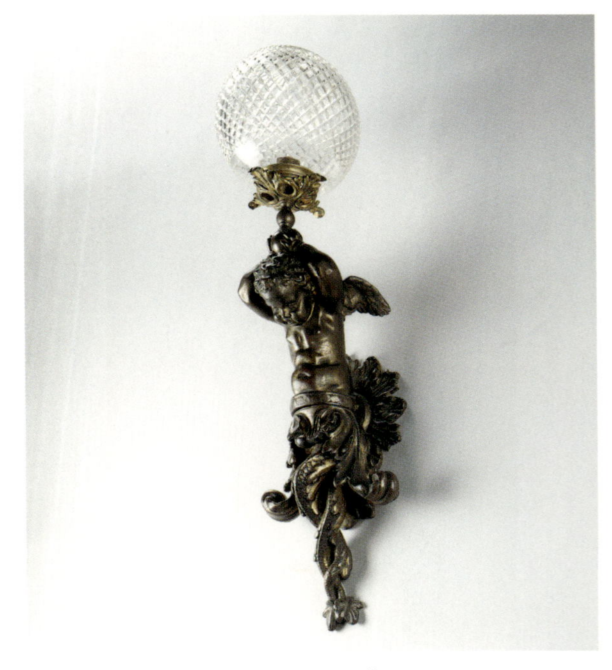

SCONCE · *American (?), c. 1891*
Brass, cut glass, $27\frac{1}{4}$ x $9\frac{3}{4}$ x $8\frac{3}{4}$ in. (70.5 x 24.8 x 22.2 cm)
*Benjamin Harrison Administration*

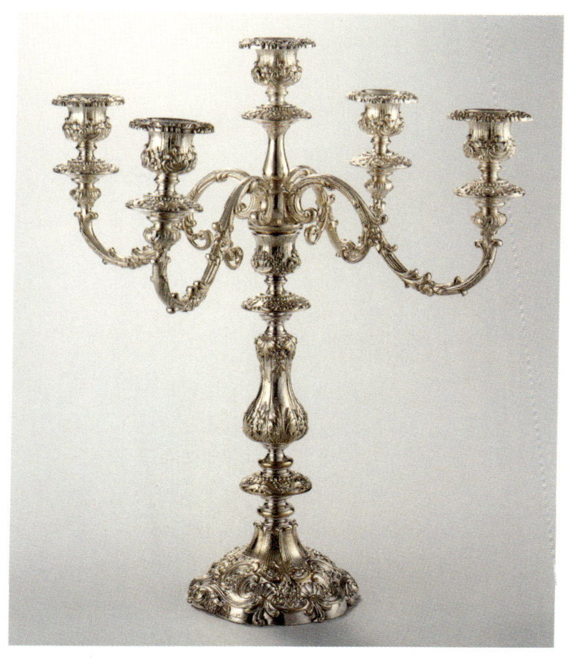

CANDELABRUM · *Gorham Mfg. Co. · Providence, Rhode Island, c. 1898*
Silver electroplate, 20 x 16 in. (50.8 x 40.6 cm)
*William McKinley Administration*

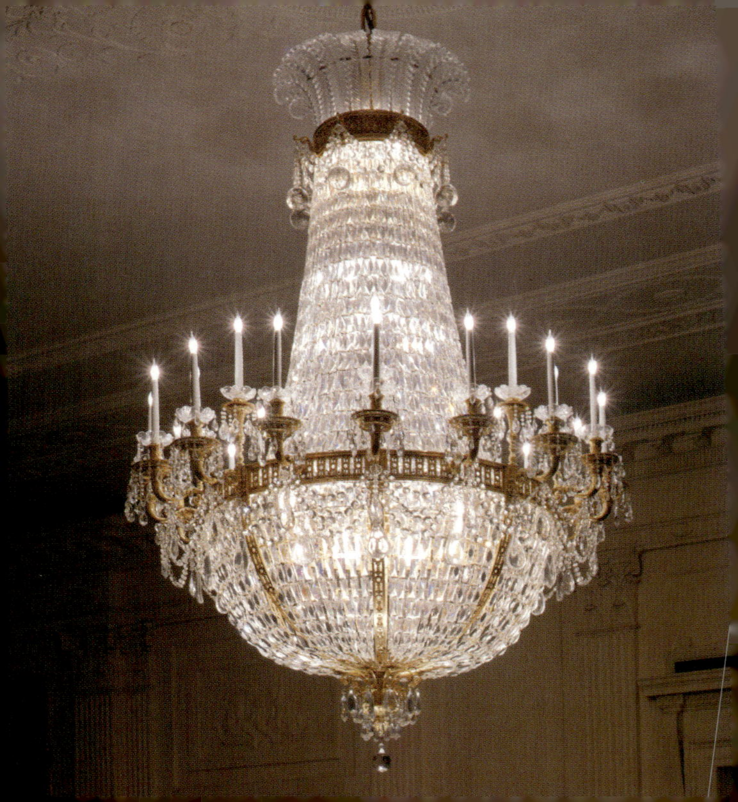

Opposite: Chandelier
*Christoph Palme & Co.*
*Parchen, Bohemia, 1902*
Cut glass, gilded brass
129 x 68 in. (327.7 x 172.7 cm)
*Theodore Roosevelt Administration*

Right: Light Standard
*Edward F. Caldwell & Co.*
*New York, 1902*
Gilded metal, cut glass marble, 123 3/8 x 29 3/4 in. (312.5 x 75.6 cm)
*Theodore Roosevelt Administration*

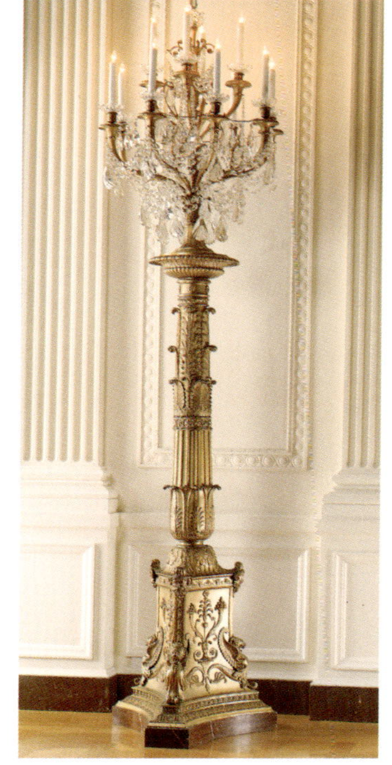

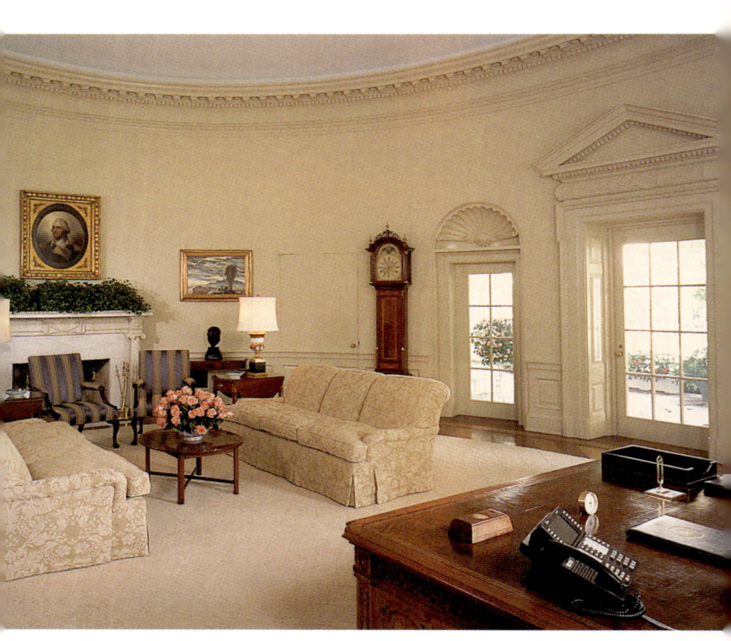

The West Wing: The Oval Office, 2001

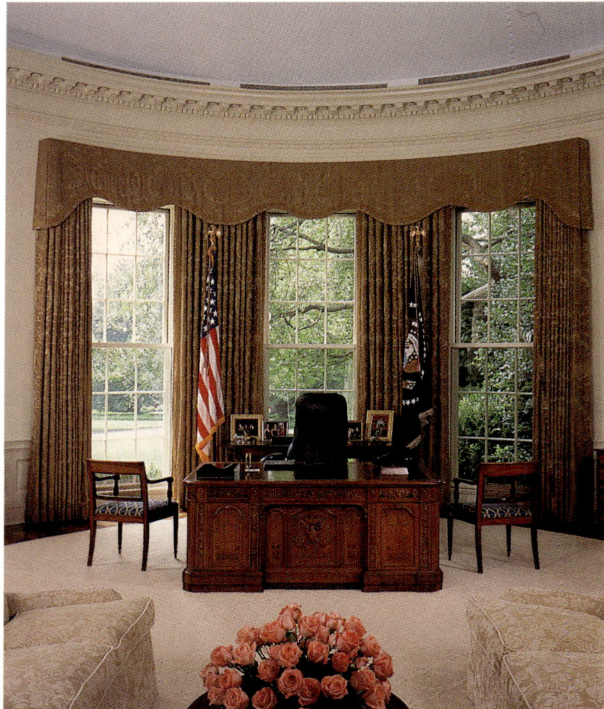

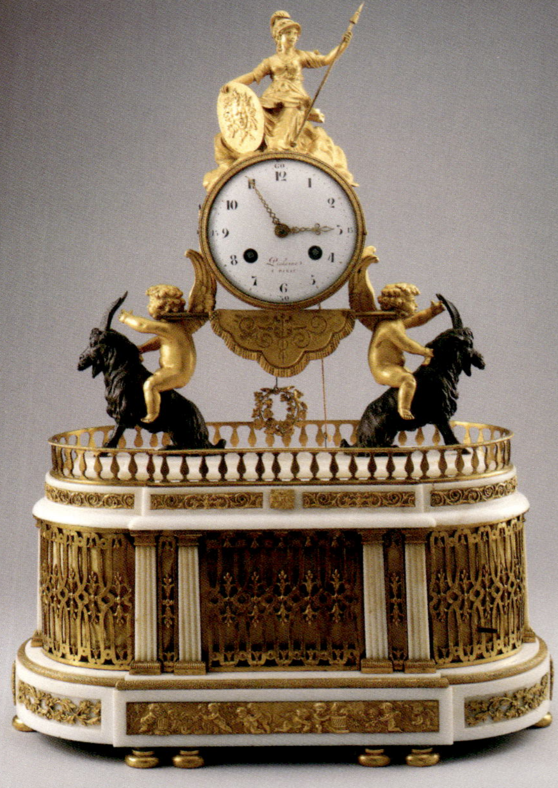

# CLOCKS

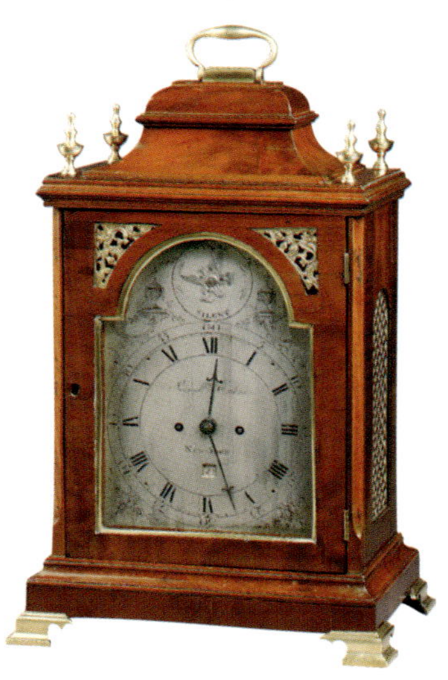

OPPOSITE: MANTEL CLOCK · *Michel-François Piolaine (working 1787–c 1810) Case possibly by Pierre Joseph Gouthière (1732/40–?) Paris, c. 1780–1800* · Gilded bronze, marble, 25½ x 18 x 8 in. (64.8 x 45.7 x 20.2 cm) · ABOVE: BRACKET CLOCK *Attributed to Thomas (?) Pearsall and Effingham Embree · New York, c. 1785–90* · Mahogany, 21¼ x 14 x 8⅝ in. (54 x 35.6 x 21.9 cm)

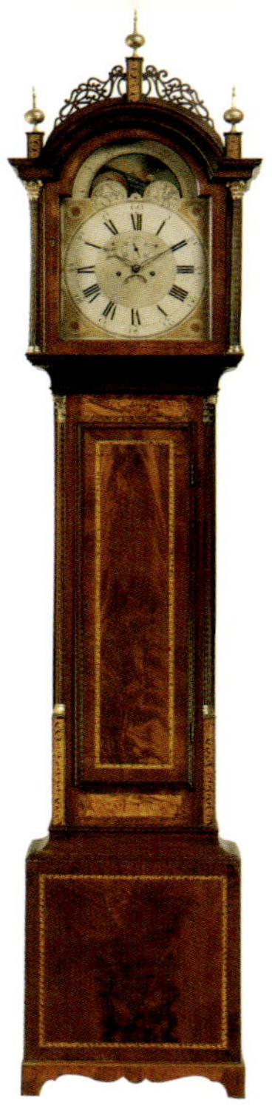

Tall Case Clock
*Case by John (c.1738–1818) and Thomas Seymour (1771–1848)*
*Boston, c. 1795–1805*
Mahogany, 106 x 23 3/4 x 10 3/8 in.
(269.2 x 60.3 x 26.4 cm)

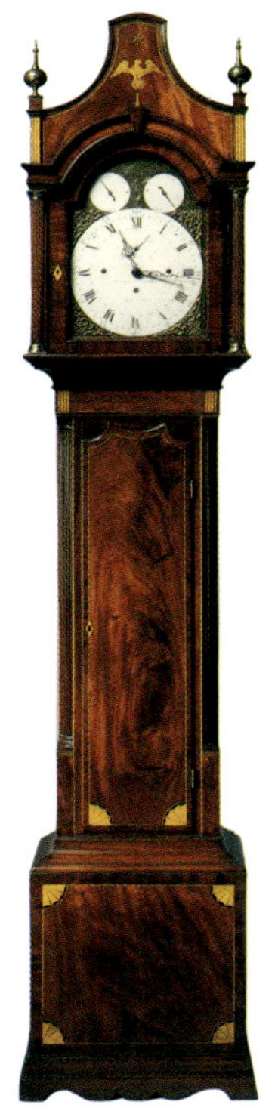

TALL CASE CLOCK
*Effingham Embree*
*New York, c. 1790–95*
Mahogany, 95 3/4 x 18 1/4 x 10 in.
(243.2 x 46.4 x 25.4 cm)

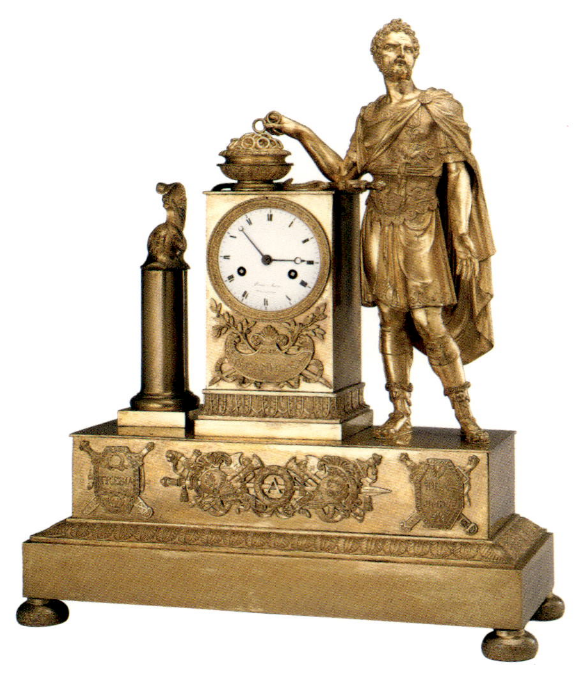

MANTEL CLOCK · *Denière et Matelin* · *Paris, c. 1817*
Gilded bronze, 23 x 18½ x 6¾ in. (58.4 x 47 x 17.2 cm)
*James Monroe Administration*

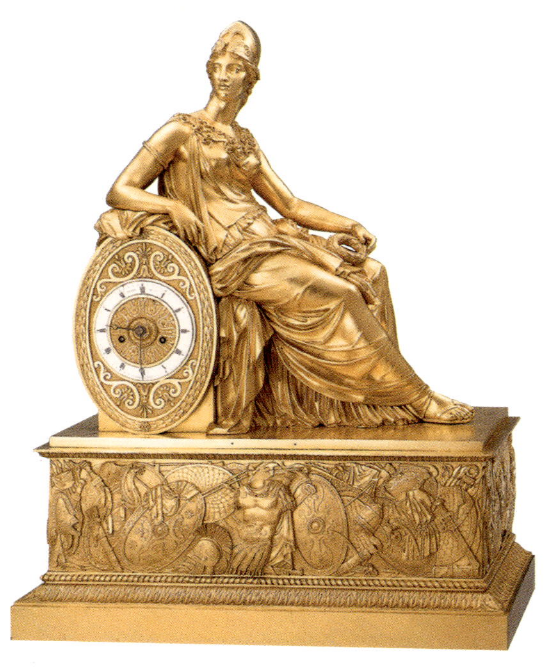

MANTEL CLOCK · *Thomire & Co · Paris, c. 1817*
Gilded bronze, 29 x 22 7/8 x 9 3/4 in. (73.7 x 58.1 x 24.8 cm)
*James Monroe Administration*

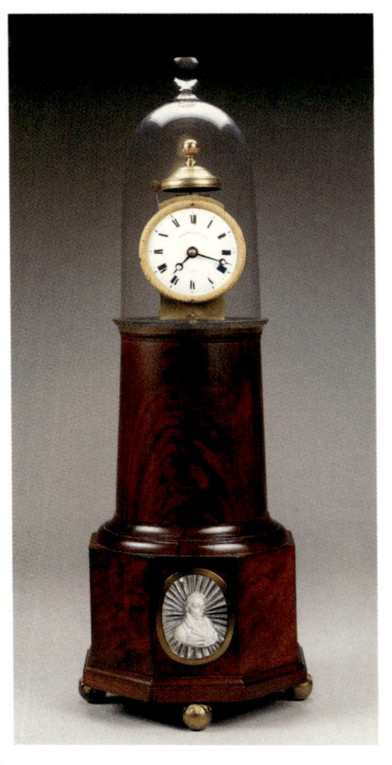

LIGHTHOUSE CLOCK
*Simon Willard & Son,*
*(1753–1848)*
*Roxbury, Massachusetts,*
*c. 1825*
Mahogany, $29^{1}/2$ x $9^{1}/4$ in.
(74.9 x 23.5 cm)

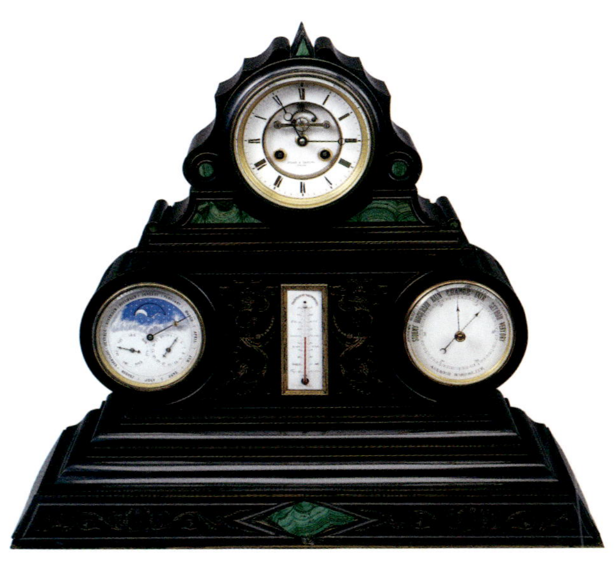

MANTEL CLOCK · *France, c. 1869*
Marble, malachite, 23½ x 26¼ x 10½ in. (59.7 x 61.6 x 26.7 cm)
*Ulysses S. Grant Administration*

# PAINTINGS

22: Gift of Mr. and Mrs. Walter H. Annenberg, 1962.
23: Gift from the collection of Mr. and Mrs. Lansdell K. Christie, 1979.
24: Gift of the Italian Republic, 1976.
25: Gift of the White House Historical Association, 1986.
26: U.S. Government purchase, 1800.
27: Gift of the Walter H. and Phyllis J. Shorenstein Foundation, in memory of Phyllis J. Shorenstein, 1996.
28: Gift of Mr. and Mrs. Paul Mellon, 1962.
29: Gift of Mrs. Vincent Astor, the George Brown Foundation, Inc., The Charles W. Engelhard Foundation, The Ruth P. Field Fund, Inc., Laurence Rockefeller, and the White House Historical Association, 1968.
30: Gift of Michael Straight, 1965.
31: Gift of Sears, Roebuck & Company, 1962.
32–33: Gift of Irwin and Francine Goldstein, in memory of Thomas and Ella Goldstein, 1999.
34: Gift of Roland S. Bond, Mrs. Alex Camp, Mrs. Maxine S. Carr, Mrs. Nenetta Burton Carter, Miss Nina J. Cullinan, Bert Fields, Mrs. William P. Hobby, Mrs. John Leddy Jones, J. W. Link, Jr., Mr. and Mrs. Roy R. Neuberger, Mr. and Mrs. John M. Olin, Mae Caldwell Rovensky Trust, Miss Margaret Batts Tobin, M. Knoedler & Co., and an anonymous donor, 1963.
35: Gift of The Morris and Gwendolyn Cafritz Foundation, 1976.
36: Gift of The Daniel W. Dietrich Foundation, 1965.
37: Bequest of Travis C. Van Buren, 1890.
38: Gift of an anonymous donor, 1978, and Mr. and Mrs. Walter Shorenstein, 1981.
39: Gift of the Alfred and Viola Hart Foundation, 1963.
40–41: Gift of the White House Historical Association, 1976.
42: Gift of Mr. and Mrs. James W. Fosburgh, 1961.
43: Gift of Mr. and Mrs. Lew Wasserman, 1963.
44: Gift of the Richard King Mellon Foundation, 1971.
45: U.S. Government purchase, 1859.
46–47: U.S. Government purchase, 1947.
48: Bequest of Mrs. Robert Todd Lincoln, 1939.
49: Gift of the Republican National Finance Committee, 1976.
50: Gift of the White House Historical Association, 1980.
51: Gift of The Barra Foundation, Inc., 1981.
52: Gift of the Armand Hammer Foundation, 1978.
53: Gift of the White House Historical Association/White House Endowment Fund, 1995.
54: Gift of C. R. Smith, 1966.
55: Gift of the White House Historical Association, 1977.
56: Gift of Mr. and Mrs. John C. Newington, 1973.
57: Gift of Mr. and Mrs. George Brown, 1964.
58–59: Gift of Arthur G. Altschul, in memory of Stephanie Wagner Altschul, 1962.
60: Gift of Dr. and Mrs. Irving Frederick Burton, 1962.
61: Gift of Dr. and Mrs. Armand Hammer, Dr. and Mrs. Ray Irani, Mr. and Mrs. John Kluge, Mr. and Mrs. Carl Lindner, the Armand Hammer Foundation, and the Milken Family Foundation, 1987.
62: U.S. Government purchase, 1903.

63: Gift of Whitney Warren, in memory of President John F. Kennedy, 1964.
64: Gift of an anonymous donor, 1965.
65: Gift of T. M. Evans, 1963.
66: Gift of Ira Glackens, 1968.
67: Gift of Joseph H. Hirshhorn, 1967.
68: Gift of Mr. and Mrs. Steven A. Spielberg—S.A.M. Trust, 1994.
69: Gift of the White House Historical Association, 1981.
70–71: Gift of William D. Rollnick and Nancy Ellison Rollnick and the Georgia O'Keeffe Foundation, 1997.

## SCULPTURE

72: Gift of an anonymous donor, 1963.
73: Gift of J. William Middendorf II and the White House Historical Association, 1980.
74: U.S. Government purchase, 1817.
75: Bequest of Travis C. Van Buren, 1890.
76: U.S. Government purchase, 1859.
77: Gift of Mr. and Mrs. James W. Fosburgh, 1961.
78: Gift of Miss Stella Matthews, Miss Elsie Matthews, and Mrs. Bertha Matthews Harrison, 1961.
79: Gift of the White House Historical Association, 1975.
80: Gift of The Barra Foundation, Inc., 1991.
81: Gift of Miss Virginia Hatfield and Mrs. Louise Hatfield Stickney, in memory of James T. Hatfield, 1973.
82: Gift of Adolph Alexander Weinman, 1923.
83: Gift of Adolph Alexander Weinman, 1923.
84: Gift of The Barra Foundation, Inc., 1991.
85: Gift of Mr. and Mrs. Saul Lerner, 1971.

## FURNITURE

92: Gift of King George VI of Great Britain, 1951.
93: One of a pair used by George Washington and John Adams in the presidential residences in New York and Philadelphia. Gift of The Barra Foundation, 1994.
94: Gift of Mr. and Mrs. Bertram Lippincott, 1976.
95: Rare maker's paper label. Gift of Mr. and Mrs. Mitchel Taradash, 1970.
96: Purchased by George Washington in 1790. Gift of Mrs. Elsie Howland Quimby in memory of Mrs. Duncan Cameron, 1962.
97: Acquired by Thomas Jefferson in France; later owned by Dolley Madison. Gift of an anonymous donor, 1972.
98: Gift of an anonymous donor, 1970.
99: One of a pair; by tradition, sold by George Washington when he left office in 1797. Gift of Mr. and Mrs. Shepley Evans and the White House Historical Association, 1975.
100: One of three examples with pedimented compartment. Gift of Vernon Stoneman, 1973.
101: Gift of an anonymous donor and the White House Historical Association, 1974.
102: Maker's label. Gift of the Hendler Foundation in memory of Lionel Manuel Hendler, 1963.
103: Gift of the White House Historical Association, 1961.
104: Suite with four armchairs. Gift of Mr. and Mrs. A. H. Meyer, 1961.
105: One of a rare pair. Gift of Yale University in honor of Frances P. Garvan, 1962.

106: Maker's bilingual paper label. Gift of Robert Knox, 1961.
107: Maker's label. Gift of the Hon. and Mrs. C. Douglas Dillon, 1961.
108–9: Intricately outfitted for sewing, writing, and painting supplies. Gift of the Richard King Mellon Foundation, 1971.
110: One of a pair. Gift of the American Institute of Interior Designers, 1961.
111: One of two, possibly a pair. Gift of Solomon Grossman, 1971.
112: Maker's label. Gift of the White House Preservation Fund, 1992.
113: Maker's label. Gift of the White House Historical Association, 1973.
114: White House Acquisition Fund, 1962.
115: From two sets en suite with sofas (110). Gift of the American Institute of Interior Designers, 1961.
116–17: Gift of Eugene W. Bolling and the Hon. and Mrs. C. Douglas Dillon, 1961.
118: Gift of the White House Historical Association, 1975.
119: Bears 1814 receipt. Gift of the White House Historical Association, 1972.
120: Gift of the Hon. and Mrs. C. Douglas Dillon, 1961.
121: Gift of the Richard King Mellon Foundation, 1974.
122: From a 53-piece suite purchased in France in 1817. Sofa—gift of the Edison Institute, 1979. Chairs—gift of Catherine Bohlen, 1961, and an anonymous donor, 1972.
123: Only piece of the Monroe suite to remain at the White House continuously. U.S. Government purchase, 1817.
124: U.S. Government purchase, 1817.
125: From a suite of 24 chairs and 4 sofas made for the East Room in 1818. Gift of Mr. and Mrs. John Ford Sollers, Sr., 1986.
126: Gift of the Hon. and Mrs. C. Douglas Dillon, 1961.
127: One of three placed in the East Room. U.S. Government purchase, 1829.
128: Only surviving example of four pier tables for the East Room.
U.S. Government purchase, 1829.
129: Listed on an 1834 Phyfe bill. White House Acquisition Fund, 1961.
130: From a suite of 42 for the State Dining Room. U.S. Government purchase, 1845.
131: From 24 for the Cabinet Room. U.S. Government purchase, 1846.
132: Carved crest rail bust of Zachary Taylor. Gift of Mr. and Mrs. Morton D. May, Jr., 1961.
133: Possibly brought from Japan by Commodore Perry, 1855, or a gift from the first Japanese embassy, 1860.
134: From 60 for the White House and Capitol grounds. U.S. Government purchase, 1852.
135: One of a pair for the Green Room. U.S. Government purchase, 1853.
136: From a Blue Room suite. U.S. Government purchase, 1860.
137: From a suite for the principal guest bedroom. U.S. Government purchase, 1861.
138: Part of a set of chairs for the principal guest bedroom. U.S. Government purchase, 1861.
139: For the principal guest bedroom. U.S. Government purchase, 1861.
140: Acquisition undocumented, possibly the Grant administration.
141: One of a pair in a Cabinet Room suite. U.S. Government purchase, 1869.
142: From the Cabinet Room suite. U.S. Government purchase, 1869.

143: From a "faux bamboo" suite used in the Hayes and Garfield bedrooms. Gift of the White House Historical Association, 1995.
144: Possibly acquired for the Garfield redecoration of the Green Room, 1881.
145: Maker's label; for the Red Room. U.S. Government purchase, 1875.
146: Only surviving chair from a Red Room suite. U.S. Government purchase, 1875.
147: Exhibited at the Centennial Exposition in Philadelphia in 1876. Gift of Edward A. Richter, 1877.
148–49: Made from timbers of HMS *Resolute* as a gift for Rutherford B. Hayes. Gift of Queen Victoria, 1880.
150: Made for the State Dining Room. U.S. Government purchase, 1903.
151: From a set, with two single-eagle tables, made for the State Dining Room. U.S. Government purchase, 1902.
152: From an East Room set of 13. U.S. Government purchase, 1903.
153: From a Blue Room suite. U.S. Government purchase, 1903.
154: Surviving example of a pair for exhibiting china. U.S. Government purchase, 1904.
155: Undocumented pre-1909 suite; placed in the East Garden in 1914. U.S. Government purchase.
156: Among seven pieces of Monroe family furniture copied for Mrs. Hoover. U.S. Government purchase, 1932.
157: Made at a shop fostered by Eleanor Roosevelt. U.S. Government purchase, 1933.
158–59: The 300,000th Steinway piano; designed for the White House. Gift of Steinway & Sons, 1938.

# METALWARE

162: Engraved "JAA" for John and Abigail Adams. Gift of Mr. and Mrs. Mark Bortman and Jane Bortman Larus, 1964.
163: One of a pair purchased by James Monroe; sold to James Madison in 1803. Bequest of James C. McGuire, 1931.
164: From a set of four from Monroe personal furnishings. U.S. Government purchase, 1817.
165: Commissioned by French volunteers in the American Revolution for George Washington. Gift of the French Republic, 1933.
166: Given by James Madison to Jacob Barker, a financier of the War of 1812, who helped save the Washington portrait in 1814. Gift of Horace W. Harrison, 1986.
167: From a set of four. Bequest of Margaret Thompson Biddle, 1957.
168: One of a pair from a service from the estate of the Baron de Tuyll, Russian minister to the United States. U.S. Government purchase, 1833.
169: One of a pair from the de Tuyll service. U.S. Government purchase, 1833.
170: From the de Tuyll service. U.S. Government purchase, 1833.
171: One of a pair. U.S. Government purchase, 1817.
172: Figures of the Three Graces; from a set of three. U.S. Government purchase, 1817.
173: One of a pair. U.S. Government purchase, 1817.
174–75: For the State Dining Room. U.S. Government purchase, 1817.
176: From a set of 36. U.S. Government purchase, 1817.
177: U.S. Government purchase, 1817.

178: Probably acquired in the early 1850s. U.S. Government purchase.

179: Made for Martin Van Buren as a bequest from his attorney-general. Gift of Helen Singleton Green, 1913.

180: From a service made for Millard Fillmore. Gift of the White House Historical Association, 1973 and 1992.

181: "Hiawatha's Boat," selected by Julia Grant at the 1876 Philadelphia Centennial Exposition.

182: Ordered by Lucretia Garfield. U.S. Government purchase, 1881.

183: Selections of tableware provided by Louis C. Tiffany for Chester Arthur. U.S. Government purchase, 1882.

184: Made with silver from old White House flatware. U.S. Government purchase, 1894.

185: Commissioned as a gift from William McKinley to the French ambassador who helped negotiate the peace protocol for the Spanish-American War. White House Acquisition Fund, 1972.

186–87: From pairs purchased for the Blue and Red Rooms. U.S. Government purchase, 1903.

188: "Minuet" pattern selected by Grace Coolidge and reordered until 1973. Gift of International Silver Co., 1926, or U.S. Government reorders.

189: From a collection of English gilded silver. Bequest of Margaret Thompson Biddle, 1957.

## CERAMICS

192: From a dinner service purchased by George Washington in 1790. Gift of Mrs. Kate Upshur Moorhead in memory of Capt. John Upshur Moorhead, 1919.

193: From a family service of John and Abigail Adams. Gift of Mrs. Charles Francis Adams, 1932, and the White House Historical Association, 1999.

194: From the Society of the Cincinnati service purchased for George Washington, 1786. Gift of Miss Mary Custis Lee, 1915.

195: From a service given to Martha Washington in 1796. Gift of Miss Mary Custis Lee, 1917.

196: From a service purchased in 1806 by James Madison. Gift of the White House Historical Association, 1976.

197: Commemorates the English capture of the French ship *La Guerrière*, later defeated by USS *Constitution* in the War of 1812. Gift of A. P. Rochelle Thomas, 1961.

198: One of a pair given to Governor William Eustis of Massachusetts by Marquis de Lafayette. Gift of Grafton Minot, 1962.

199: Monroe state dessert service. Gift of Mrs. R. C. Goetz and Mrs. Hugh Bullock, 1962, and an anonymous donor, 1986.

200: Scenes of Passy where Benjamin Franklin lived as U.S. minister to France. U.S. Government purchase, 1817.

201: Scenes of Greek poet Homer and Byzantine general Belisarius. U.S. Government purchase, 1817.

202: Portraits of George Washington and John Adams. Gift of the White House Historical Association, 2000.

203: Purchased from the effects of John Tyler. Gift of Henrietta Bates McKee Brooke, Elliott McKee, Caroline Farnsworth, Frances Stone, and Fredrick H. Brooke, Jr., 1957.

204: Portrait of Andrew Jackson after John Vanderlyn, c.1819. White House Acquisition Fund, 1979.

205: From a rare pair of American vases; portrait of Andrew Jackson. White House Acquisition Fund, 1988.

206: One of a pair from a John Quincy Adams family service. Gift of Miss Mary Louisa Adams Clement, 1906.

207: Gift of Mr. and Mrs. Raymond G. Grover, 1962.

208: Image after an English engraving. Gift of Mrs. Harry M. Ullman, 1961.

209: Polk state dinner and dessert service. Gift of Mrs. Daniel Digges and Miss Mary Forsyth, 1909, Mrs. Jeanne Delattre-Seguy, 1964, and an anonymous donor, 1987.

210: Pierce state service. Gift of an anonymous donor, 1986.

211: Only piece of the Pierce state service to remain at the White House. U.S. Government purchase, 1853.

212: Lincoln state service. U.S. Government purchase, 1861.

213: Lincoln state service. U.S. Government purchase, 1861, or 1866 reorder.

214: Grant state service. U.S. Government purchase, 1870, or 1874 reorder.

215: From 23 plates acquired in the 1882 Tiffany redecoration. U.S. Government purchase, 1882.

216: One of two "wild turkey" dinner platters, Hayes state service. U.S. Government purchase, 1880.

217: Hayes state service. U.S. Government purchase, 1880.

218: Benjamin Harrison state service. U.S. Government purchase, 1892.

219: One of a pair presented to William McKinley on the inauguration of a new Franco-American telegraph cable. Gift of the French Republic, 1898.

220: Theodore Roosevelt state service. U.S. Government purchase 1903.

221: Silver wedding anniversary gift to President and Mrs. William Howard Taft in 1911. Gift of Charles P. Taft, 1966.

222: Wilson state service, the first made in the United States. U.S. Government purchase, 1918.

223: Franklin D. Roosevelt state service. U.S. Government purchase, 1934.

224: Truman state service. U.S. Government purchase, 1951.

225: Lyndon B. Johnson state service. Gift of an anonymous donor, 1968.

226: Reagan state service. Gift of the Knapp Foundation, 1982.

227: Clinton state service commemorating the 200th anniversary of the White House, 1800. Gift of the White House Historical Association, 2000.

## GLASSWARE

230: Given by Andrew Jackson to a friend. Gift of Russell Wetmore, 1970.

231: One of a pair given to James Madison in 1816. Gift of the White House Preservation Fund with funds from Mr. and Mrs. Lloyd E. Rappaport and funds in memory of Lila Acheson Wallace, 1986.

232: Jackson state service. U.S. Government purchase, 1829.

233: Jackson state service. U.S. Government purchase, 1829 or 1833.

234: Probably ordered to supplement the Jackson service. U.S. Government purchase, 1849–53.

235: Image after an English print. Gift of the White House Historical Association, 1993.

236: Decanter reportedly purchased at a 19th-century White House sale. Gift of Mrs. Charles W. Richardson, 1918. Bowl and glass descended in the James K. Polk family. Gift of Mrs. George M. Fall, 1907.
237: Pierce state glass service. U.S. Government purchase, 1853, and gift of Mrs. Daniel C. Digges and Miss Mary Ann Forsyth, 1909, and the White House Historical Association, 1971.
238: Lincoln state service. U.S. Government purchase, 1861.
239: Lincoln state service. U.S. Government purchase, 1861 or reorders.
240–41: Lincoln state service. U.S. Government purchase, 1861 or reorders.
242: Benjamin Harrison state service. U.S. Government purchase, 1891 or reorders.
243: From a set of six. U.S. Government purchase, 1894.
244: "Strawberry Mansion" pattern. Transfer from the United States New York World's Fair Commission, 1940.
245: Service made for the Federal Building at the 1939 World's Fair. Transfer from the United States New York World's Fair Commission, 1940.
246: Franklin D. Roosevelt state service. U.S. Government purchase, 1937, or reorders.
247: Kennedy state service. U.S. Government purchase, 1961.

# LIGHTING FIXTURES

250: One of a pair by the foremost late-18th-century London maker. Gift of an anonymous donor, 1946.
251: One of a pair; presented by Lafayette to Major General Henry Knox in 1784. Gift of the American Institute of Interior Designers, 1962.
252: One of a pair. Gift of the Richard King Mellon Foundation, 1971.
253: One of a pair purchased by James Monroe; sold to James Madison in 1803. Bequest of James C. McGuire, 1931.
254: From a set of four once owned by the Dukes of Hamilton. Gift of Mrs. Dorothea S. Wiman, 1963.
255: One of a pair. U.S. Government purchase, 1817.
256: Female figures derived from French Empire designs of "Victory." U.S. Government purchase, 1817.
257: One of a pair given to Andrew Jackson. Possible gift of Robert Patterson.
258: Reportedly given by Dolley Madison to one of her freed slaves. Gift of Mrs. Edward W. C. Russell, 1976.
259: From two pairs from Tiffany & Co. U.S. Government purchase, 1880.
260: From a set of four installed in the Family Dining Room during the introduction of electricity. U.S. Government purchase, 1891.
261: From a set of six. U.S. Government purchase, 1898.
262: One of three for the East Room. U.S. Government purchase, 1902.
263: One of four made for the East Room. U.S. Government purchase, 1902.

## CLOCKS

266: Gift of President Vincent Auriol of France, 1952.
267: Gift of the White House Historical Association, 1974.
268: Gift of the White House Historical Association, 1972.
269: Musical chimes. Gift of the National Society of Colonial Dames in America, 1973.
270: Carthaginian general Hannibal. U.S. purchase, 1817.
271: Roman goddess Minerva. U.S. Government purchase, 1817.
272: American form; commemorative portrait of the Marquis de Lafayette. Gift of Mr. and Mrs. A. H. Meyer, 1961.
273: Barometer, thermometer, and perpetual calendar mechanism. U.S. Government purchase, 1869.

## EXPLANATORY NOTE

In the captions, objects associated with presidents are credited in two forms: "administration" for objects acquired by the government and "belonged to" for personal property later added to the collection. At times government property has been sold, and these objects that have been returned have an original "administration" in the caption as well as a donor credit in the catalog.

## FURTHER READING


Klapthor, Margaret Brown. *Official White House China: 1789 to the Present.* 2d ed. New York: Harry N. Abrams, 1999.

Kloss, William, et al. *Art in the White House: A Nation's Pride.* Washington D.C.: White House Historical Association and the National Geographic Society, 1992.

Monkman, Betty C. *The White House: Its Historic Furnishings & First Families.* Washington D.C.: White House Historical Association; New York: Abbeville Press, 2000.

Seale, William. *The President's House: A History.* 2 vols. Washington D.C.: White House Historical Association, 1986.

Spillman, Jane Shadel. *White House Glassware: Two Centuries of Presidential Entertaining.* Washington D.C.: White House Historical Association, 1989.

# INDEX

 The text of this book was set in Requiem. Printed and bound in Hong Kong.
First edition

10 9 8 7 6 5 4 3 2 1

*Library of Congress Cataloging-in-Publication Data*
Monkman, Betty C.
Treasures of the White House / by Betty C. Monkman ; principal photography by Bruce White.
p. cm.
"A tiny folio."
Includes index.
ISBN 0-7892-0738-9
1. Art, American—Catalogs. 2. Art, European—Catalogs. 3. Art—Washington (D.C.)—Catalogs. 4. White House (Washington, D.C.)—Catalogs. I. White, Bruce. II. Title.

N6505 .M583 2001
709.153—dc21 2001033499

## About the Author

Betty C. Monkman has worked in the White House curator's office since 1967, first as museum registrar, then associate curator, and since 1997 as curator, a position initiated by Jacqueline Kennedy and made permanent in 1964 by Executive Order by Lyndon B. Johnson. She planned and curated the first exhibition on the White House in 1992 and continues to work closely on other exhibits at the White House Visitor Center. She has written books and articles on White House decorative arts and has lectured throughout the country.

## About the Photographers

Bruce White, the principal photographer, specializes in works of art and architecture and has been engaged by some of the country's leading cultural institutions. He was formerly a staff photographer at New York's Metropolitan Museum of Art.

Erik Kvalsvik, who photographed the paintings and sculpture, contributes his work to publications covering art, architecture, interiors, and gardens.